Praise for *The 2,000 Percent Squared Solution*

The 2,000 Percent Squared Solution is a brilliant distillation of essential management principles that everyone, and I mean <u>everyone</u>, can use to drive dramatic acceleration of performance. It's packed with great stories that make the principles easy to understand, embrace, and apply. Whether you're a leader in a big, small, for-profit, or not-for-profit organization, you need this book.

> Rosabeth Moss Kanter — Harvard Business School, best-selling author of *Confidence: How Winning Streaks & Losing Streaks Begin & End*

A 400 times increase in results! Is that an outrageous claim? Not if you know how. It's all about leverage – finding the point where small incremental efforts create enormous returns. Coles and Mitchell provide the insights, examples and experience to help you find those leverage points – a compelling read.

> David P. Norton — Author, *The Balanced Scorecard*

If you want greater profits and more efficiency, read this book. I found many breakthrough concepts for growing and streamlining all of our companies in this book. It made me aware of a lot of things we were not addressing and we are now.

> Jack Canfield — Co-author of *The Success Principles™*, and Co-creator, *Chicken Soup for the Entrepreneur's Soul®*

The 2,000 Percent Squared Solution provides proven strategies that really get you thinking about how to improve your business. Even more important, it gives you provocative stories that stick in your brain and then pop out at you the next day when you're least expecting it! All in all, a lot of food for thought.

> Roger von Oech — Author of *A Whack on the Side of the Head* and *Creative Whack Pack*, and Inventor of the "Ball of Whacks"

The 2,000 Percent Squared Solution is a must-read for any organization or individual seeking to maximize effectiveness and opportunity. While we all have only 24 hours in a day, this book reveals the strategies to be 2,000 percent more effective in 96 percent less time. Implement this advice to create the time to make dreams a reality.

> Brook Noel — CEO of Champion Press, Ltd. and Author of *The Change Your Life Challenge: A 70 Day Life Makeover Program for Women*

Remember the old advice that goals should be "challenging but attainable?" Today the new advice is – reinvent, re-imagine, reengineer. Tomorrow the advice will probably be more aggressive as global opportunities explode. *The 2,000 Percent Squared Solution* provides the ideas, examples and tools which will help you make big, bold improvements in your business. This book is a "must-read" for every business leader.

> Paul B. Thornton — President, Be the Leader Associates and Author of *Leadership: Best Advice I Ever Got*

The 2,000 Percent Squared Solution combines audacity and practicality into a one-of-a-kind guide for improving performance. Whether you're leading a large organization or running your own shop, you will benefit from the advice and guidance in this book.

> Daniel H. Pink — Author of *A Whole New Mind*

Mitchell and Coles continue to offer readers creative examples and guidance for achieving performance breakthroughs. Their recommendations are supported by numerous examples of how companies and nonprofits leverage their scale for greater impact.

> Robert S. Kaplan — Baker Foundation Professor, Harvard Business School

Most of the things you can do to improve your business are actually common-sense, small innovations. They're relatively easy to put into practice, but we don't – because they feel unfamiliar. *The 2,000 Percent Squared Solution* suggests, persuasively, that doing this kind of improvement doesn't just add up, but multiplies your capability. The winners do exactly that. This book shows what they do.

> Art Kleiner — Editor in chief, *strategy+business*

Don Mitchell and Carol Coles have found a great way to help you take your business to the next level and beyond! I highly recommend you immediately read and apply the principles contained in this empowering book!

Coach Zev — Founder of www.EmpoweringMessages.com

If you're ready to make quantum leaps in your business, run out and get *The 2,000 Percent Squared Solution*. Mitchell and Coles give you the ideas, tools and practical examples you can apply, right now, to make significant improvements and catapult your business to new heights.

Jim Donovan — Author of *Handbook to a Happier Life*

An old preacher once said that "Hell will be discovering what you could have done with your life." If you want to avoid that awful fate read *The 2,000 Percent Squared Solution*. In this gratifyingly practical book Mitchell and Coles take away all excuses and literally take you step by step to the full and profitable potential of your life and your business.

Ian Percy — Author of *The Profitable Power of Purpose*

One of the most important concepts in life is leverage. "Leverage" allows us to do a lot with a little and to look for ways that not only solve the problems, but make the problems disappear. *The 2,000 Percent Squared Solution* is one of those paradigms that shows you how to work with leverage. Kudos to the authors.

Mike R. Jay — Master Business Coach

Fantastic! This awesome book will expand your mind by 2,000 percent and then some. It will reveal enormous "zero-to-infinity" growth ideas which are so simple it's uncanny. You will be equipped for high-speed exponential growth — virtually to infinity, at costs as low as zero. Read it fast, and zoom far ahead!

Frank Feather — Business futurist and Author of *BIZNETS: The Webopoly Future of Business*

A powerful and highly practical roadmap for business model innovation — the authors draw on many interesting examples from a wide range of organizations to illustrate their ideas clearly and concisely.

Michael A. Roberto — Author, *Why Great Leaders Don't Take Yes For An Answer*

If your competition buys this book and implements its recommendations and you don't, your organization could become obsolete and virtually invisible. *The 2,000 Percent Squared Solution* sounds like a mystery, yet the authors write more lucidly than any business experts you have read elsewhere. I have never called a business strategy book "exciting." However, this one merits that description — and more acclaim. Mitchell and Coles explain their business formula with intriguing illustrations from their international consulting practice. You will welcome the Socratic approach of posing provocative questions that awaken your creativity. I rate *Squared Solution* a "must buy" for everyone wanting to jet-propel their business.

Bill Lampton, Ph.D. — Author, *The Complete Communicator: Change Your Communication, Change Your Life!*

By disregarding today's limitations to seek 2,000 percent squared improvements, you'll be aiming higher than ever before. Who knows what you can accomplish until you start thinking that way?

Michael J. Birck — Chairman and co-founder, Tellabs

If you want to cut your learning curve by half so you can progress more quickly on your road to BUSINE$$ SUCCE$$, do yourself a favor and make the investment in Don & Carol's book now! Just be ready to get whacked on the side of the head and kicked in the seat of your pants because this is not a book you merely read, it's a book you experience!

Daniel St-Jean — Founder of The BizzBoosters, Inc. and Host of www.YourMarketingToolsForSuccess.com

Change your thoughts and you change your world, Norman Vincent Peale, once said. Carol Coles and Donald Mitchell have done their part in this well-written and well-told book. The book is packed with stories, examples, and concrete advices on how to make entrepreneurial leaps by changing your thoughts.

Tom Karp — Director of The KaosPilots, Norway and Associate Professor at Oslo School of Management

The 2,000 Percent Squared Solution is that rare combination of common sense and accumulated wisdom that provides simple, easy-to-implement advice. Your time with this book will give the equivalent of several degrees in entrepreneurship without all the effort and buzz words!

Rick Frishman — Co-author of the *AUTHOR 101* series of books (www.author101.com), President, Planned TV Arts

Let's face it. Most business books aren't worth reading. They tell you things you already know in long-winded passages filled with obscure jargon. *The 2,000 Percent Squared Solution* is a happy exception. Who knew that a book about growing profits 400 times faster could be filled with uncommon good sense, interesting examples and simple directions? If you only read one business-improving book this year, make it *The 2,000 Percent Squared Solution*!

Alan Guinn — Managing Director of The Guinn Consultancy Group, Inc and Author of *Psyched for Life*

Are you serious about wanting to create solutions that deliver 400 times more benefits? Do you want to learn how to increase sales by more than 20 times while increasing profit margins by 20 times? Then look no further than *The 2,000 Percent Squared Solution*. The book has everything you need to systematically learn, and more importantly, apply all the concepts in your unique context. The book is filled with stories and examples to keep you engaged. This is a must-read for business leaders, small business owners and people leading and managing non-profit organizations.

Srikanth Srinivas — CEO, Opex Partners, Inc. and Author of *Shocking Velocity! Rapidly Achieve More With Less*

I am a big fan of *The 2,000 Percent Solution* series. Why? Those books helped me achieve more than 20 times my prior success. *The 2,000 Percent Squared Solution* provides a further exponential improvement in your ability to succeed with your business challenges and opportunities. The book is filled with practical know how and examples you can use to make enormous breakthroughs.

Hiroshi Fukushi — Director of Ajinomoto Thailand; President of FD Green, Thailand; Author of *A Strategic Approach to the Environmentally Sustainable Business*; and Coauthor of *We Will Make the World Green*

I can't wait to implement the ideas in *The 2,000 Percent Squared Solution*. Donald Mitchell and Carol Coles take "the poetic road less traveled by" to bring you brilliant solutions to difficult problems. The beauty of this? Anyone can make changes that produce 20 times an increase in the usual results with 96 percent less time and effort in 6 months or less. Count me in.

Susan Harrow — Author of *Sell Yourself without Selling Your Soul* and CEO of PRsecrets.com

The 2,000 Percent Squared Solution, a sequel to the worldwide best seller, *The 2,000 Percent Solution,* is a wake up call for anyone who wants to attain exceptional success in life. Nothing is more urgent or important than knowing we can be more, do more, and make a greater impact for the good of our families, our business, our world. By giving us the power tools to do this with their timely and timeless writing, Don Mitchell and Carol Coles have hit the nail on the head. *The 2,000 Percent Squared Solution* has bestseller written all over it.

Elijah Chingosho — Author of *African Airlines in the Era of Liberalisation*, available at www.afraa.org

If your company has less than perfect morale, misses its goals and experiences disappointing financial returns, *The 2,000 Percent Squared Solution* is compulsory reading. Why earn 4 or 5 percent return on your money when you could be earning at least 20 times as much? I improved my investment return in a small investment company by 1,000 percent, and my partner and I turned our company around implementing these principles. Take off your blinkers, stop stalling and start reading and acting!

Bill Kempen — Director, Impact Human Resources

The 2,000 Percent Squared Solution dramatically demonstrates the power of working on the right tasks in the right order to gain exponential breakthroughs.

Aron J. Ain — Chief Executive Officer, Kronos Incorporated

You did a first rate job in helping many business owners with this book. In today's world with all the challenges, you made help simple as 1, 2, 3. One read the book, two answer the questions and three discover solutions to some of the business challenges that have been obstacles that in some cases seemed like mountains unable to cross.

John Beaton — Corporate Development, Initiate School of the Canadian Rockies

In this book Don Mitchell and Carol Coles offer unique insights into overcoming distrust among potential customers and adding improvements in performance that can help you take your business several levels ahead of your toughest competitors. Just use the sequence in this book that (i) shows you specific levers of your business model you can pull to expand the scope of your offerings, (ii) helps you find out why people don't buy from you and (iii) gives you ideas for improving the delivery of your offerings and you'll be way ahead of where you could hope to reach on your own.

Each of the book's two parts is supposed to help you achieve a 2,000 percent improvement in performance. I think that's too modest. In my view, 2,000 Percent Squared (400 times) improvements represent the lower limits of what you can achieve by putting their ideas to work for you. I draw that conclusion because this book helps you see untapped potential that is thousands of times your current level of performance.

Samuel J. Okoro — CEO, Leapfrog Alliance Ltd

By opening our minds and hearts to new paradigms, ideas and beliefs, we can make quantum leaps in achieving any endeavor. *The 2,000 Percent Squared Solution* challenges us to think bigger about what is possible and how we can achieve our goals with less time, effort and money than we ever imagined possible.

This book should be required reading for anyone wanting to succeed!

Annette M Bau — CFP, Founder of TheMillionaireSeries.com and Author of *The 7 Principles of Becoming a Millionaire for Life: Powerful Lessons to Help You Create Wealth, Abundance and a Phenomenal Life*

Introducing a new technology into a market can take time because there are so many possible things to focus on. With *The 2,000 Percent Squared Solution* you'll find breakthrough ideas faster for changing the way customers identify and solve their problems. You'll soon realize that the market for your technology may be exponentially greater than you first imagined.

Doug Scott — President, Avitar, an Oral Fluid Diagnostics Company

This is a stimulating, compelling and easy read for anyone challenged with making major improvements in operating performance. It really makes you think about what is going on in your business and the competitive threat if another company beats you to making changes.

David R. A. Steadman — President, Atlantic Management Associates, Inc.

Only the most proactive and properly focused will flourish in tomorrow's global economy: That's the powerful message of *The 2,000 Percent Squared Solution*. If you want to transform your industry and your future, the simple steps in this incredibly proactive book will take your business anywhere you want to go.

Randy 'Dr. Proactive' Gilbert — Founder of InsideSuccessRadio.com

Donald Mitchell and Carol Coles are both Customer Passion Evangelists who have created amazing ways to gain perpetual answers to all your problems in *The 2,000 Percent Squared Solution*. I've critiqued many books on Amazon.com but none that I can inspire my customers with as deeply as this book. Read it and finally once and for all solve all your problems.

Deremiah — Consumer Passion Evangelist, Speaker/Author and Nightingale Conant "Acres of Diamonds" Award Winner

In this masterful book, Donald Mitchell and Carol Coles lead you to ask yourself an efficient and effective combination of powerful questions. As you turn inward for answers, you will tap into a wealth of information that you already knew, but didn't know you knew. This book will certainly awaken you to the path toward better, faster, smarter, and more productive results!

Pamela Garcy, Ph.D. — Clinical Psychologist and Author of *The Seven Steps to Smart Inner Guidance* and http://www.myinnerguide.com

Customer binding is an old mantra but how do you do it? Then there are competitors who will offer your product at a fraction of your price. How do you stay ahead of all these challenges? *The 2,000 Percent Squared Solution* will give you practical ideas how to stay far ahead of those pressures.

Arun Kohli — CEO, True Global Limited

If you've been looking for the master key to unleash your true potential beyond your wildest dreams, you're going to love the secrets Mitchell and Coles share with you in *The 2,000 Percent Squared Solution*. They magnify the already incredible results-producing lessons of the first book, *The 2,000 Percent Solution*, and lead you to your own unlimited reservoirs of creativity. Follow their advice and get ready to enter the world beyond your imagination!

Teresa Bolen — Author of *Master Plan to Master Exams: How to Discover Your Hidden Abilities to Create the Success You Desire* (www.MasterPlanToMasterExams.com)

In *The 2,000 Percent Solution* we learned that no matter how successful we are, no matter how smart we think we are, we are way below achievable potential. *The 2,000 Percent Squared Solution* brings us practical ideas and examples helping us to reset our mind to achieve this 2,000 percent growth and even more.

Alain Pierre Mignon — Chairman, PT Fratekindo, Chairman of the Indonesian-French Chamber of Commerce & Industry, Government advisor and member of the French Parliament (AFE)

This book is innovation on steroids. It definitely shows you how to develop more creative ideas AND implement them more creatively, yielding unimaginable results. I recommend *The 2,000 Percent Squared Solution* 100 percent.

Stephen M. Shapiro — Author, *24/7 Innovation* and *Goal-Free Living*

Mitchell's and Coles' *The 2,000 Percent Squared Solution* is the user-friendly, comprehensive owner's manual for intelligently and profitably growing your business in 2007 and beyond. Told through on-point case studies and examples, its primary message is that for business to expand it must have a thoughtfully and synergistically developed plan that is customer- and purpose-centered as well as outcome-based. This plan requires, for example, those who are part of the process, from customers and beneficiaries to employees, suppliers, and distributors, to participate. Their roles? That can vary from brainstorming to user consultancy focused on capturing invaluable perspectives and insights on what changes should be made; what new products are needed; what new uses old products can serve; and the why, how, when, and where of effectively and efficiently creating positive outcomes. The authors have hit the bull's eye again. I highly recommend this book.

Signe A. Dayhoff, Ph.D — Self-Presentation and Personal Marketing Coach, GetYourIdealClients.com

Many people seem to live to work. And the work expands to fill so many parts of their lives that they cannot make improvements in what's important to them. With Don Mitchell's and Carol Coles' *The 2,000 Percent Squared Solution*, work can be made simpler and more pleasant so that truly self-improved beautiful living can follow.

David Riklan — Founder, SelfGrowth.com, The # 1 Self Improvement Site on the Internet

The 2,000 Percent Squared Solution is an ideal travel guide on the road to success. Packed with practical strategies and outstanding analogies, this book serves as a proven road map to accomplish stunning results in any business venture. Outstanding case studies and insightful exercises round out this fantastic resource. I can't recommend it highly enough.

Deanna Davis — Author, *Living With Intention: Designing a Wildly Fulfilling and Remarkably Successful Life* (www.deannadavis.net)

Filled with interesting case studies on subjects ranging from Jell-O Jigglers to NASA's Mars Rovers, the heavy hitter suggestions in this book will help you improve your business profits by 2,000 percent squared.

Steve W. Martin — Author, *Heavy Hitter Sales Wisdom*

The 2,000 Percent Squared Solution is a proven model of leverage in action. If you are serious about creating solutions which deliver 400 times more benefits, you won't put this book down.

Jodie Shaw — Chief Marketing Officer, Action International, The World's #1 Business Coaching Team

The 2,000 Percent Squared Solution is a delightful and worthwhile kick in the creative pants.

Sheldon Bowles — Coauthor, *Raving Fans*, *Gung Ho!*, *High Five!* and *Big Bucks!*

For the 30 years I've known him, Don Mitchell has always had a remarkable understanding of what works. In *The 2,000 Percent Squared Solution*, he's articulated, with examples aplenty, what makes the REAL difference in business today.

Philip Lader — Corporate Director

Fasten your seat belts as *The 2,000 Percent Squared Solution* whips you down the road to new ideas and opportunities. The journey is fun, informative and fast-paced. You'll cover a lot of ground from learning how to publish a book to understanding the key to how customers think to what it takes to be an entrepreneur.

Andy Cohen — Author, *Follow The Other Hand: A Remarkable Fable That Will Energize Your Business, Profits and Life*

Imagine expanding your market to 21 times its current scale. Imagine decreasing your costs by 96 percent. Now imagine a resource that will ask the right questions and expand your thinking to help make both possible within the next six months. That is *The 2,000 Percent Squared Solution*. Prepare to dazzle your stakeholders and dwarf your competition with Donald Mitchell and Carol Coles' roadmap to success.

Larry Hehn – Author, *Get the Prize: Nine Keys for a Life of Victory* (www.larryhehn.com)

Everyone's doing more listening to customers today. But are they asking the right questions? Donald Mitchell and Carol Coles in *The 2,000 Percent Squared Solution* have found many new and intriguing questions that will help an organization attract and retain more customers. If leaders respond properly to what they learn, the results can be mind-boggling breakthroughs.

Richard C. Whiteley — Whiteley Group and Author, *Customer-Driven Growth*

Often a company's prime motivation for change is the presence of red ink. On the other hand, black ink complacency can blind a company to abundant opportunities. In their new book, *The 2,000 Percent Squared Solution*, Mitchell and Coles are the business alchemists for today's vibrant economy. Accelerate organizational growth with the creative and innovative approaches found in this essential handbook.

Brian E. Walsh, Ph.D. — Author, *Unleashing Your Brilliance*

The first sentence of the second paragraph of Chapter 9 is worth a hundred times the price you pay for this book. Buy it for your management team and encourage them to read it twice!

Alex Mandossian — Founder and chief trainer of www.TeleseminarSecrets.com

Psst. Can you keep a secret? You can accomplish more by applying *The 2,000 Percent Squared Solution* than most entrepreneurs achieve in 400 lifetimes.

Mark Hughes — Author/CEO, *Buzzmarketing*

You can pay a consultancy $1 million to analyze your business, or get terrific value by having your team read *The 2,000 Percent Squared Solution.* The authors coach you, through exciting and descriptive examples, on how to slice and dice your business from every possible angle. And instead of just finding "solutions," Mitchell and Coles inspire you to find 2,000 percent squared solutions.

Dr. Brad Smart — Author, *Topgrading: How Leading Companies Win by Hiring, Coaching, and Keeping the Best People*

Mitchell and Coles have produced an excellent work replete with actionable ideas. I'm going to add a few of them to my list right now....

Donald C. Wunsch — M.K. Finley Missouri Distinguished Professor, Dept. of Electrical & Computer Engineering, University of Missouri, Rolla

In the fast paced internet business I'm constantly looking for an edge over the competition. After reading *The 2,000 Percent Squared Solution*, I walked away with practical ideas of how to create unique solutions for my clients using resources that were already right at their fingertips. If you want to exponentially grow in your business by showing your clients what they don't know they have, read this book!

Jamie Markizon — CEO, StrategicWebsites.com

Entrepreneurs and business leaders continually seek the next new thing. That search can take them away from the basics of adding customers and improving customer experience. Mitchell and Coles show in *The*

2,000 Percent Squared Solution that the road to exponential success is paved with attention to saving customers time and money while improving the use and value of what you offer. Avoid that critical lesson and experience continual crisis, rather than astonishing success.

Roger E. Herman — Certified Management Consultant, Author, *Impending Crisis*, and CEO, The Herman Group, Greensboro, NC

The fathering of one's heart's desire can change the entire world. Truth is what works. If it works for you, it's your truth, your reality.

R. Winn Henderson, M.D. — Host of *Share Your Mission* and Author of www.theultimatesecrettohappiness.com

The 2,000 Percent Squared Solution

The Fast, Effective Road Less Traveled for Creating 400 Times Greater Profits and Effectiveness

Donald Mitchell
Carol Coles

Mitchell and Company Press
Weston, Massachusetts
United States of America

The 2,000 Percent Squared Solution
The Fast, Effective Road Less Traveled for Creating
400 Times Greater Profits and Effectiveness

For information address:

Mitchell and Company Press
P.O. Box 302
Weston, Massachusetts 02493
http://www.mitchellandco.com

ISBN: 978-0-6151-4276-0

The 2,000 Percent Solution was originally published by AMACOM,
an imprint of AMA Publications, which is a division of the American
Management Association.

Published in the United States of America.

This book is dedicated to our readers who are using the 2,000 percent solution process to become world heroes by lifting millions out of despair, hunger, illness, homelessness, poverty, and illiteracy.

Contents

Part Two: Follow the High-Speed Road Inexpensively to Enjoy Increased Benefits for 96 Percent Less Cost   100

Background Briefing 1
What Is a 2,000 Percent Solution?

No problem of human destiny is beyond human beings.
— John F. Kennedy

Reader's Note: *The following material reviews key concepts from* The 2,000 Percent Solution *(reissue edition, Authors Choice Press, 2003) and* The 2,000 Percent Solution Workbook *(iUniverse, 2005). If you've already read those two books, you are welcome to skip ahead to Part One's introduction instead. If you want a brief refresher or haven't read those books, read on.*

An emergency room (ER) nurse kept hearing complaints from patients who had been waiting for hours to see a doctor. After reading *The 2,000 Percent Solution*, she began to keep track of how long it took various kinds of patients to get the attention they needed. She was shocked to find that those who were too sick or injured to explain their problems but who appeared to be okay sometimes waited for more than 10 hours — even if they needed immediate treatment. This nurse shared her concerns with the other ER nurses and physicians. They discussed possible solutions and decided to train the guards at the door to spot people who couldn't explain about themselves and bring a triage nurse immediately to check the patient. Waiting time for these vulnerable, hard-to-diagnose patients dropped to less than 10 minutes. Although her colleagues didn't know it, they had just put in place a 2,000 percent solution.

A *2,000 percent solution* **is any method of accomplishing what your organization does now with zero-to-four percent of the current time and resources, or accomplishing an increase of 20 times in results while employing the same or fewer resources.** *A combination of those results can also be a 2,000 percent solution.*

That much improvement probably sounds pretty extreme to you. It shouldn't. We've all seen 2,000 percent solutions, but we don't usually label them as such. For instance, a slow reader takes a course in better reading methods. Reading speed increases from 100 words to 1,100 words a minute while comprehension of what is read doubles. The reading speed increase is a 10-fold improvement, $[(1,100 - 100)/100 = 10]$, and the doubling of comprehension allows twice as much to be comprehended in whatever reading time is involved. When you multiply reading 10 times faster by double the comprehension, you have a 2,000 percent solution — a 2,000 percent increase in reading comprehension per minute from the same time and effort.

What brought 2,000 percent solutions to our attention? We were attracted to this subject of creating 2,000 percent solutions because both of our families depended on small businesses when we were growing up, and 2,000 percent solutions made an enormous difference in these operations and in our lives. We hope this book will do the same for you and your business or nonprofit organization, whether you lead it or simply work there.

Let's look at some more examples to help you grasp what a 2,000 percent solution is. Technology often helps us speed results without increasing resources. For example, you can send material halfway around the world now in an e-mail for a tiny fraction of the cost and time of sending an air courier package. E-mail is also a 2,000 percent solution compared to the best method commonly available 20 years ago: sending a facsimile.

Thinking more clearly about the implications of what needs to be done can have a similar effect without waiting for technology to advance. For instance, many electronic products are now designed to have many fewer parts than the products they replace. Consequently, repairing products with fewer parts takes much less time and reduces costs. For more expensive products, the parts are often monitored electronically to note when they are about to fail. The message that failure is imminent is sent to the repair person before the failure. The part is replaced, and the customer never experiences a problem. Repeat sales and profits improve as a result. For less expensive products, online resources allow customers to diagnose their problems, implement the proper solutions, and receive faster results at much less cost than providing hands-on repairs.

Sharing information throughout organizations has had similar effects. Many organizations now use business intelligence software that allows everyone to know what performance is in the activities each person influences. As a result, fewer problems occur and the solutions come faster and less expensively.

More recently, organizations have learned to access better ideas inexpensively by involving large numbers of experts through online contests. Goldcorp was a pioneer in this effort when it sponsored the Goldcorp Challenge in March 2,000. Hundreds of the world's best geologists looked at Goldcorp's exploratory drilling results online and produced a number of excellent suggestions. By spending a few hundred thousand dollars for a Web site and prizes, Goldcorp located new gold reserves worth hundreds of millions.

Topping that success, Larry Huston, vice president of R&D, Innovation, and Knowledge for Procter & Gamble (P&G), reported in October 2005 that P&G had run more than 200 versions of the Goldcorp Challenge since 2,000. These contests had yielded innovations with a success rate of over 80 percent, increased the company's R&D productivity by 45 percent, and provided 35 percent of all of P&G's successful innovations in recent years.

From these examples, you can see that breakthroughs are possible for providing 2,000 percent solutions to the most important organizational tasks. By considering these examples, we hope you'll be able to see possible variations on their themes to establish 2,000 percent solutions for important tasks where no one yet dreams of such improvements.

Background Briefing 2
Why Are 2,000 Percent Solutions Available for Almost Any Activity?

Each problem has hidden in it an opportunity so powerful that it literally dwarfs the problem. The greatest success stories were created by people who recognized a problem and turned it into an opportunity.
— Anonymous

When first creating a 2,000 percent solution, many people report discovering that their solution could have been implemented at any time during the prior 50 years. But no one had. Why is that?

Let us tell you a story that helps explain such delays. One of our students works in a business where 95 percent of the ingredients were once discarded at the end of the production process. That's like taking a piece or two of a large wedding cake and then throwing the rest of the cake away. The organization first called the unused ingredients "waste" and dumped that material into the ocean. A new treaty in the 1970s prohibited this kind of dumping, and the "waste" went into landfills. Environmental laws were later enacted that made it more attractive to do something else with the "waste," and the leftover ingredients were turned into "by-products" that didn't have much value. The student redefined those used ingredients as "products" and discovered that with a little upgrading they became valuable forms of organic fertilizer that many were anxious to buy. Soon the student had developed a large fertilizer business and was successfully making similar upgrades of waste into valuable products for other manufacturers.

From this experience, our student learned that people only pay a lot of attention to "products," seldom focus on "by-products," and hardly ever examine their "waste." Similarly, people pay a lot more attention to 2,000 percent solutions than to efforts to meet the annual budget increase of 10 percent. Why? It's more exciting and rewarding to develop 2,000 percent solutions. When you accomplish that first 2,000 percent solution, your self-esteem reaches a higher level than you ever thought possible. You've done it once and you know you can do it again.

A parallel observation to Pareto's Law (referred to by many as Pareto's Principle, or the 80/20 principle, meaning that 80 percent of the results can be observed to come from 20 percent of the people doing an activity) states that 80 percent of the results of any economic activity come from 20 percent or less of the efforts. Let's look at an example of this principle to see why 2,000 percent solutions are naturally abundant.

Imagine that a business has 100 salespeople selling 100,000 units a year. Consistent with the parallel observation to Pareto's Law, 20 of those salespeople produce total sales of 80,000 units per year while the remaining 80 salespeople produce total sales of only 20,000 units per year. The most productive 20 salespeople average selling 4,000 units per year while the 80 less productive average sales of 250 units per year. The 20 most productive salespeople create on average 16 times (4,000/250) than the average of the 80 remaining sales people. Matching the performance of the remaining 80 sales people to what the most productive 20 salespeople accomplish is a 1,500 percent solution.

Within the group of 20, some are more productive than the others. Let's assume that the most productive salesperson produces annual sales of 7,000 units. That amount is 28 times what the 80 less productive salespeople average. If the less productive people can move up to the productivity of the most productive salesperson, that's a 2,700 percent solution.

Within the group of 80, some are less productive than others. Let's assume that the least productive salesperson who won't be fired sells merely 100 units per year. If that person could match the most productive salesperson, that would be a 6,900 percent solution.

The nature of which customers are served may have something to do with why these two salespeople vary so much in productivity. But if the least productive salesperson can increase performance to even half the average of the most productive group, that's still more than a 2,000 percent solution

Let's also assume that the company has a more effective competitor where the most productive salespeople sell on average 10,000 units per year. Within that group, let's also assume that the most productive person sells 18,000 units per year. If some of this success is based on selling methods that the least productive salesperson in the first company can emulate but doesn't use now, that relatively low performing salesperson would only have to capture one-eighth of the results of this most productive competitor's salesperson to achieve a 2,000 percent solution.

In addition, there are probably better performing salespeople in other industries who could also show the lowest producing salesperson in the original company how to improve. By drawing on those examples, the least productive salespeople can expand their productivity further.

From the first company's management perspective, notice that the challenge is different. Only if the salespeople in total improve their productivity by 20 times does the company enjoy a 2,000 percent solution. Even if the methods and personal qualities of the best salesperson can be duplicated in the rest of the sales force, such a 2,000 percent solution cannot be achieved. That's because the company would still need eight salespeople to equal the 100 current salespeople in performance. Only by dropping the sales force to four people and keeping the same sales level could the company achieve a 2,000 percent solution. Reaching that level of performance would mean exceeding the productivity of the competitors' best performer. What's the solution?

The odds for creating a 2,000 percent solution for the whole sales force are improved by another factor we haven't discussed. Few of the top performing salespeople will be using identical methods. As a result, you can combine highly productive techniques to exceed the performance of even the most effective salesperson.

There's also hope for improvement from other sources. The parallel observation to Pareto's Law also applies to every other activity that a person does in a company: Twenty percent of the employees will produce 80 percent of the results. By learning from the best inside and outside the company and combining those lessons in new ways, the most productive employees can improve further.

Likewise, 20 percent of the customers will produce 80 percent of the earnings. So it's as important whom you sell to as it is how efficiently you perform. Some organizations will find that their highest volume salespeople are mostly bringing in business from relatively unprofitable customers. As a result the most profitable best practice may be found among a so-called average performer who only produces high margin sales. Cross-fertilize the methods of the high volume salesperson with the high-margin one, and you should increase the profit-productivity of sales efforts by much more than 2,000 percent.

For a given organization, simply determining who are most productive and what they do differently that may account for their success is a very powerful starting point for expanding effectiveness. That's why the few organizations that do such benchmarking within their company are quick to find ways to make enormous improvements.

At Mitchell and Company (the management consulting firm we manage to help leading companies create the next generation of best practices), we measured a large number of companies performing the same activities to see how each company's effectiveness compared to its competitors. Much like what the parallel observation to Pareto's Law suggests, companies were highly effective compared to other firms in only a few areas … usually fewer than 5 percent of their most important activities. Companies were about as effective as the average firm in about 30 percent of their important activities. And these same companies were well below average in the remaining important activities.

That measurement made us realize the enormous potential of outsourcing. If you have some activity where you are well below average throughout your company, you may have the potential for a 2,000 percent solution by simply outsourcing that same activity to a top performing outside organization.

Here's a lesson to keep in mind now that you understand that you can recognize 2,000 percent solutions virtually wherever you look: Pick the highest payoff opportunities first! We all know that each activity varies in its significance. For instance, developing new medicines at a pharmaceutical company is much more valuable than most other activities. If your company is below average in such an important activity, the company-wide benefits of either improving to become above average or outsourcing to an organization that is above average can result in a 2,000 percent solution for the entire company's profits. As a result, those who are wise in selecting the activities to improve first can make much faster progress than those who focus in less significant activities.

You should consider an even more important lesson: Some companies are making tremendous strides by developing skill throughout their organizations in designing and implementing 2,000 percent solutions. Such organizations will have vast advantages over those who simply look at the internal best practice or the industry best practice, or outsource to a highly effective outside organization. Such 2,000 percent solution expert companies will be able, instead, to advance beyond the future best practice toward the theoretical best practice. Implementing beyond the future best practice usually creates at least 5,000 percent solutions. Coming close to a theoretical (or ideal) best practice often creates 10,000 percent solutions. If you create a 2,000 percent solution that also serves to greatly expand the market by adding new users of your offerings, the gains can be exponentially larger. If your solution goes into common practice by many organizations, you may spawn a worldwide revolution in effectiveness as inventions like the wheel, the printing press, the telephone, and e-mail have done.

From that perspective, you can see that achieving a 2,000 percent solution is often a modest target … even though at first blush a 2,000 percent solution would seem to be the opposite, a stretch goal. Clients and students who have worked on creating 2,000 percent solutions were often able to reach 20 times higher performance levels within six months of implementing this solution development process. Rarely does it take longer than two years to stimulate performance to these higher levels through implementing the new practices. Individuals who have developed 2,000 percent solutions usually report being able to create the plan for one solution with less than 60 hours of effort over a few weeks. Hardly anyone ever requires more than 120 hours of personal effort.

If you would like to learn more about the 2,000 percent solution development process, see *The 2,000 Percent Solution* and *The 2,000 Percent Solution Workbook*. The rest of this book will be much more valuable if you are familiar with both those books and have applied their lessons.

Prologue

What is now proved was once only imagined.
— William Blake

It's time to take the training wheels off for those creating 2,000 percent solutions. We wrote this book, *The 2,000 Percent Squared Solution*, for those who want to create solutions that deliver 400 times more benefits, rather than the 20 times more benefits that a conventional 2,000 percent solution provides.

We realized the need for this book when one of our students began looking at how to increase consumption by more than 20 times while increasing profit margins by 20-fold. He quickly developed a business model to help joint venture partners move from serving their home apparel markets to all of the world's markets by producing high-quality fashion goods in low-cost locations. Within a few months, the potential value of his company soared from tens of thousands of dollars to several million dollars … with the opportunity to soon become several hundred million dollars, a 2,000 percent squared solution if he succeeds.

And so we wrote to this book to help others develop paths to such potentially huge advances. We wish someone had outlined this approach for our families' businesses when we were young.

In most cases, the plan for a 2,000 percent squared solution can be created with fewer than 150 hours of effort over six months or less. This experience will make you the equivalent of a Ph.D. in the subject of running your organization to be more effective. Your stakeholders and you will create the benefits of an enormous improvement that most organizations would need an army of Ph.D.s to create.

Like good parents, we wanted to make sure that you are not alone in your first attempt to create a 2,000 percent squared solution. We've written this book to be simpler and easier to use than either *The 2,000 Percent Solution* or *The 2,000 Percent Solution Workbook*. You will also find more how-to advice and examples of key points.

Our examples emphasize relatively small situations. That's deliberate. Most people work in such circumstances or are familiar with them. By looking closely at these situations, you will more readily appreciate the ideas and be able to apply the lessons. Since large organizations are usually made up of lots of small situations, these examples will be equally valuable for larger companies and nonprofit, nongovernmental organizations (NGOs).

We look forward to writing about your successes in future books. Please share those successes with us so we can learn more about creating 2,000 percent squared solutions. You may contact us by e-mail at ultimatecompetitiveadvantage@yahoo.com. Be sure to mention the title of this book in your subject line as follows: "Successful Example of Applying The 2,000 Percent Squared Solution."

Acknowledgments

Work hard, be brave and allow yourself no excuses.
— Marco-Pierre White

This book wouldn't exist without Peter Drucker's insistence that we share our method for breakthrough progress with the world. Following this path has been an incredible adventure so far. Thank you, Peter. We are sorry that you didn't live to see this book in print.

Peter's brilliant insight was that almost all organizational problems could be better solved by using the processes described in *The 2,000 Percent Solution*. Here's how he described the advantage. Rather than learn hundreds of problem-solving processes to be effective in various circumstances, people could master this one method and apply it broadly. That focus means that practitioners would be more effective by developing more skill by using this one process than those who have to apply many methods can be. Because the 2,000 percent solution methods also produce larger results, practitioners have access to more resources to make further gains. Those who become skilled in making 2,000 percent solutions soon have unstoppable advantages over organizations that do not have this capability, and the practitioners' success spreads this method into universal application.

As always, we are deeply grateful to our clients for being the first to use these concepts. We thank you also for helping us refine our ideas and presentation.

Several of the ideas for this book were developed in response to the needs of executives who take online tutorials with us. We appreciate the many remarkable solutions these dedicated knowledge seekers have shared with us. Thank you for showing us how many of the world's most difficult problems can be alleviated by knowledgeable people who live in the midst of deprivation and want to make a crucial improvement to their neighbors' lives. Since many of you prefer to labor anonymously on behalf of humanity, we have decided not to single out anyone from this group for recognition by name.

During the writing process, a number of people pored over the text. These dedicated advance readers added interesting examples, helped us smooth out our points, found ways to eliminate confusing material, and identified errors to correct. While dozens of people helped in various ways, we are especially grateful for the efforts of Elijah Chingosho, R. Dewkurun, Oliver Haggenmüller, Tom Karp, Bill Kempen, Bob Kudyba, Ikandilo Kushoka, Bill Lampton, Alain Pierre Mignon, Thabo Mosala, Sam Okoro, Athanasios Papantoniou, Roy Rissanen, Cam Scholey, Jacob Yesaya, and Mercy Yesaya.

Our wonderful editor, Bernice Pettinato of Beehive Production Services, again achieved wonders through turning our often turgid prose into lightly tripping language. This is the fourth book she has edited for us, and we continue to learn volumes from her with each successful experience.

We are pleased to again honor our coauthor of *The 2,000 Percent Solution*, Robert Metz. Thanks for showing us how to share our ideas with grace and humor. Hopefully, we've applied those lessons equally well in this book.

Thanks, also, to you, our readers. We would not keep writing books on this subject without your encouragement. Your enthusiastic support is what drives us forward to improve on what we have already shared.

Finally, we would like to recognize one another. Few people will ever know the joy that our collaborations have brought us.

Although many people made great contributions to *The 2,000 Percent Squared Solution*, we accept that the responsibility for any errors or omissions is ours alone.

*The
2,000
Percent
Squared
Solution*

Introduction

In Search of Great Solutions

Before creating the 2,000 percent solution process, we noticed that most of the world's best solutions to important problems were put into use by a few people more than 400 years before broad adoption. Consider the mortar in Roman roads. Visit Italy and you see roads that are still in use after more than 1,500 years. Watch the new concrete highways near your home, and they will soon be crumbling from ice damage, leaving endless potholes. True, the Romans didn't have large semis carrying heavy loads on their roads. But the Romans were clearly ahead of their time when it came to making roads built to last.

The Romans knew that ice is the enemy of roads. Water needs cracks to get into before it freezes and causes damage. The Romans drew from the pumice that had spewed out of Mount Etna to create finely ground, glass-based powder. When mixed into their mortar, the material became ice resistant.

By contrast, the local contractor building your concrete highway wins the bid based on the lowest price. In that environment, contractors are un-likely to insist that better roads be built. The contractor usually puts coarse material (like sand and finer bits of gravel) into the concrete. Water finds it easy to penetrate, freeze, and expand, thus destroying the concrete contain-ing these coarse materials. Some contractor then gets to rebuild the road and make a second profit, and a third, and so on. You and I pay the bills through higher gasoline taxes. We also have to align our cars more frequently.

Recently, some governments have grown wiser. They specify that the concrete has to use fine-grained material like fly ash from coal-fired plants. Fly ash is very cheap, even less costly than sand, so look for your roads to last longer in the future. How long will these roads last? We won't know for decades, but it's a nice prospect to consider.

If a solution that obvious has been overlooked for so long, we won-dered "What else are we missing?" It turns out that there's a huge backlog of great ideas we can use to make exponential progress in overcoming impor-tant problems. Let's consider the ways to make such exponential progress in more detail.

Here's a reminder of what a 2,000 percent solution is: Any meth-od of producing a 20 times increase in the usual results with the same amount of time and effort, or producing the same results with zero-to-four percent of the current time and resources ... *or some equally effective combination of both approaches.* The road example may have the potential to fit that description; you may be able to build some roads that last 21 times as long for less money and effort.

Here's what else we learned about making large improvements. Most people apply the 2,000 percent solution process to one improvement oppor-tunity at a time. The three most popular choices for creating such solutions have been:

1. Speeding up a sluggish process that's filled with unnecessary delay
2. Accelerating a slow rate of making cost reductions
3. Eliminating errors in an ineffective process

By themselves, such improvements provide remarkable benefits for stakeholders (those who are affected by the organization's or the individu-al's efforts) and delight those who develop the solutions. We congratulate all who have accomplished such fine results.

Relatively few, however, take the poetic road "less traveled by" to seek first expanding usage by 21 times ... but that road makes "all the dif-

ference." Why is that more desirable road usually avoided? We think it has something to do with low self-esteem. New 2,000 percent solution creators often tell us during the early stages of their investigations that they lack confidence they will succeed. Unless they cannot find a real mess in an existing activity that seems easy to fix, these new solution creators are unlikely to want to tackle expanding usage. Paradoxically, such expansions usually also deliver astonishingly better ways to speed up sluggish processes, accelerate cost reductions, develop better offerings, and eliminate errors. This opportunity to greatly expand usage seems to be one of those rare cases where you can have your cake and eat it too!

When both usage and delivery effectiveness improve, stakeholders can gain 20 times more benefits than from either improvement alone. When that combination happens, these two complementary 2,000 percent solutions acquire the power of 20 or more individual 2,000 percent solutions. That's what we mean by a 2,000 percent squared solution. You can also think of this concept as developing a 40,000 percent solution, or a 400 times increase in benefits.

To some, that goal may seem remote. Keep an open mind while we share some examples of our experiences in creating 2,000 percent squared solutions for inexpensively attracting more readers to our books.

In 1998, a best-selling author friend told us that it was important to distribute tens of thousands of free copies of business books either just before the book is published or right after publication. Tom Peters, coauthor of *In Search of Excellence* (reissue edition, Warner Books, 1988), tells the same story about one aspect of how that book became a blockbuster.

When *The 2,000 Percent Solution* was being written, we heeded that advice. Before publication, we sent out thousands of draft copies for advance reading. After publication, we sent out thousands more free copies of the completed book to influential readers. In addition, we created a Web site for the book and put all but two chapters online there for free reader access. The cost to do this sampling was over $40,000. We estimate that these activities have directly yielded 20,000 people who have read some part of that book. That means our cost per reader for just this activity was about $2.00. Since royalties on books like ours are usually around $2.00, this was a money-losing proposition unless this distribution yielded sales of at least 20,000 additional books. In the case of our friend, this was no concern because his company had paid this sampling expense. Our costs, however, came out of our personal pockets. We needed to do better.

For *The Ultimate Competitive Advantage* (Berrett-Koehler, 2003), we decided to create a 2,000 percent squared solution for advance distribution. For that book, we only provided free advance copies to those who helped us create the book. Our cost for those copies was about $1,200. We then wrote brief articles based on the book and arranged to have them published in prestigious journals and magazines such as *Leader to Leader, Chief Learning Officer,* and *The Journal of Business Strategy.* We next condensed the articles and turned them into brief guides that Amazon.com publishes for free. In the first two years, we estimate that over 30,000 people read some part of that book through these efforts. We estimate that total readership through this approach will swell to 100,000 people by the time *The Ultimate Competitive Advantage* has been in print as long as *The 2,000 Percent Solution* has been. If that occurs, we will have produced 100,000 readers at a cost of $1,200. That means our cost per reader will be $0.012. The first book's campaign cost us 166 times as much per reader as what the latter campaign did, and we will actually draw more readers with the new, less expensive effort. These estimated results will provide us with a 66,000 percent solution compared to our first approach (16,500 percent lower cost per reader multiplied by 400 percent more readers).

For a forthcoming book we are developing, that sampling solution has been further enhanced. The prelaunch involves a daily blog in which the material is tested for reader reaction. We estimate that more than 200,000 people will have read some part of the book through the blog before the book is published, and our cost is only the electricity to post the blog entries. We will also reuse the Amazon.com guides that worked well for *The Ultimate Competitive Advantage* to add another 100,000 readers at limited cost. Publication publicity will probably draw another few hundred thousand people to the blog samples. We also plan to send millions of excerpts for free by e-mail to people who subscribe to various complementary newsletters. We should be able to increase our total readers by several hundred more percent. Since we carry advertising on the blog, we have a revenue offset to our costs. If enough clicks occur from our blog to advertisers' sites, this sampling program may well turn out to be free to us. As you can see, repeating such a process on the same or a similar problem can be profoundly valuable in making further improvements.

To put these 2,000 percent squared solutions into perspective, you need to know what Peter Drucker taught us: Surveys show that only about 10 percent of all business books that are purchased are actually read by anyone. Even more surprisingly, only one in a hundred business books sold is read cover to cover. As a result, a massive business best seller may have only 20,000 readers, and almost all of those have read just part of the book. Our 2,000 percent squared solution activities allow us to easily and effortlessly share our message with far more people than business best sellers do at a minimal cost that almost anyone can afford. If anyone buys our books based on these low-cost previews, we definitely have an economic gain.

Reading Directions

In this book, we build on what you have learned by reading and applying *The 2,000 Percent Solution* and *The 2,000 Percent Solution Workbook*. Although *The 2,000 Percent Squared Solution* was written as a stand-alone book, you will gain much more benefit from this book if you are already familiar with its two similarly titled predecessors.

Like those books, this book, too, is designed to be applied. You will gather less than 1 percent of the potential benefit until you apply this book's lessons for creating two complementary 2,000 percent solutions.

While the earlier books emphasized business examples from the United States, in *The 2,000 Percent Squared Solution* we also explore global humanitarian examples for those who provide social services to the needy and hurting. We made this addition to assist all those who are applying the 2,000 percent solution process in nonprofit organizations.

In Part One, you learn how to create a 2,000 percent solution that expands usage by more than 21 times. In a for-profit enterprise, expanding usage means increasing revenues by 21 plus times. In a humanitarian organization, expanding usage means that 21 times as many recipients enjoy benefits.

In many cases, optimal solutions involve leading both kinds of expansions. For-profit customer increases create cash flow to provide more free services to poor people for organizations like Aravind Eye Care System in India (see *The Fortune at the Bottom of the Pyramid* by C. K. Prahalad, Wharton School Publishing, 2005, pp. 265-286). Such free services offer the potential to reduce costs for all those served and make serving paying customers more profitable. That cost improvement adds more cash flow to provide free services, and so on.

In Part Two, you find a powerful guide for making large cost reductions independent of the expansion size involved. This subject is important because cost reductions are a primary source of the money required to attract more customers and to serve more needy people.

Following the theme of the road less traveled, Part One uses the metaphor of planning and building a new, high-speed highway ... one that no one has traveled before but that will appeal to many people once they try it. In Part Two, we use the metaphor of traveling more efficiently in a car on that high-speed road to explore successful application of a cost-reduction focus.

Each chapter describes helpful steps to take. Read and apply each step. Chapters contain questions that you should be sure to answer in order to best apply the steps. We suggest that you record your answers in a notebook or computer file. You will find it helpful to review what you first noted when you repeat the process.

Be sure to pay attention to all the examples. Each story was chosen to demonstrate one or more principles that almost any organization can adapt for its own use. If at first you don't see an application for anything described in a story, be sure to reread such examples until an application occurs to you. To grasp the opportunity, you may have to increase or decrease scale, substitute terms or conditions, adjust incentives, or combine methods among examples. Feel free to let your mind move laterally from what's great or important about an example to tailor an approach that fits your situation like a personalized item of apparel.

Here's more about something we mentioned in the earlier section, "What Is a 2,000 Percent Solution?," to show you how to apply the examples. In *The Ultimate Competitive Advantage* we described how Goldcorp, the gold mining company, found much more gold and at less cost by running a worldwide contest for geologists than by doing exploratory drilling of its self-perceived best prospects. The key concept behind the Goldcorp example is to engage as many more people as you can who have potentially valuable new perspectives, while spending less time and money than you do now to improve your most valuable activities. Any method that pursues this principle could be an appropriate application of the example. If you work in a mining company, you could also have a contest for geologists, but an aerospace company might have a contest for engineers. Such a contest could easily be unethical if conflicts of interest arise, so an application where that risk exists might have to be avoided. In other cases, such as where investment bankers are involved, perhaps no one would be willing to compete unless contingent fees are provided for the winners as prizes.

The questions within each chapter are designed to help you connect the dots from the examples to a solution that fits your situation. Our goal is to make you more adept at connecting your own dots. We've learned that almost everyone can draw on their own perspectives and experiences to develop superior solutions to those of an outside expert through using this process. No two dot-connectors will draw the same image, and that variety usually opens the door to more gains.

Some strategic management scholars who reviewed this book noted that we do not cite a number of popular conceptual and how-to books in that discipline. That choice was deliberate. The books we reviewed that are related in intent are either very dated in their approach, ignore the lessons of continuing business model innovation (which we reported for the first time in *The Ultimate Competitive Advantage*), assume a top-down approach is the only method that will work, limit their focus to large for-profit enterprises, or are constrained by assumptions that are easily overcome by the 2,000 percent solution process. Instead, we are defining for you a breakthrough approach that any for-profit or nonprofit organization, regardless of size, can apply. To mention those less helpful works would needlessly complicate our simple, but detailed, story. Where management books contribute theory or examples that further our message based on our decades of experience in this field, we have cited those references to help you.

If you want to see the new concept of this book in context, let us offer this brief commentary. Two major waves of management methods for seeking more perfect solutions preceded the 2,000 percent solution and the 2,000 percent squared solution. The first search lasted for many decades and emphasized finding problems within an organization and eliminating those problems. The early work of the various quality movements emphasized this approach. While many benefits came from this work, the focus eventually proved to be too narrow to unleash the highest levels of potential performance. The second wave of seeking solutions was to focus instead on processes and eliminate dysfunctions from those processes. One weakness of this approach related to picking optimization targets that compromised performance in terms of stakeholders who were not being considered. In addition, it proved to be difficult to implement the process changes that were sought. Our approach shifts focus from those earlier approaches by selecting outcome-based principles to guide the efforts and considering the whole environment in which the organization operates as the realm within which to optimize cooperation and mutual benefit among stakeholders. Outcome-based principles show great promise for continually lifting our horizons into more valuable, more satisfying, and more effective improvements. To learn about those differences in the nature and scale of improvements, compare the solutions this book leads you to create with the solutions that your past improvement methods would have produced.

Part One

Build the High-Speed Road to 21 Times More Availability

Speed, it seems to me, provides the one genuinely modern pleasure.
— Aldous Huxley

Our first trip on a German autobahn was an experience we'll never forget. There's no speed limit on these well-engineered and flawlessly maintained roads. Many people drive high-powered Porsches, BMWs, and Mercedes that are designed to almost fly over these routes.

The CEO of a prominent German company loaned one of us his personal car and driver for a quick jaunt to the airport. Thank God for that favor: Otherwise, one of us would have been driving and neither had driven faster than 120 m.p.h. before. On the autobahn driving at 120 is like poking along at 55 m.p.h. on an American freeway. We passed that speed within a few seconds. Before long, the speedometer topped 250 kilometers an hour (roughly 160 m.p.h.). It was exciting, but that initial reaction began to turn into fear. Fortunately, the driver glanced back and noticed a slightly green passenger … and the car slowed. At 140 m.p.h. the anxious passenger relaxed. That lower speed then felt comfortably slow even though it was much faster than prior experiences. This trip proved that you can get used to anything pretty quickly. And the faster you adjust, the sooner you make more progress and enjoy the process.

Some people experience the same sense of combined excitement and fear when they first think about making benefits available to 21 times as many people. In this part of the book we start at a slow pace and accelerate gradually past your current experience to make it easier for you to adjust to this faster journey.

Let's think about scale for a moment. The average business serving individuals has fewer than 1,000 customers. The average business addressing the needs of companies has fewer than 30 customers. If you compare those numbers to the world's population (over 6 billion) and the number of businesses (many millions), you quickly appreciate the untapped potential for the average business to expand. By comparison, many schools, hospitals, local charities, and town government departments directly serve no more than a few hundred people a week. Even if one of these organizations suddenly expanded its scope by 2,000 percent, the resulting scale would still be small compared to global potential.

Similarly, the largest companies and nonprofit organizations are serving considerably less than 1 percent of the world's population at any moment. Clearly, these larger organizations also have substantial opportunities to expand their delivery of goods and services.

For now, just enjoy thinking about how much delight you will gain from providing your own offerings in 21 times greater volume … especially if you can reach that level at your own comfortable pace.

Here's a look at the road to increased usage you'll follow in Part One.

At the beginning of your journey, you need to decide what kind of performance you want to expand by 21 times. Sometimes the answer is obvious. Other times, you have to look beyond the obvious. For instance if you currently sell furnaces, you could decide to sell furnaces to 21 times more people to reach 21 times greater volume. That's fine. But if you look around, you may find a better choice. Since people buy your furnaces to make their homes warmer, you may choose to also help them improve their warmth in other ways as well (such as by installing needed insulation) and gain some of your increased volume from your expanded scope of offerings.

Likewise, a nonprofit organization may be providing food for poor people who are looking for work. You could decide to feed 21 times as many people. Or you could also decide to help unemployed poor people find jobs. Even better, you can help the unemployed find great jobs serving other unemployed people to find great jobs as well.

Chapter 1 can help you consider whether you want to deliver more of the same benefits or a better combination of benefits.

Chapter 2 addresses why some people refrain from buying or using your offerings. These limiting factors may include personal stalls such as ignorance, misconceptions, disbelief, sloth, lack of time, being short of money, and emotional discomfort with what you offer. You can uncover the hidden barriers to expansion by asking this question: "How much would I have to pay you to take and use my offering?" Yes, even many free services are so unattractive to potential users that you would have to pay them a significant amount to take and use the offering. By asking how much and why people want to be paid, you'll find powerful flaws with what you're offering.

In Chapter 3 you consider how to eliminate the barriers to expanded usage that you found in Chapter 2. First, brainstorm with others to accumulate as many ideas as possible. Second, thrash those idea grain stacks to separate out just the choicest seeds of potential improvement. Third, compare those best barrier-busting opportunities to select the methods that match your resources.

Chapter 4 discusses how to implement barrier-busting plans. By anticipating what could go wrong and preparing for those issues, you will finish paving your faster route sooner so you can begin serving more people.

In Chapter 5 you learn how to speed up progress by applying some 2,000 percent solutions for expanding awareness and usage of your offerings. You also explore how to ensure that everyone will be delighted with your expanded availability.

Chapter 1

Find the Ideal Route
Determine What Benefits
to Make More Available

If you ever plan to motor west,
travel my way,
take the highway that's the best ...
Get your kicks on Route 66.
— Bobby Troup

From space many places on Earth look pretty flat. From the ground more obstacles become apparent: Granite mountains loom in places where chasms divide neighboring areas. Both perspectives tell you something you need to know. The space view shows you the most direct route as the proverbial crow flies, while the close-up view shows you obstacles that are well worth avoiding where that's possible. In this chapter, the broadest perspective, like that from space, is emphasized. That perspective encompasses expanding your business model in volume-improving ways.

In considering how to expand your business model's delivery of offerings and benefits, you should be guided by what will be easily understandable and desirable by your stakeholders ... and where the adjustments will provide more profit for businesses and more effectiveness for nonprofit organizations. Business model innovation is something that many organizations struggle with. In this chapter, we've broken out the elements and added continuing examples to make innovative business model thinking and analysis easier to do. This chapter's material will, however, be clearest to those who have already read *The Ultimate Competitive Advantage*.

Expand What You Do Now

Unless you are providing a very small percentage of the needs of each customer or beneficiary, growing by 21-fold requires adding customers or beneficiaries. Because so many organizations can expand to provide 21 times the number of customers or beneficiaries, that's a great place to begin. You should start by considering who you will serve as these added customers and beneficiaries and where those benefits will be delivered to make the expansion more practical.

Let's share a story with you that we first examined in *The Ultimate Competitive Advantage* to help make that point about who and where clearer. A young married couple, Mr. William and Ms. Dorothy Hustead, bought a small store in a tiny town near the South Dakota Badlands. From 1931 to 1936, they struggled through the Depression serving the town's 326 impoverished residents.

One day in 1936, Ms. Hustead, bothered by the sound of cars on the nearby highway heading for Mount Rushmore, persuaded her husband to expand their business to serve these travelers. Mr. Hustead put up signs on the highway to draw visitors to their store, making a unique appeal. The signs said, "Free Ice Water … Wall Drug." In those days before automobile air conditioning was common, that offer was a powerful appeal. Beginning from this humble expansion of its customer base, Wall Drug now serves more than 20,000 visitors a day during the summer in its Wall, South Dakota, store and many more on its Web site, www.walldrug.com.

Who Is Served and Where

Let's begin considering volume-expanding business models by looking at "who" is served. The lesson is to keep it simple. Change as little as possible while becoming more efficient and effective as an organization for your customers and beneficiaries. The simplest way to do this is to put more volume through an existing organizational structure without adding fixed costs or increasing the ratio of variable costs to sales.

In a for-profit organization you will naturally first want to attract the most profitable potential customers. If current customers buy a very small percentage (say 1 to 2 percent) of their needs from you, such a profitable expansion may simply be possible by selling 40 to 50 times more to selected current customers. You are already spending time and money to gather a small part of these customers' total requirements. In many cases your overhead costs to provide more products and services would not increase.

Let's assume your current pretax profits are 10 percent of sales and your contribution to profits before overhead costs is 30 percent of sales. This circumstance means that selling more of the same mix of offerings at the same price to an existing customer would almost triple the profit contribution margin on the increased sales. Were that to occur, a 20 times increase in volume would lead to a 60 times increase in profits! See Example 1 if you want to explore how this could happen.

Example 1: Adding 20 Times More Revenues Without Increasing Overhead Costs Speeds Profit Growth

If corporate overhead cost remains constant while profit contribution grows to $6.3 million from $0.3 million, pretax profits expand by $6.0 million (60-fold) while earning the same profit contribution as a percentage of revenues.

Annual Pro Forma Financials Before Volume Expands

Revenues	$1,000,000	100 percent of revenues
Cost of providing offerings	700,000	70 percent of revenues
Profit contribution	300,000	30 percent of revenues
Corporate overhead cost	200,000	20 percent of revenues
Pretax profit	100,000	10 percent of revenues

20 Times Volume Increase with No Additional Overhead Expenses

Revenues	$21,000,000	100 percent of revenues
Cost of providing offerings	14,700,000	70 percent of revenues
Profit contribution	6,300,000	30 percent of revenues
Corporate overhead cost	200,000	1 percent of revenues
Pretax profit	6,100,000	29 percent of revenues

In a nonprofit organization there's a similar savings incentive to provide more of the same offerings to the same recipients. Let's consider an organization that carries donated food by truck to distribution centers serving needy families. Most such distribution centers provide a small portion of a family's total weekly needs — perhaps as little as one meal a week. The families may be visiting 10 to 30 different distribution centers weekly to fulfill all their needs. The trucks carrying the goods to a given distribution center are often owned and operated by that center, may be in use for only a few hours a week, and could be operated much more often.

Let's assume that more volunteers can be found to load the food, and drive and unload the trucks. Both the nonprofit organization and the needy families will benefit economically if 21 meals weekly are delivered and distributed at one time to a distribution center. See Example 2 for a quantification of this point.

Example 2: Adding Trip Volume for an Underutilized Truck to Increase Food Available to Needy Families for Each Pick Up

When a truck isn't driven very much, its capital costs (depreciation of its value from the purchase price) exceed the operating costs. Put that truck into use more often and you are able to divide the capital costs over more miles. As a result, your cost per trip of the same distance will become much smaller.

Truck Beginning Point — 1 Truck Trip per Week

Annual truck capital costs	$52,000
(5,200 miles per year)	
Capital cost per trip	1,000

20 Times Truck Volume Increase — 21 Truck Trips per Week

Annual truck capital costs	$109,200
(109,200 miles per year)	
Capital cost per trip	100

Note: Annual capital cost is higher because service life is reduced by driving more miles a year.

Recipients' automobile operating costs, by comparison, vary directly with use. Driving 21 times as much results in spending 21 times as much. If they can reduce their driving, however, their operating costs per week go down.

Automobile Operating Costs Beginning Point for Recipients — 21 Pickups per Week

Weekly gas, oil, and maintenance	$21.00
Cost per pickup	1.00

Automobile Operating Cost — 1 Trip per Week

Weekly gas, oil, and maintenance	$ 1.00
Cost per pickup	1.00

By contrast, if an organization picks people and organizations to serve who are located far away and desire less profitable offerings, this choice of who is served and where to serve them can increase costs to serve each customer and beneficiary versus doing more with the same customers. For instance, if the for-profit company seeks to serve new customers globally who require local support, the company's overhead and the cost of offerings may grow faster than revenues. In that case, absolute profits may decline or even turn into a loss. See Example 3 which quantifies this circumstance. Or if the nonprofit's food distribution truck has to serve families all over a large country and recipients still receive only one meal per week, the cost to deliver the food will increase from the expanded volume case described in Example 2 even though the same number of people are served in both cases. Look at Example 4 to see details of why this cost increase can occur.

Example 3: Adding Less Profitable Revenues in Diverse Locations Increases Offering and Overhead Costs

More volume doesn't automatically translate into more profits. If you have to sell items with less profit contribution as a percentage of sales due to new customer preferences and your overhead costs grow, you'll more than offset the profit gain you hoped to obtain. In this example, the corporate overhead cost remains almost constant as a percentage of sales through the need to support more geographic areas with administration, while the profit contribution percentage drops from 30 percent to 20 percent. However, if overhead costs go up enough as a percentage of revenues, the effect can be to turn a profit into a loss.

Annual Pro Forma Financials Before Volume Expands

Revenues	$1,000,000	100 percent of revenues
Cost of providing offerings	700,000	70 percent of revenues
Profit contribution	300,000	30 percent of revenues
Corporate overhead cost	200,000	20 percent of revenues
Pretax profit	100,000	10 percent of revenues

20 Times Volume Increase with Higher Offering Costs and Overhead

Revenues	$21,000,000	100 percent of revenues
Cost of providing offerings	16,800,000	80 percent of revenues
Profit contribution	4,200,000	20 percent of revenues
Corporate overhead cost	4,150,000	20 percent of revenues
Pretax profit	50,000	<1 percent of revenues

Example 4: **Adding Truck Trip Volume but Expanding Miles Driven per Trip by a Large Factor and Keeping Food Received per Family Pickup the Same**

While driving more miles can reduce capital costs per year for a vehicle, there's a limit to how far this efficiency goes. In this example, you drive such longer distances that you actually wear out your vehicles and have to buy new ones. In addition, your operating costs of fuel, oil, and maintenance would also be higher from taking longer delivery trips. In this example, the longer and more frequent trips lead to a slower rate of reduction in capital costs per trip than in Example 2.

Truck Beginning Point — One Truck Trip per Week

Annual truck capital costs	$52,000
(5,200 miles per year)	
Capital cost per trip	1,000

20 Times Truck Volume Increase with Tripling of Miles Driven per Trip

Annual truck capital costs	$327,600
(327,600 miles per year)	
Additional truck operating costs	81,900
Capital cost and additional operating costs per trip	400

Notes: Annual capital cost is higher than in Example 2 because service life is reduced by driving more miles a year. The $400 capital cost and additional operating cots per trip is three hundred dollars more per trip than in Example 2.

Automobile Beginning Point for Recipients — 21 Pick Ups per Week

Weekly gas, oil, and maintenance	$21.00
Cost per pickup	1.00

Since pickup frequency remains the same, recipients receive no benefit in reduced costs.

What Is Served

Selling or providing more of what you already offer can be a big help in creating efficiencies. But sometimes you are serving virtually all of someone's needs for those items as the Husteads were doing in Wall Drug during 1931 through 1936. Another part of Wall Drug's success came later from continually expanding its offerings. The current store offers much increased choice compared to 1936 in its 76,000 square feet (almost the size of two football fields).

The application to a for-profit organization is obvious. What else can you profitably sell or provide at a fair price with desirable qualities and service that the customers you already have want to buy? The advent of the Internet makes this evaluation much more potentially rewarding because postal, air freight, and electronic delivery choices enable you to serve most of the world. If Wall Drug doesn't already, the firm will eventually offer some items and services on its Web site that wouldn't be profitable enough to place in the South Dakota store.

As with the previous examples, this for-profit challenge requires considering the potential volume and the effects on overhead costs and profit contribution margins. Example 5 shows the kind of effect that a positive change in volume can make by adding volume through more profitable items that do not increase overhead costs very much.

Example 5: Adding More Profitable Items to Expand Revenues Without Increasing Overhead Costs as Rapidly Further Speeds Profit Growth

This example shows the profit multiplying potential of increasing profit contribution margins from 30 percent to 40 percent while decreasing corporate overhead costs from 20 percent to 3 percent of revenues. The result is a 7,700 percent profit solution. If revenues could be grown even more, a 40,000 percent solution (a 2,000 percent squared solution) could result.

Annual Pro Forma Financials Before Volume Expands

Revenues	$1,000,000	100 percent of revenues
Cost of providing offerings	700,000	70 percent of revenues
Profit contribution	300,000	30 percent of revenues
Corporate overhead cost	200,000	20 percent of revenues
Pretax profit	100,000	10 percent of revenues

20 Times Volume Increase with Higher Profit Contribution Products and Limited Additional Overhead Expenses

Revenues	$21,000,000	100 percent of revenues
Cost of providing offerings	12,600,000	60 percent of revenues
Profit contribution	8,400,000	40 percent of revenues
Corporate overhead cost	600,000	3 percent of revenues
Pretax profit	7,800,000	37 percent of revenues

A similar effect occurs in food trucking by the nonprofit organization if items dense in nutrients and weight are shipped instead (e.g., old-fashioned oatmeal versus potato chips). See Example 6 for a quantification of this factor.

Example 6: Adding Helpful Nutrient Volume Through an Underutilized Truck and Increasing Food Available to Needy Families

Capital costs can be lowered greatly if we carry food that contains more helpful nutrients per volume. By shipping foods with 10 times as many nutrients, we are able to lower the capital cost per trip/unit of helpful nutrients by another 90 percent.

Truck Beginning Point — 1 Truck Trip per Week

Annual truck capital costs	$52,000
(5,200 miles per year)	
Capital cost per trip	1,000
Capital cost/unit of helpful nutrients	0.10

20 Times Truck Volume Increase with Denser Nutrients — 21 Truck Trips per Week

Annual truck capital costs	$109,200
(109,200 miles per year)	
Capital cost per trip	100
Capital cost/unit of helpful nutrients	0.001

Note: Annual capital cost is higher because service life is reduced by driving more miles a year.

Increasing nutrient density has a similar effect on the recipients costs. The 96 percent cost-reduction from fewer trips is improved by providing 10 times more nutrient-dense foods.

Automobile Operating Costs Beginning Point for Recipients — 21 Pick Ups per Week

Weekly gas, oil and maintenance	$21.00
Weekly gas, oil and maintenance/	
Unit of helpful nutrients	0.21

Automobile Operating Cost — 1 Trip per Week for Denser Nutrients

Weekly gas, oil and maintenance	$ 1.00
Weekly gas, oil and maintenance/	
Unit of helpful nutrients	0.00084

Alternatively, if a for-profit company's overhead and waste grow too rapidly as a result of adding potentially more profitable items (such as offering dozens of flavors of ice cream and frozen yogurt during the winter in a cold climate), profits will decline from that kind of growth. Example 7 shows a quantification of this risk.

Example 7: Adding More Profitable Items to Expand Revenues Hurts Profits When Overhead and Waste Costs Grow Too Rapidly

The potential profit gains from higher profit contribution percentages (going from 30 percent to 40 percent in this example) can be more than offset if waste and overhead costs grow too rapidly in providing required items. Perishable, high-tech, and fashion items often have this problem as time causes value to decline, resulting in waste or markdown charges. Higher profit contribution offerings often require more administration and service to support them.

Annual Pro Forma Financials Before Volume Expands

Revenues	$1,000,000	100 percent of revenues
Cost of providing offerings	700,000	70 percent of revenues
Profit contribution	300,000	30 percent of revenues
Corporate overhead cost	200,000	20 percent of revenues
Pretax profit	100,000	10 percent of revenues

20 Times Volume Increase with Higher Profit Contribution Items and Faster Growth in Overhead and Waste Expenses

Revenues	$21,000,000	100 percent of revenues
Cost of providing offerings	12,600,000	60 percent of revenues
Profit contribution	8,400,000	40 percent of revenues
Added waste and markdowns	3,150,000	15 percent of revenues
Corporate overhead cost	5,200,000	25 percent of revenues
Pretax profit	50,000	<1 percent of revenues

If you consider the nonprofit trucking example for food distribution, a similar point becomes readily apparent. Trucks that haul frozen foods are different from those that haul refrigerated foods and dry goods. Most distribution centers for poor people provide only dry goods. If the distribution centers add frozen foods, a special truck will have to be purchased and a freezer added. Electricity costs will soar, and there will be less space for dry goods. Unless a lot more volume goes through these new facilities, the added costs may exceed the value of the benefits to food recipients compared to sticking with dry goods providing the same nutrient volume. If the foods transported are less nutrient dense, the cost of delivering a unit of helpful nutrients may increase compared to what is shown in Example 6. The economics of this reduction in beneficiary value delivered are displayed in Example 8.

Example 8: Adding Less Nutrient-Dense Volume with Frozen Food to Increase Food Available to Needy Families

In this example, a change in what is delivered increases capital costs in total by sixfold. This shift in costs is made worse by a 90 percent reduction in nutrients being delivered.

20 Times Dry Goods Truck Volume Increase with Denser Dry Nutrient Foods — 21 Truck Trips per Week

Annual truck capital costs (109,200 miles per year)	$109,200
Capital cost per trip	100
Capital cost/unit of helpful nutrients	0.001

Note: Annual capital cost is higher because service life is reduced by driving more miles a year.

20 Times Volume Increase with Less Nutrient-Dense Foods Including Frozen Items — 21 Truck Trips per Week

Annual truck and storage capital and added operating costs	$655,200
Capital cost per trip	600
Capital cost/unit of helpful nutrients	0.06

Note: Driving requires two trucks (one for dry goods and one for frozen foods), a freezer, more dry storage space, and added electricity costs.

When the Offering Is Provided

If Wall Drug had begun 24 hour a day operations in the early 1930s, that action would have added costs for electricity and staff, but probably little more volume. The town's residents knew that they could buy from the only pharmacy in town during the day. If they had an emergency need in the night, they could always knock on the door at the Hustead's house. After the highway signs began to attract a larger customer base, being open longer hours did begin to pay off. Likewise, the Wall Drug Web site wouldn't make as much profit if it were open less often than 24 hours a day, every day of the year.

Profit-making businesses can run tests to see when sales volume increases enough to pay for added overhead, operating, and capital costs. The analysis of this situation can be put into the format displayed in examples 1 and 3 after tests have been run.

A nonprofit organization will often see great enhancements to benefits received by stakeholders from being open more hours, when additional donated goods and services and volunteers are available. In the food distribution example, working poor families may be able to reduce pickup costs by timing trips to match daily commutes to and from work when the distribution centers are open before and after normal working hours. The analysis of this opportunity can be displayed using the format in examples 2 and 4. Like the for-profit organizations, the demand for such expanded hours can be tested and the benefits received compared to the added electricity and other added operating and overhead costs. Obviously, the potential for recipients taking excess goods and reselling them is present, and that risk will have to be managed. An electronic card system, similar to that used in university cafeterias, might be used to monitor frequency of access and quantities taken.

How the Offering Is Provided

If Wall Drug had delivered ice water to cars in the parking lot during the 1930s, those coming for the free ice water would have been thrilled. Wall Drug might, however, have earned less if some potential customers left with the ice water without entering the store. Once inside, many people looking for free ice water also bought small items and ate ice cream cones.

For-profit businesses should always be testing to see how different ways of supplying an offering affect demand and costs. Pizza parlors in college towns wouldn't sell nearly as many pizzas if they didn't offer dorm delivery. Students are willing to pay more to have a pizza delivered, so the added cost doesn't hurt the business's volume. Enterprising owners of such take-out pizzerias have been known to send their drivers out stuffing menus under dormitory doors on slow nights. Volume quickly picks up when the menus are delivered.

Examples 1 and 3 again provide a useful format for analyzing the results of such tests involving how the offering is provided for the impact on volume and costs.

Nonprofit organizations often find that demand increases geometrically if the offering is provided in more convenient ways. For instance, needy patients who live a long way from hospitals seldom return for tests, even when the tests are free, because the patients often have limited access to and funds for transportation. Mobile clinics that provide testing services in the evenings can increase the quality and frequency of health care for those with the most serious conditions at limited cost. Similarly, if the food distribution centers were willing to provide free home delivery at recipient-selected times, few needy families would fail to avail themselves of the service. For those who are ill, such a service may be essential to receiving the food. If volunteers are willing to use their own cars, gasoline, and time to deliver the food, a nonprofit organization can increase its reach greatly by coordinating such improved accessibility.

Examples 2 and 4 can again be used as a format to evaluate the economic impact of the changed method after a test has determined how usage and costs are affected.

Why the Offering Is Used

Adding new reasons to use an existing product or service can provide an enormous business improvement. Our mothers used Arm & Hammer® Baking Soda in cooking when we were young. We knew that good eating was ahead whenever one of our moms took out her orange box. From the company's point of view, moms couldn't bake often enough. But one teaspoon of baking soda would produce eight dozen cookies. Church & Dwight, which made this brand of baking soda, needed new reasons why people should use their product. Someone discovered that bicarbonate of soda also made a good air freshener in a refrigerator. Suddenly, a family was using as much of the product to deodorize its refrigerator for six months as went into over 9,000 cookies. Revenues and profits soared.

Literacy programs often provide free services to the poor. Many such programs falter, however, when all they offer is remedial reading aimed at helping the student read at a fourth-grade level rather than a third-grade level. These are adults, and they have limited need to add one year of elementary school reading skill. Some programs overcome this lack of relevance by letting prospective students influence their curriculum to achieve some personal purpose. Parents want to be able to help their children with homework. Some readers want to learn how to fill out job applications. Others need to know how to fill out forms to apply for government benefits. Still others want to be able to read the Bible. When the literacy programs are customized in these ways to serve the student's purpose, attendance improves and learning accelerates.

How Much the Offering Costs to Use

Many for-profit manufacturers and service providers concentrate only on influencing their own prices and costs. In the process they ignore or are insensitive to what customers and end users pay to use these offerings. While this narrow viewpoint may be profitable, much more profit is missed because demand is dampened due to soaring costs incurred by customers and end users.

For example, our banker called to suggest that we open new personal checking accounts. These accounts are free. We didn't really need these checking accounts, but our interest was piqued when he told us we would each receive a free Blackberry® portable digital assistant (PDA). We don't need Blackberry® PDAs, but figured that we could sell them on eBay and make a profit to put into our new checking accounts. After signing up for checking accounts, we learned that we would only receive the Blackberry® PDAs if we subscribed to a service costing $720 for a year. Suddenly, we had checking accounts and "free" certificates for PDAs we didn't want to spend $720 to use. The bank had wasted its time and money on us, and we had checking accounts we didn't need.

Presumably enough other people signed up who used the accounts to make the promotion successful. The bank may have thought that it had won. But here's what it had missed. If the bank had instead offered a $200 off value on the PDA and six months of free service, we probably would have tried the Blackberry® PDAs. If we had liked the product and service, we would probably have continued to use the PDAs and think favorably of the bank when we did. Or if the bank had offered us $100 off the PDA's price and no required service, we could have pursued our original plan and sold these products on eBay for a profit.

Nonprofit organizations can have similar problems of not taking all costs into account. A country's health ministry decided to help limit the spread of sexually transmitted diseases by making condoms available. But there were not enough condoms to match the demand in some distribution centers. When the condoms were unavailable or unaffordable, many men began washing the condoms and reusing them, in some cases even sharing used condoms with other men for additional reuse. Having become accustomed to these practices, some men favored the convenience of reusing condoms even when new ones were available for free. This government policy may have unintentionally helped spread sexually transmitted diseases by giving their citizens the false impression that sexual partners were safe as long as a condom was used.

Go Beyond the Scope and Concept of What You Do Now

Let's return to Wall Drug in the 1930s to explore expanding a for-profit business's scope and concept. People heading for the Black Hills also needed services. Wall Drug could have checked car radiators to see if they needed more water and could have helped tired travelers make motel reservations, plan side trips to little-known attractions, obtain referrals to South Dakota physicians and dentists, and acquire local towing insurance for their cars.

While the free ice water was welcome to hot, tired travelers, Wall Drug failed to appreciate that such travelers were primarily trying to enjoy a nice vacation and would have welcomed many reasonably priced, vacation-enhancing services. Wall Drug could have offered some of those services for free to the travelers by relying on commissions from motels, attractions, and insurance companies. While checking the radiators, Wall Drug would have found plenty of cars that needed gasoline, oil, filters, windshield wiper blades, spark plugs, and other minor items that could have been provided after the radiator water was checked. The Husteads would have benefited by realizing that they were also in the business of improving vacation travel, rather than only selling pharmacy items.

Nonprofit organizations are often similarly too narrow in their thinking. We have visited many food distribution centers for needy families, but don't recall ever seeing such a center that provided a way for the unemployed to find work. While hundreds of families are lined up for the groceries, a separate set of volunteers could be helping match people to available jobs in the area. Volunteers could help those with limited reading and writing skills to explore lists and fill out applications. Cellular phones could be shared to make job interview appointments. These centers should see their role as helping the needy to be able to provide for their own needs. As the Chinese proverb says, you do more good if you teach someone to fish rather than just providing a fish for today's meal.

As an example of how more can be accomplished by thinking about other ways to help, Habitat for Humanity found that it could multiply its global efforts by encouraging national organizations to send one-tenth of the money they raise to other countries. While a new home in the United States might cost $50,000 to build, an African home might cost only $500. By sharing 10 percent of the money they raise, a U.S. affiliate can increase the number of families served by their funds as many as 10-fold. In addition, the Habitat families and volunteers learn to build homes, take care of the homes, and help others build their homes. In many cases, the families and volunteers can then find work in home building and related trades. As the no-interest mortgages are repaid, poor families are also providing funds for other poor families to use.

What's missing to have the right scope and concept? Organizations are focused on providing more of what they do today rather than considering what those who receive the products and services really want and need. Naturally, organizations need to focus. As the examples earlier in this chapter demonstrate, taking on the wrong additional products and services can create havoc with the economics of a business or nonprofit organization and leave everyone worse off.

For now, let's set aside those economic obstacles. We'll return to overcoming those limitations in Chapter 2. Focus instead for now on what the optimum scope of operations should be for a business or nonprofit organization.

Who Else Needs Your Products or Services?

Most organizations answer the question of who else needs their offerings by describing more of the same kinds of customers or beneficiary recipients in some other location. That answer is helpful as far as it goes, but it doesn't exhaust the potential.

Keep going. Who else? Rather than just scratching your head, invite customers, suppliers, distributors, partners, employees, and those in the communities you serve to help you. Procter & Gamble (P&G) got a tip from an employee's family member about a great product available in Asia for removing scum from bathroom tiles. On further investigation, the product was discovered to be made of automobile insulation produced by BASF, which was already a P&G supplier. It's highly likely that BASF didn't think of P&G as a potentially large user for its automobile insulation material. The story ends happily for BASF thanks to that P&G family tip.

We once met a marketing specialist for a large company whose job was to find new uses for the company's products that would attract more customers. When asked how many new customers this activity had attracted, the specialist stroked his chin and softly said, "One." When asked how much product this one customer had bought, the quantity turned out to be tiny. Based on its track record, this company would have done better to have abandoned its inside-out search.

Here are some questions that may help you find new users:
- What other attributes does your offering have that no one is yet using?
- What new, valuable attributes could be added to your offering?
- How could your offering be adjusted to substitute for something else?
- How could your offering be combined with something else to add benefits for new users?
- What can you eliminate from your offering to make it less expensive to use than a currently preferred alternative?

What New Uses and Adjustments Will Delight Users?

A number of years ago, Jell-O® marketers were looking for a way to expand volume for the brand's gelatin. The product was one of the most profitable food products ever, but volume growth was weak. The marketers decided to follow gelatin purchasers into their kitchens to see what they used the product for. Undoubtedly, they expected to see moms and kids making bowls of gelatin like their own moms once made for them. Not so in some kitchens. Here, inventive moms put highly concentrated gelatin into cookie cutter molds, and children played with this new form of the well-known food before eating it. This investigation was the beginning of how the Jell-O Jigglers® promotion was ultimately developed. These delightful edible toys made gelatin making and eating more attractive for moms and kids, and helped the company by encouraging a much higher use of their gelatin.

Companies that have active help lines and online bulletin boards often get similar ideas from those sources. Many businesses also hold customer councils of their largest and most advanced users to find ideas to improve what they offer. Be sure to also seek out nontraditional users to find the most innovative opportunities.

Like the Jell-O® example, some of the best ideas come from trailing beneficiaries and customers around to see what they do with the product and what other problems they have. A patient was recently sent to the hospital for new types of diagnostic tests. Settling down into a multimillion dollar piece of equipment, the patient trustingly followed the technician's orders to lie face down with a pillow for comfort. Within 20 minutes, the pain in the patient's neck became very unpleasant. Within 30 minutes, the patient was losing feeling in the feet and legs. Within 40 minutes, the patient asked to stop the test. Gutting it out for another 2 minutes, the test was completed. The patient said that enough was enough. The technician said that another 30 minutes was going to be needed starting in an hour. The patient obligingly agreed to come back as long as the test could be taken lying face up. With that agreement, the patient came back and was told to hold a certain pose while lying face up. Within 10 minutes, new forms of pain came in waves. And so on. Face up was even worse!

If any engineer had ever watched a patient suffer with this expensive form of a medieval torture device, the engineer would soon have figured out that no patient in his or her right mind would ever agree to take that test again ... and would tell everyone to avoid that test like the plague. Did any engineer ever try out this awful device? We doubt it.

Anyone who had ever seen a massage table would know that great comfort can be provided for the face-down prone position by putting in a cushioned holder that lets one's face descend below table level while one's arms are either prone next to the body or hang downward. Such a solution would have provided blessed relief for patients and probably boosted sales for the manufacturer by hundreds of millions of dollars.

Nonprofit organizations can be equally insensitive. In downtown Boston there's a homeless shelter that is open during the days for women only. That rule is followed because many of these women have been abused by men and don't feel safe at shelters where men can come and go. While visiting this shelter, it soon became obvious that many women were reluctant to come in the shelter because there were men lurking on the street near the entrance. If the shelter's organizers had simply provided an imposing female escort to help women enter and leave the shelter, many more women would have spent the day inside on that blustery December day.

Here are questions designed to help you uncover adjustment opportunities for your offering. What makes your offering
- boring?
- frightening to some people?
- painful or uncomfortable?
- embarrassing?
- sadden people?
- a needless expense for the user?

When Are Better Times to Make Your Expanded Offerings Available?

Many organizations will expand their offerings to new types of customers and stakeholders, but fail to appreciate that those expanded offerings require a shift in when the offerings are available. With increased global commerce, many regions of the world are experiencing more visits by foreign business people and tourists. Yet the regions may remain unresponsive to the needs of the new stakeholders. Here's an example: A trip to Mexico City can require adjustments for those from other countries. Many banks and businesses are closed for much of the afternoon; it's siesta time. If you usually dine at 7 p.m., you're also in for a surprise. Most fine restaurants don't open until 10 p.m. If organizations were to shift their hours to accommodate their new foreign customers, they would see significant added demand as long as their competitors adhered to traditional practices.

Many banks in every part of the world unintentionally create the same inconveniences for customers by scheduling employees to eat lunch when customers are on their lunch breaks. That schedule means that more customers come in when there are fewer people to help them. When it gets to be 5 p.m. on a weekday, most banks are closed. If you need to see someone about a loan application or to get into a safe deposit box, you either have to plan to take time off from work or come in on Saturday morning. If Saturday is your Sabbath, that's an even worse problem. It's not surprising that when one bank started offering branch services inside supermarkets on Sundays that customers were ecstatic. You could now combine banking and grocery shopping if you wanted to. Notice that if the banks had simply opened up on Sundays in some existing locations, the solution wouldn't have worked as well as by combining a new type of location and new hours that fit the schedule of many customers who come to that location.

When are most businesses open in the United States? You can go there when everyone else is at work. This timing is a leftover from the days when most people lived in two-adult households and only one adult worked outside the home. Increasingly, retail stores are offering longer hours to adjust for households where all the adults work outside the home and many of the teenagers work when they aren't in school.

By contrast, if your customers are mostly at work from 9 a.m. to 5 p.m., you may do more business with them if you are open from 6-9 a.m. and from 5-8 p.m. and are closed in between times. That's the case if they have to come to a special location to use your services. One chain of discount providers of at-work clothing for women professionals found it could earn the most by only being open on Friday nights and for long hours on Saturday and Sunday. Their customers and employees were very occupied during the week with work and family responsibilities.

Women used to have their fertility issues treated in physicians' offices and in hospitals. A few years ago, specialty practices emerged. They quickly found that traditional doctor's hours brought loud complaints. Fertility clinics for women are often open now from 6 a.m. to 9 p.m., seven days a week with the women professionals taking the bulk of the 6-8 a.m. and 7-9 p.m. slots while the stay-at-home women take up most of the rest of the time.

If customers don't need to come to your location, being open 24 hours a day, seven days a week will almost always be a better choice if you can automate your offerings. Online sites naturally have that quality and can be set up to operate through self-service software with a minimal nighttime backup staff. If you outsource to an organization on the other side of the world, even your nighttime backup staff works at a more convenient time.

We are often amused by restaurants that are open long hours, but fail to appreciate the full implications of providing better customer access. There's such a restaurant near us. One of their strongest offerings is brunch … but brunch is only served on Sunday during two-and-a-half hours. Who said that people don't want to eat brunch on other days? Brunch items are easy to prepare on short notice, as diners and coffee shops have been proving for years by offering breakfast 24 hours a day.

You may be laughing about how silly these problems are and how your long hours work well for your customers. But think again. If you have global customers, some of them are wide awake and needing your services at all times. You probably just have your expert staff members available from 7 a.m. to 7 p.m. in your own time zone. As a result, customers 12 time zones away have little access to your top people unless they want to call during the middle of the night.

Here are questions designed to help you uncover time-based opportunities:

- When do your customers buy your offerings?
- When would your customers like to buy your offerings?
- When are your customers using your offerings?
- When would your customers like to use your offerings but cannot now?
- When is it inconvenient to use your offerings?
- What potential customers won't consider buying your offerings because of timing issues?
- When do customers need special services from you?
- When do competitors make their offerings and special services available?

Where Are Better Places to Provide Your Offerings?

We live in Massachusetts, a state known for its endless and seemingly bottomless potholes in streets and highways; perhaps that's why we became interested in better concrete for roads. Driving over such potholes can result in bent tire rims. When that happens, you have a constant leak in tire pressure unless you buy a new rim (at a cost of several hundred dollars) or have your rim straightened (a much cheaper alternative). We had heard rumors that there was a reputable company that straightened rims. Annoyed by the most recent flat tire due to a bent rim, one of your authors was able to track down the organization. An appointment was made during which complex driving directions were received. The location was in the next town over from our offices, in a suburb well-known for its low crime rate. Imagine our chagrin when we ended up in a neighborhood that looked like a military target after bombing practice. But that wasn't the worst of it. Going inside, the facilities were filthy and cluttered. Sure enough we eventually had a straighter rim, but we wouldn't ever suggest that anyone go there for that service. It was thoroughly unpleasant. Undoubtedly, the company was saving money by being in that location. But in a more pleasant surrounding, we would have sent hundreds of customers to them, rather than keeping mum about the company. The company could have overcome this problem by moving to a smaller inexpensive site in the same town that was more desirable to customers. If that wasn't possible, the company should have offered a service to pick up, straighten, and return rims during the evenings when customers are at home.

A little-appreciated fact is that many businesses receive a disproportionate number of their customers from those who live and work nearby. For instance, a neighborhood restaurant located away from major roads might gain 85 percent of its sales from those who live and work within a half mile. Despite this fact, many people will operate their business or nonprofit organization from only one location. A food bank will distribute groceries next to its warehouse, rather than distribute near where its recipients live.

Here are questions designed to help you uncover location-based opportunities:

- Where are competing offerings provided?
- How long does it take customers and recipients to reach your location?
- How expensive is it for people to reach your location?
- How does your location compare to the areas where these people normally spend their time?
- How do the expenses of a better location compare to what you pay now?
- Can you efficiently provide pickup and delivery services?
- Can you efficiently operate more locations?

What Are Better Reasons to Use Your Offerings?

As consultants, we are used to potential clients evaluating our services in terms of the size and frequency of the benefits they are seeking for their organization. Such an examination is usually done through reference checking with our past and current clients who have had similar issues. Once satisfied that we can help them with their specific issue, an engagement almost always follows.

We quickly learned, however, that clients were using us for what we perceived to be the wrong services. What clients thought were their most pressing issues were usually not their biggest opportunities. We compared the results clients received from having us help them identify and implement their opportunities with those clients who had us work on a narrow area of the client's choice. The clients who received our help with identifying opportunities came out way ahead. From that measurement we learned and were able to share a powerful reason for clients to use our opportunity identification services. As a result, our total revenue expanded rapidly and our opportunity identification work grew even more rapidly. Our clients were happier, told more people to use us, and enjoyed better results.

A local government agency, which received most of its money from the U.S. government, had a problem similar to our potential consulting clients. Faced with a relatively fixed budget for providing services, the agency felt that it could accomplish the most by continually funding the same activities and suppliers. In that way, bureaucracy and disruptions in service could be minimized. Where the agency went wrong was in failing to understand what level and quality of services its suppliers were delivering. Due to faltering leadership in partner organizations, service delivery was dropping rapidly even though the budgets were being maintained. Since no complaints were making their way to the agency, the problem was invisible until measurements were put in place and the track records of alternative suppliers were investigated.

A new policy was established to take the lowest performing suppliers and substitute new suppliers who had impressive track records in the same areas. Within a few years, benefit effectiveness more than doubled even though the budgets didn't change much.

From these two examples, we want you to be sensitive to the fact that customers and recipients may not be receiving the right offerings from you. When that happens, it's your responsibility as an expert to find out what's best for all concerned and change your marketing and offering processes to better inform and support your customers' and beneficiaries' interests.

Here are questions designed to help you uncover marketing- and support-based opportunities:

- Which customers and beneficiaries benefit most from your offerings?
- How do those who benefit most differ from those who benefit less?
- How do your marketing and support affect selections and uses of offerings?
- What do your customers and beneficiaries need to know that they don't know now to make better use of your offerings?

- What is the most effective way to provide that knowledge?
- Who needs that knowledge now?

Play a More Central Role in Peoples' Lives

Positioning your offerings as playing a more central role is the heart of this chapter. Most organizations have defined their role in serving customers and beneficiaries in a much too narrow way. That's like an airline only offering to sell vacation travelers a one-way ticket.

Here's an example: One of our students wanted to develop a 2,000 percent solution for flying relief supplies in war-ravaged and drought-stricken areas. He initially focused on flight safety, on-time arrival at the landing strips, and other flight-related measurements. One of us pointed out to him that what he was focusing on didn't make any difference if the food, medicines, and supplies didn't rapidly get to the people who most needed them. Responding to that observation, the student chose instead to see his job as supervising a system for delivering the supplies to those who needed them. This focus meant coordinating with those who trucked and carried the food from the airstrips and being sure that distribution methods were effective in refugee camps and other disaster relief areas. With that shift in focus, food and medicine began arriving sooner and in greater quantities for those who had the greatest need.

Here's an example from Asia: An organization had been providing wheelchairs to disabled people living in an institution for 10 years. During a visit by the head of the organization to check if more wheelchairs were needed, a young lady who was sitting in one of the wheelchairs shyly noted, "Mister, thank you for your help but we would like to work … we do not want to have to beg all of our lives." That comment opened his eyes to what the real needs of the recipients were. Today, the organization also provides teachers to the institution so that job skills can be learned. Several people have been placed in office jobs where a wheelchair isn't a draw back, such as receptionist and typist. With time, this shift in role by the organization will lead to a 40,000 percent solution as those who need the wheelchairs become economically self-sufficient in respectable jobs and can leave the institution, thus allowing many more people to be served by the institution.

Let's look again at one of the earlier examples in this book to see this point from another perspective. You probably remember Jell-O Jigglers®, the gelatin dessert that was fun to play with. For the Jell-O® team, that promotion could have spurred them instead into a new role … providing healthier, more playful food that parents and adults could prepare and enjoy together in portion-controlled sizes. A look at other General Foods brands during the era when Jigglers® were introduced shows what could have been done. Birds Eye® Frozen vegetables could have been diced to make components for Lego®-like structures baked into tasty treats based on designs put into frozen vegetable packages. Feeding the dog could have been made into more fun by pressing the soft-moist Top Choice® extrusions into amusing molds provided in packages. Dry Jell-O Pudding® could have been sold with containers suitable for filling with protein-reinforced pudding to make humorously shaped frozen treats. Vitamin enriched Kool-Aid® could have been frozen into the same shapes using the same molds. Sugar-reduced Tang® could have come with recipes to make colorful layered breakfast drinks like dessert parfaits you see in fine restaurants. Stove Top Stuffing® could have been reformulated to lower its glycemic load and made easier to pack in molds for making whimsical structures that would fit onto a plate.

New and expansive roles are often the right place to be searching. Organizations are moving in to take over broad areas of companies' and individual needs. The first enterprise to seek such an expanded role often develops a disproportionate advantage … if performance is good. Think of this expansion as similar to driving alone on a new high-speed autobahn while everyone else has to fight bumper-to-bumper traffic on expensive toll roads.

What do we mean by new and expansive roles? Perhaps someone is already playing each of the following roles. But whether or not anyone has done so, these potential roles should help you identify ideas that you should be racing down the innovation highway to provide.

- Life coaches who work continually with those aged 13 to 26 to help them effectively pursue their educations and careers.
- Divorce managers who facilitate the transition from marriage to becoming single again while helping ensure that parental and financial performances are optimized.
- Career enhancement marketers who help their clients decide on which skills to develop, which jobs to take, and how to manage a career track while obtaining favorable publicity for their clients.
- Supplier-design optimizers who work with your organization's suppliers to come up with new and redesigned offerings that will be more effective and lower cost than what you provide now.
- Community developers who establish best practice groups to

provide voluntary expert help to your organization.
- Venture capitalists who invest in developing poor people with high potential.

Here are some questions designed to help you define broader, more valuable roles for beneficiaries and customers:
- When and where are customers and beneficiaries wasting time or resources?
- How can such waste of time and resources be overcome?
- What roles might be accepted by those who need the most help?
- How can adequate resources be obtained to provide these offerings?

What Are the Highest and Best Directions for Your Offerings and Talents?

Too many of us stop thinking about what we are doing as soon as we finish a task. We happily turn to our to-do list and quickly check off another completed item before moving onto the next task. That "job done" satisfaction has been a problem with those who create 2,000 percent solutions. Such solution creators are more likely to move on to learn some less effective process than they are to deepen their knowledge by creating another 2,000 percent solution. These talented innovators are even less likely to repeat the 2,000 percent solution process on the same problem or opportunity. Worst of all, even those who do repeat the process are then less likely to teach the process to anyone else. Yet such teaching would deepen the teacher's understanding of the process while enhancing an organization's ability to prosper in the future from having more 2,000 percent solutions.

In the same way, most of us stop thinking about our offerings as soon as they leave our sight. That's what happened to the pilot who managed the flights for relief supplies. Although he had certainly seen food and medicine distributed in relief camps, he didn't usually think about that important aspect of creating value from his transporting of supplies.

Now is a good time to change your myopic focus to a longer-sighted one. Hundreds of business books advocate becoming customer centered, but that's only part of the answer. Instead, you have to become purpose centered in serving a fuller extent of your beneficiaries' and customers' needs in your areas of current and potential expertise and resources.

Here are questions designed to help you identify the highest and best use of your offerings, resources, and talents:

- Which customers and beneficiaries receive the least benefit now? Why?
- Which beneficiaries and customers enjoy the most benefit now? Why?
- How could you add much more benefit at little or no cost?
- Why don't beneficiaries and customers demand those benefits now?
- Where do customers and beneficiaries misunderstand the value they could receive from your offerings and talents?
- Why do those misunderstandings exist and persist?

What Is the Simplest Route to Add the Most Value?

People usually overestimate their own abilities and potential. In so doing, they often make the mistake of creating a complicated solution to something that can be accomplished more simply. Go for the simple and easy instead. Consider the Procter & Gamble (P&G) example of conducting hundreds of Goldcorp-like challenges in a short period of time that was described previously in the section "What Is a 2,000 Percent Solution?" The alternative for P&G was to try to outperform the rest of the world's R&D and product development professionals, even though P&G could never expect to employ more than a very small percentage of those professionals. The chances of that road being a high-speed lane to success were very slim.

Here are some ideas that may stimulate your thinking:

- Start helping beneficiaries and customers before any harm is done to them.
- Stay in constant contact with customers and beneficiaries to be able to prepare them for situations before such circumstances arise.
- Create a simple communications routine that leaves no room for error.
- Make as much of the process "serve yourself" as possible.
- Systematically examine how to eliminate problems for beneficiaries and customers.
- Make implementation foolproof by providing warning signs and relevant instructions when the customer or beneficiary is off course.

How Can Progress Be Safely Accelerated?

To safely accelerate progress, start with your concept for an initially expanded role and a process. Lay out the concept's operation one step at a time like the instructions for a model car kit you are building. Insert the likely delays that will occur. Investigate how those steps and delays can be replaced with simpler and faster methods. Repeat the process.

Here's an example: A marketing consultant approached us many years ago about developing and implementing the marketing for some of our services. The idea intrigued us because we were very busy, and neither of us wanted to take the time to develop new marketing programs and carry them out. We readily agreed to work with the consultant. He made this agreement even easier by making his compensation contingent on his success.

We soon discovered that whatever the consultant knew about marketing, he didn't know much about how to gather and work with information. He began sending us endless lists of questions, spending long days reviewing our answers with us and rehashing the same ground. Since he didn't understand the technical side of how we delivered our services, he began to feel like he couldn't work on marketing our offerings until he acquired that technical knowledge. Unfortunately, learning that much about the offerings was a formidable intellectual challenge that wasn't worth the effort for any of us.

This seemingly endless series of communications and meetings went on for months before we finally asked the man to stop. Otherwise, we might still be pursuing his process. Since his perceived problem was that he wanted to understand the service delivery process, this information gathering effort could have been made faster by gathering client information about what they understood and thought about the process. Clients didn't really understand the process either … but that wasn't a concern to clients as long as they could use the results of the process and have confidence that they were on the right track. The fact that we always checked out the recommendations through confidential interviews with investors provided the credibility that established the necessary client confidence. We could have easily arranged for the consultant to have spoken to a few clients, with or without us around, and he would soon have found out all he had to know.

Next, he could have surveyed a reasonable-size sample of those who needed and knew our services but who hadn't purchased those services to find out how these executives had decided not to purchase. Having discovered the gap between what the satisfied customers thought and understood and what the undeveloped prospects knew and understood, the marketing consultant could then have started to develop test programs to change understanding among the prospects. Following the results of a few successful tests, the consultant would then have begun to implement programs that improved our marketing effectiveness.

With such a process, the consultant could have been producing improved marketing for us in less elapsed time and by taking up less of our time. Why didn't he? It was clear that he was a Socratic learner; that is, he needed all of his questions answered by an expert before he could come to any decisions. The consultant could not step back and redesign his own process to make it faster and better. As a result, we lost confidence that he could improve our marketing process or save us any time.

Here are some questions designed to help you perceive a faster, more direct route for your beneficiaries and customers:

- What's the minimum information needed to act?
- Where and when is unnecessary information being developed?
- What is the minimum offering needed to provide most of the desired benefits?
- Which delays in the sales and offering delivery cycle can be eliminated? How?
- Where are mistakes being made that can be drastically reduced? How?
- What assumptions are being made that should be challenged?

How Can You Deliver the New Offerings in the Most Pleasant Way?

A rapid ride can be unpleasant unless the rider's comfort is secured. Perhaps that first trip on the autobahn would have been less daunting if we instead had been listening to soothing music or watching a humorous video. Unexpected change is equally disruptive for many people. Turn that unexpected change into a delightful ocean cruise, and everyone will praise the change. For instance, an equally high-speed ride a few years later on France's TGV train turned out to be an amusing pleasure for us.

Beneficiary and customer comforts are often a low priority for those developing a better offering. Instead, the intellectual elegance of the final result is emphasized ... often at the expense of pleasant coddling and polite help.

You frequently see this problem in shelters for homeless people. One such shelter in Boston is well equipped with marvelous facilities including showers, a great choice of new clothes, bright classrooms where people can learn new skills, a large kitchen, pleasant dining tables, and counselors who help with specific problems. But most of the homeless people who come into the shelter don't have a positive experience there. On a cold winter day, people are required to sit quietly between meals in uncomfortable chairs at long tables situated in large rooms. If these homeless people want to have a pleasant social conversation with their friends, they have to go back outside. Inside, they spend most of the day like people who are on a brief break from prison cells.

Hospital outpatient departments are seldom much better. You show up for an appointment, and you are lucky if you see the physician within an hour of the scheduled time. While you are in the waiting room, chances are good that one or more of the people will be sneezing, coughing, and wheezing in a good imitation of having contracted a fatal plague. You begin to wonder why you came.

Compare these problems with delays experienced while flying on jet-Blue Airways. While seated on that low-cost and low-priced airline, you have dozens of channels of current television programming to watch. Unless passengers have something they have to do right after the scheduled arrival time, most won't even notice if the flight is a little late. A delay may simply give passengers time to see the rest of their favorite television program. Many customers pick their flights by what television shows they can watch on the airline.

Here are some questions to help you make your new offerings potentially more delightful:
- How can you turn delays into delights?
- How can you help people look forward to experiencing your offering?
- What improvements will make the time fly while your offering is being enjoyed?
- What positive experiences can you add that people will tell others about for years to come?
- How can you make beneficiaries and customers feel rewarded by employing your offering?

How Can You Make It a Joy to Provide the New Offerings?

Suppliers, partners, and employees need to enjoy your new offerings as well, or their bad moods will spoil the experience for customers and beneficiaries.

If you go to a restaurant where the host and servers are all having a ball, don't you have more fun too? After you check into a hotel late at night and the desk clerk looks at you like a enemy invader who is spoiling his nap, you probably don't sleep as well as you might wish.

Management texts often encourage those working on designing new offerings to involve those who will be critical players in providing the benefits. In that way, it is thought that employees, suppliers, and partners will pursue the opportunity with more enthusiasm. A better reason for such involvement is to be sure that the new roles are a delight to those who will play the key roles.

Little differences can be important. The people working at a Disney theme park often compete quite hard for acting roles in hot, uncomfortable costumes, even though many don't pay much more than the legal minimum wage rate. But the work feels like a step up from other jobs in the parks, and may be the only acting job available to that person.

Let's extrapolate that observation into a principle: People like to step up to bigger, more rewarding roles. For example, partners like being consulted about what they are normally required to accept. Suppliers like having a chance to design their piece of an offering rather than simply being asked to come up with a low price for their part of the task. Employees like to learn new skills, entertain people, and feel appreciated.

Naturally, it doesn't do anyone any good if those who design the offering are gone and create something that no one wants to provide. So you also want to think ahead for future generations of those who will be asked to help.

We recently saw a fascinating example of this principle at work in a new type of high school. At The Metropolitan Regional Career and Technical Center in Providence, Rhode Island, a high school only has 100 students in it. Because of the smaller size, every student is treated as an individual. Students take responsibility for their own educations by finding internships involving work the students think they might want to do as adults. Interns are mentored by adults who do that sort of work in the community, and teachers serve more as advisors in helping the students design their studies. Reading, writing, math, and the other typical high school subjects are pursued solely in terms of the internship the student has chosen. Two days a week the students are away working on the internships, returning to the school in between to develop skills in what they are learning. One teacher works with the same 15 students for four years. Students and their teacher get to know one another quite well and develop more trust than you observe in most high schools. Principals, teachers, and staff look excited and happy as they go about their appointed rounds. When I compare that observed enthusiasm to how many teachers and staff members describe their work in high schools now, it's not hard to see the benefits of this new concept. The new approach blossoms because it works for all stakeholders … not just the students. Of course, the students look purposeful, focused, and happy. When we visited, we could hardly believe that we were in a high school.

Here are questions to help you add more joy for stakeholders other than customers and beneficiaries:

- Who are the stakeholders who will be affected by the new offerings?
- How will new roles compare to existing roles?
- How can the new roles be redesigned to make them more attractive than existing roles?
- What other stakeholders can be added who will prefer the new roles?
- How can these stakeholders redesign the roles to make those roles even more attractive as well as better for beneficiaries and customers?

Share Your Vision by Telling Your Story

By now you should have an image of your path to expanding use. If you don't have that image, reread this chapter, and sleep on what you read, and think about it until you do have that image. Feel free to talk over your thoughts with family members, friends, colleagues, and stakeholders.

When you formulate your idea, turn that image into a brief, interesting story, of less than 150 words, that you can tell others to describe the opportunity presented by your idea. A good resource for developing that story can be found in Stephen Denning's book, *The Springboard* (Butterworth-Heinemann, 2001).

Here are the elements you should put into a positive story:

- A short statement of the problem ("Refugees were starving for lack of timely food arrivals … ")
- Wording that puts the listener into the story to feel the bare bones of the predicament (" … and officials didn't know what to do to improve.")

- A protagonist people can relate to who is like themselves; for example, missionary pilots want to hear about their colleagues ("A missionary pilot … ")
- A protagonist who employs the indicated offering (" … took a course based on *The 2,000 Percent Solution* and learned that his focus on flight safety had been too narrow.")
- A description of the solution to the problem ("He shifted his focus from running efficient flights to ensuring that food, medicine, and other critical supplies were received in a timely fashion by the refugees.")
- A real or potential happy ending ("Food deliveries at the refugee camp improved and starvation risk ended.")
- A statement that alerts the listener or reader to the potential of this resolution ("Imagine if everyone took a similarly broad view of being sure that results are improved for those most in need.")
- An ending that leaves the listener to draw her or his own conclusions about what to do next

Tell your story and use the feedback you receive to improve your story. Also keep track of the concerns that people raise about your story. Those concerns will give you clues for the issues you encounter in Chapter 2.

Chapter 2

Locate Obstacles
Along the Ideal Route
Identify the Barriers to Universal Usage

Do you know there's a road that goes down to Mexico and all the way to
Panama?... and maybe all the way to the bottom of South America ...?
Yes! You and I, Sal, we'd dig the whole world with a car like this because, man,
the road must eventually lead to the whole world.
Ain't nowhere else it can go ... right?
— Jack Kerouac

In the 1950s many people dreamed about the unlimited potential of being able to drive from Alaska in North America to Patagonia in South America. In those days, only a small percentage of people had flown, and the open road offered a special allure.

With such broad appeal and discussion, you would think that many people took that exciting opportunity. Yet very few did. Why? The road was a long and hard one, and many dangers lay along the way.

For North Americans, the challenges included car insurance that often didn't extend south of the United States, a lack of repair parts in many locations, an inability to speak and understand Spanish and Brazilian Portuguese, problems with dysentery, concerns about bandits, ignorance concerning local accommodations, and fear induced by stories of people having become lost in jungles along the way. Surely it was easier to drive across one's own familiar country than to take on such seemingly limitless challenges in pursuit of unspecified, although abstractly intriguing, benefits.

The opportunity to expand your sales level or beneficiary support by 20 times can be equally daunting ... but in different ways. Here are some questions that might go through your mind: Will a foreign government seize our property? Will a currency collapse leave the investment worthless? Will our executives be kidnapped for ransom? Will we be able to sell or deliver enough to cover the high overhead costs of having many new operations? Will our cash flow remain positive enough for the organization to be financially sound? Will the return on investment satisfy investors, lenders, and donors? Will people steal from our organization? Will terrorists attack our operations? Will politicians denounce what we are doing? Will competitors be able to bribe corrupt officials to put pressure on us?

Only time will tell what all of the risks, barriers, and delays will be. However, it is an enormous advantage when you can find the largest and most difficult obstacles first. You can then have more time to either consider those obstacles or strategically avoid them. For example, Jack Kerouac could have eliminated many of his potential problems in traveling the length of the Americas by bringing enough travelers checks to buy another car if necessary; carrying spare parts for what was most likely to fail; learning how to make his own repairs; storing extra water, fuel, and oil in the car; treating local water and food to make them hygienic; and including a passenger who spoke Latin American Spanish well.

Find Out Why Most People
Don't Buy or Use Your Offerings

While you probably think that daunting dangers are your biggest problems, chances are that while these challenges loom large in your mind, these dreaded risks actually cast a relatively small shadow compared to other challenges. What is your biggest obstacle? For most organizations the overwhelming barrier to progress is that most customers and beneficiaries wouldn't use your offerings even if you paid them to!

While this is not a market research book, it's a good time to share a little secret that everyone knows who performs much market research. Relatively few people ever consider using the offerings of any given company or benefit supplier, except for a few behemoth operators like Wal-Mart. Without being considered as a possible choice, you have the same chance of succeeding that a soccer player does who cannot enter the stadium where the match will be played. For example, let's consider U.S. institutional investors and the stocks of the Standard & Poor's 500 companies. Here you have a public market dominated by large investors and large companies. That sounds like a match made in Heaven for the public companies. Right?

Wrong. Most portfolio managers are expected by investors to follow a promised style. If the style is to buy small capitalization companies, that portfolio manager shouldn't be holding any large company stocks. Oops! Also, the style usually excludes companies that the manager doesn't know well. Since the average portfolio manager only knows about 50 companies well, that excludes 450 large companies right there. And on it goes.

If a big American company has trouble attracting portfolio managers investing lots of money to pay attention to them, what chance does a smaller operation have of appealing to small, diverse, and less well-informed beneficiaries and customers? Very little.

Let's look at some of the common sources of the disconnect between offerings and their intended customers and users. Our research has shown that ignorance, misperceptions, harmful complacency, disbelief, and mistrust are often the foundations of why people reject helpful offerings.

Sources of Ignorance

Many potential beneficiaries and customers are ignoring you because they don't know enough about you to consider what you offer. Busy lives and schedules allow relatively little time for searching out better alternatives — except when it seems there is no choice but to do so.

You, like your potential customers and beneficiaries, know relatively little about the businesses and benefit organizations in your immediate vicinity. If you doubt that, make a list that details everything you know about every such organization you can think of within a 5-mile radius of your house. Then go for a drive and notice how many organizations you didn't even remember to put on your list.

Let's consider some of the most common causes of such harmful ignorance. The barriers to knowledge include how our brains work, the psychology of being too easily satisfied, challenges with finding useful information, and a misguided understanding of what needs to be learned. When you overcome these barriers, you can quickly find yourself becoming aware of and employing vastly more advantageous choices.

Your Reticular Activating System Creates Tunnel Vision The tendency to exclude options is enhanced by the way our brains focus on only a small percentage of what we see around us, a function of the reticular activating system. That mental process assures that our conscious minds focus on only what we are looking for. Tell someone not to think about green, and all they will notice is green. In a famous experiment, researchers put together a brief film of teens passing basketballs. Before the film starts, viewers are asked to identify how many passes occur. People diligently count. Despite paying attention, less than half find the right answer. Next, researchers ask if anyone noticed anything unusual. Around a third of the people will comment that someone dressed in a gorilla suit walked through the basketball players. The rest don't remember seeing a gorilla suit at all. We were most impressed when we recently recreated that experience and found ourselves with the wrong number of passes and having missed the gorilla suit ... despite knowing about the film and the experiment before watching.

As a result, someone might literally drive by your place of operation every day for years and never notice that your establishment is there. This lack of awareness is especially likely to occur whenever there's a distraction nearby that's of more interest. In fact, it was drivers' focusing on reaching Mount Rushmore quickly that caused all but a handful of motorists to bypass the little town of Wall, South Dakota, where Wall Drug was based until the famous signs offering free ice water were added along the highway.

Even worse, our modest knowledge quickly weakens as the radius expands away from our residence and place of employment. And only a small percentage of people have been in more than a handful of the regions in their own part of the world.

Once Satisfied, We Happily Drive Past the Competition   Let's consider a more optimistic case. Assume that a potential customer or beneficiary is fully aware of an organization and what it does. What are the chances that an individual with such knowledge will actually buy or seek benefits from the organization?

Less than 15 percent of those with such good knowledge will bother to step inside the premises. Why? They don't think they need what the organization offers. Here's an example: There are dozens of dry cleaners within a 5-mile radius of our home. Because business styles have emphasized more casual dress for a number of years, we don't often need dry cleaning. All dry cleaners in our area have signs with price specials in their windows. The prices are all about the same.

Where do we take our dry cleaning? We go to the same dry cleaner we've been using for more than 20 years. They do good work, win awards, and are not any more expensive than anyone else. (You may remember that we wrote about them, Jaylin Cleaners in Newton, Massachusetts, as a successful business model innovator in *The Ultimate Competitive Advantage*.) Why should we try out other dry cleaners?

But just a few months ago, we did try another dry cleaner. We needed some alterations made. Jaylin's tailor was about to go on vacation and couldn't handle the job in time. We walked 100 feet away to another dry cleaner whose tailor was on the premises, and the work was done on time and in a way that was indistinguishable from Jaylin's. We will remember that experience, and the second dry cleaner will probably be getting some of our business from time to time when the parking lot is full at Jaylin or their tailor is out.

Having found two perfectly acceptable dry cleaners, there's not much chance that either of us will now go in search of a third choice. Our ignorance will continue about those other choices … until we need a third choice. Should a third choice be needed, a more convenient location will probably determine that selection.

Looking for Choices Can Put You in an Information Traffic Jam
Notice how the Internet makes the problem of overcoming ignorance both better and worse. If you search for a new supplier, you will probably find more choices than you want. Chances are that you won't look past the first page of your search engine results. Yet there may be tens of thousands of competing vendors. So although our potential to find an optimal supplier or benefit provider is now greater, we are so choked with choices that we are unlikely to look very hard for one. Why? The potential that we perceive can be gained by taking on one versus another will seem to be less than the value of our time that would be needed to select the optimal one.

You May Not Be Able to Find People Who Give Reliable Directions For those who do want to make a better decision, there's a shortcut available: You can ask someone who is very knowledgeable for their recommendation. Among friends, word-of-mouth referral works well. Since your friend knows that you will come back to complain if the recommended organization doesn't perform, your friend will try to share what she or he knows without overstating the case.

On the Internet, however, finding trustworthy providers through online referrals is more difficult. First, you probably don't know much more about the organization or person you are asking for advice than what their marketing says. So although you may have done business together for some time, you don't know much about them when it comes to quality of their referrals. Second, Internet providers are well aware that word-of-mouth is golden, and many provide outsized payments for such referrals. It's not usual for half the price of an offering to be paid to the person who makes a referral. When that's happening, many people will be inclined to recommend those who pay the highest referral fees ... rather than those who objectively perform best.

You May Be Asking Directions for the Wrong Destination Beyond the problem of getting good directions, "out of sight is out of mind" can afflict beneficiaries and customers in a more subtle way. Beneficiaries and customers probably don't know what categories of offerings and benefits would help them the most. Take the overweight person who diets all the time but doesn't know about how high glycemic foods cause the body to store fat even when consuming relatively few calories. Until that person learns this important lesson, she or he will continue to be overweight despite good intentions and lots of self-discipline.

Here are questions to help you appreciate the major sources of ignorance about your organization and its offerings:

- Which potential users and beneficiaries of your offerings are totally ignorant that your offerings exist?
- Why are these potential users and beneficiaries ignorant of your offerings?
- Which potential users and beneficiaries of your offerings are aware of your offerings but don't think they need your offerings?
- Why do these potential users and beneficiaries think they don't need your offerings?
- Which satisfied users and beneficiaries for your offerings don't recommend your offerings to others?
- Why don't these satisfied users and beneficiaries recommend your offerings?
- Who are the people doing most of the referring of potential users and beneficiaries for your type of offering?
- Why do those active referrers not support your offerings?

Sources of Misperceptions

Social workers anywhere in the world will tell you that they spend most of their time trying to persuade those who need help to seek the right aid. Those who are poor, ill, abused, unemployed, and overwhelmed have such strong negative emotions about their circumstances that they often reject helpful choices because these people don't believe anything can be done.

In the business context, a perceived slight that occurred decades before may cause a potential customer to shun a valuable offering.

In any context, the manner in which an offering is made will disproportionately affect how people perceive the offering's appropriateness for them.

Let's consider organizational names and descriptions as a starting point for our investigation of misperceptions. Imagine that there are two appliance repair companies listed in whatever source you consult. One company calls itself "Mr. Fix-It" and the other calls itself "Quick Service Repairs." Without knowing anything about either one, you might be inclined to favor Mr. Fix-It when something major has gone wrong (such as a short in your stove's microwave oven) and Quick Service Repairs when you need the appliance back running again as soon as possible (such as your freezer when it's full of frozen food).

The suppliers' capabilities may be quite different. Mr. Fix-It may be lousy at microwave ovens, but fast in arriving for freezer emergencies. Quick Service Repairs may be slow in arriving for any problem, but does excellent work on site once they do arrive. If both companies keep the same names and the same performance attributes, both companies will disappoint many of their new customers … many of whom will never use the company again.

Consider instead the performance perceptions created by these companies if they exchange names. The renamed Mr. Fix-It will soon have a tremendous following of people who need help with on-site repairs while the renamed Quick Service Repairs will soon dominate the freezer repair market.

Now that you see how branding and performance attributions have to be aligned, let's look at a different source of misperceptions … the way the offering is presented by those who provide that offering. Our home's furnace was falling apart, and our fuel oil service and delivery man told us that we would have to replace the furnace soon. When heating oil prices increased rapidly in late 2005, we realized that a new furnace might also be more fuel efficient. At the same time, we knew that the old furnace had other problems. Strange creosote-like odors leaked into the house in unexpected locations. Our fuel oil serviceman told us that nothing could be done about the odors. He also recommended a friend of his to install our new furnace. The recommended man had installed the serviceman's furnace, and the serviceman had been very pleased with the results.

We called the recommended installer, and he ignored us. We asked our serviceman to call the installer on our behalf … and that call also did no good. After waiting a month, we decided to contact other installers. We started with our plumber because he had experience with boilers. He reluctantly agreed to look at our job, came right away, and provided a quote that seemed pretty fair. We asked him if he could come down a little on price, and he said he couldn't. Because he never buys furnaces, he could not get a volume discount like frequent furnace installers can. We thanked the plumber and kept looking. One company sent the firm's president, all dressed up in a classy suit and tie. The man was very impressive and showed us why we had the odors, pointing out that extra work would be needed to fix the problem. Responding favorably to his expertise, we asked him to quote on everything that would need to be done. Weeks passed, and no quote appeared. Finally, we browbeat him into giving us an oral quote. It was almost double that of the plumber's. We found that other bidders also varied in their appearance, their ability to diagnose our problem, and the prices they quoted. A few told us to be sure to clean our air ducts before installing the new furnace; otherwise, our house would be filled with soot because the new furnaces have stronger blowers to circulate the air. That was new and valuable information.

At the last moment, the first man, the one recommended by our serviceman, called to say he would be over in 15 minutes to look at our job. He walked through in less than 3 minutes, and faxed back a bid within 30 minutes. It was the low bid. He didn't mention anything about cleaning air ducts or fixing the odors.

We decided to have the air ducts cleaned on our own and hired the recommended man to put in the furnace. It just didn't seem worth it to spend several thousands of dollars extra hoping to fix the odors. We sent the down payment check to the installer, and he called back the day he got the check to schedule installation for two days later. The duct cleaner and the contractor's removal man nicely coordinated so that the duct cleaning could be done faster. The duct cleaner gave us a deal and provided us a lot of extra services because his job was made easier by the removal man. The installer located all of the problems that were causing the odors and simply fixed the problems without asking for any extra money. The new furnace was soon operating, and the installer did a great job of cleaning up from the mess. The unpleasant odors were instantly gone. We were delighted!

What are the lessons here? The installer we chose is obviously a prince and wizard among furnace contractors, but his method of dealing with potential customers makes him seem unreliable. Clearly, the people who made a good impression on us with their knowledge and willingness to share that knowledge caused us to want to work with them. It was only when these impressive people either wanted double the price or failed to follow through in a timely fashion that we dismissed them. Had they only asked for a 20 percent premium and been timely on follow through, we probably would have hired one of them.

Had the first man shown up to look at our job within two weeks of our first call, we wouldn't have contacted anyone else. But we still would have had a problem with soot being blown into our house from the dirty ducts. We would have been annoyed. So we were well served by the delay in our installer's reply to our request for a quote. The installer needs to take a few more minutes to talk to prospects and explain about duct cleaning. He can probably charge more money if he does, and his profits will grow as customer satisfaction soars.

Here are questions to help you appreciate the major sources of misperceptions about your organization and its offerings:

- Does your organization's name capture the essence of your most valuable attributes?
- What organizational name would better communicate those attributes?
- Do the names of your offerings capture the essence of their most valuable attributes?
- What brand names would better communicate those attributes?
- How does your performance not meet the standards of what beneficiaries and customers often need?
- Would it be worthwhile to customers and beneficiaries for you to provide more performance in those areas … even if prices and time involved for your offerings increased?
- With whom does your organization have a bad reputation that doesn't reflect your current performance?
- How can you change your name and reputation to remedy that out-of-date bad reputation?

Sources of Harmful Complacency

We have always found that the world pretty neatly divides itself into those who understand and act on optimizing performance of almost everything they come into contact with … and those who ignore optimization. Maintaining automobile and motorcycle tire pressures is a good example. Keep your tires at the right pressure and you gain advantages: The ride is smoother; your brakes work better; you are less likely to have a blowout; fuel economy is better; and the tires last longer. Many filling stations offer free air to inflate your tires. Invest about a dollar into an air pressure gauge, and you have everything you need to benefit. It will help, though, if you remember that air pressure varies with altitude and temperature. You will need to deflate tires when you suddenly encounter hot days in the mountains and inflate tires when you experience cold days at sea level. How much time will it take? You will probably spend less than 15 minutes a year unless you have a leaky tire. Yet most people can be observed to be driving around with tires that are over- or underinflated.

Why? The sources of this harmful complacency are many. Some older drivers grew up during a time when almost every filling station would check and automatically adjust tire pressure. Having enjoyed that benefit, these drivers unconsciously rely on automobile service people to do the same today. Some places where you have your oil changed will do this automatically … and some will not. Such drivers are assuming that all such service organizations do. Wrong!

Other drivers grew up in families where one person in the family took care of all mechanical aspects of cars, trucks, and motorcycles. Then these drivers married spouses who had the same history. Neither spouse takes care of mechanical issues until the vehicle literally won't move.

Some drivers feel so rich that they would rather wear out tires than take care of them. It's psychologically easier for these people to think about buying new tires than tire care. Interestingly, the time it takes to pick out and purchase tires and retorque the lug nuts on a new set of tires is usually longer than just keeping the proper pressure. But if you purchase or lease a new car every year, it's not a problem. The depreciation cost of such rapid trade-ins often amounts to over a third of an average person's annual income. If the main reason you change cars is to avoid vehicle maintenance, that's an expensive way to save time. You could save enough money to enjoy the equivalent of paying yourself several thousand dollars an hour to provide or buy the services you need.

Some drivers avoid checking tire pressure because they are fastidious about their clothing and cleanliness. Unless you keep some hand cleanser in your car and are careful when you kneel to check the tires, you can definitely pick up a little grime. As a result, many people check and inflate tires when they have on their old clothes while doing errands. But those who are concerned about their appearance at all times will just avoid the whole thing.

Some drivers are just unaware. What tires? "My tires work just fine," replies the oblivious driver when asked about tire pressure on her virtually flat tires.

The basic problem in each case is that the person doesn't know or care enough about the potential benefits of proper tire pressure to do something about it. One of the major limitations of the human brain is that it has a hard time accurately imagining anything that hasn't been experienced yet. If you have ever had a tire blowout at high speed, you definitely will go to some effort to avoid another one. But if you haven't had such a blowout, you assume that it won't happen and that it won't be that bad if it does.

If you do have a blowout due to improper inflation, you will probably assume that your tire vendor sold you a bad tire and start thinking about contacting a lawyer. It will probably never occur to you that your failure to maintain the proper tire pressure was the primary cause of the blowout.

What's missing? In each case, those who are knowledgeable and can easily provide the needed service should educate and encourage drivers to take care of tire pressure. Oil-change providers are the obvious place for this educating to occur … assuming that you are dealing with drivers who change their oil. Some people ignore even that necessity. But the places that tout such oil change services often charge 50 to 75 percent more than places that don't mention that they check and adjust tire pressure. The inexpensive providers could probably eliminate the expensive competitors with a prominently advertised maintenance-checking program that adds little extra cost.

Here are questions designed to help you identify the major sources of complacency about your organization and its offerings:
- In what costly or harmful ways do beneficiaries and customers misuse your offerings?
- What bad assumptions are customers and beneficiaries making about your offerings?
- What valuable attributes of your offerings are beneficiaries and customers ignoring?
- Why are customers and beneficiaries ignoring those valuable

attributes?
- What are inexpensive ways to educate and encourage beneficiaries and customers to overcome these sources of complacency?

Sources of Disbelief

We had dinner with good friends a few years ago. The husband described with great enthusiasm how he had just agreed to buy his wife a brand-new minivan. He spoke confidently about the many advantages it would provide: more room for passengers; better visibility while driving; and greater safety.

We politely commented that perhaps he hadn't checked minivan safety records lately. In those days minivans had terrible safety records. While minivans looked big and safe, they weren't as safe as other types of vehicles. We mentioned that he could achieve his objectives better with a Volvo station wagon. He immediately disagreed. How could a Volvo be safer than a big trucklike minivan?

We explained that part of the problem was that people felt overconfident in minivans and drove them too aggressively. In addition, it's easier to roll a minivan than a Volvo station wagon. Volvos were also designed to handle such rollovers more safely for the passengers than minivans were. Further, it's easier to be thrown out of a minivan in a crash than a Volvo. Many deaths occur when drivers and passengers are expelled from the vehicle during a collision.

Our friend thought about what we had to say and said he would check out the facts. We could tell that he was still very skeptical of our "facts" that Volvos were safer for his family than minivans were.

It made us smile in future years every time we saw that family's Volvo station wagon.

Danger Sign: Misleading Appearances Ahead Without Warning
What went wrong for Volvo? Minivans outsold Volvo station wagons by an enormous margin. Volvo station wagons clearly had the safety edge. Most people were buying minivans for families that included young children and planned to transport even more children. Safety had to be important to these owners. Volvo station wagons were more expensive, but rich people were also buying many more minivans than Volvo station wagons.

Volvo had historically emphasized that its vehicles were safer. That advertising had, however, mostly focused on its sedans ... the company's biggest revenue source. A little-known fact at the time was that Volvo's executives had decided not to build a minivan because they couldn't make one that would be safe enough to meet their internal standards.

Volvo did little to compare its station wagons to minivans. You may recall that station wagon sales, which had been dropping for years, plummeted as minivans gained popularity. Volvo's decision not to act was probably driven by a perception that station wagon sales were unavoidably headed down in a major way. Why spend money on a loser?

With no countermessage from Volvo to explain its station wagon's advantages, many people who could afford a Volvo mistakenly bought minivans that served their safety objectives less well.

Appearances can certainly be deceiving. That's a major lesson of the Volvo example. Here are a few other examples of where aspects of vehicle appearances and performances can give the wrong impression:

- Bigger is better (not when it comes to parallel parking)
- More expensive is better (a Ferrari just won't carry six adults comfortably)
- What you see is what you get (many two bench truck cabs can be converted to carry more cargo internally where the back bench is)
- It's how much steel there is between you and the outside world that determines safety (a roll bar can keep you from being crushed by all that steel if you flip over ... otherwise the steel can become your enemy)
- 0 to 60 miles per hour in 4.5 seconds (but how fast can you stop this vehicle in a straight line on ice at 60 miles an hour?)

Danger Sign: Believing You Know What You Want Can Be Deceiving More significantly, beliefs can be deceiving. Here's an example of what we mean: Many people mistake what their interests truly are by framing the issue in the wrong way. Given the choice between flying and driving from Las Vegas, Nevada, to El Paso, Texas, few people would choose to drive except to save money. After all, a discounted one-way air ticket is usually available for just a little over $100. The distance is more than 700 miles and would require over 10 hours of driving, which excludes time for rest and refueling stops. For an individual, flying seems to have a clear advantage.

At some point, enough people in a family are involved that driving starts to have the cost edge.

If you change your perspective, the question looks a lot different. Between Las Vegas and El Paso you can see some of the most beautiful natural wonders and delightful anthropological sites in the world. You can go to the Grand Canyon and the large meteorite crater in Arizona to start. From there, you can take a side trip north to see the gorgeous vistas of Monument Valley and the stunning ruins of Mesa Verde. Swing east from there, and you can go through Canyon de Chelly to see a sort of Southwestern Eden before heading south towards the subterranean splendors of Carlsbad Caverns. On your way to Carlsbad stop for a UFO milk shake in Roswell, New Mexico, and read the road signs that make jokes about the Roswell incident. From Carlsbad Caverns, it's just a short drive to El Paso.

Naturally, such an amazing trip requires some advance planning, takes more time, and costs more money than flying or driving through as fast as possible. But for those additional investments in time and money in taking the road less traveled, you can have the family experience of a lifetime. The only thing you will miss is the magnificent aerial view of the Grand Canyon. But you can make up for that oversight on your next cross-country flight to or from Los Angeles by flying during the daytime … or you can take one of the many tourist flights for this purpose from Las Vegas before you start your drive.

Whenever we believe that we know exactly what we want, chances are that we are selecting a route through life that misses all the best choices. Both as suppliers and users of offerings, we owe it to ourselves and one another to overcome our facile beliefs and become aware of more choices and act on any better choices. We need to believe that there's a better way than the best way we know today. Otherwise, disbelief owns our destiny and will guide us down less rewarding roads.

Here are questions to help you identify the major sources of disbelief about your organization and its offerings:

- What does each current and potential customer and beneficiary believe are the major benefits and drawbacks of your offerings?
- Where those beliefs are incorrect, what are the reasons for the incorrect beliefs?
- How have your actions and communications fed those incorrect beliefs?
- How can you make current and potential beneficiaries and customers aware of the true benefits and drawbacks?

- How can you make your actions and communications more credible?

Sources of Mistrust

Some scientists claim that we are born with few fears. Fear of heights is one, but our families, friends, and acquaintances help us appreciate the benefits of caution in many other circumstances. In some cases, we learn to avoid certain things on a general basis, such as fire. These learned aversions can be based on misleading overgeneralizations. Fire can certainly burn us, but you can pass your hand quickly through a candle's flame and not be harmed. You can also walk barefoot over 30 feet of glowing coals and not be burned either (but we don't recommend you try it without proper instruction, preparation, and supervision).

Experience can be the source of other avoidances. If someone once said "Trust me" while selling you some shoddy merchandise that later failed, you may be wary of those who ask for your trust in other buying situations.

A lot of mistrust is based on large reactions to subtle clues ... many of which clues may not really mean what we take them to mean. For instance, you go into a store that is decorated in horribly clashing colors. You are immediately repelled and want to get away. In addition to the colors making your visit unpleasant, you wonder about the competence of any business that would make such an obvious mistake. But are they actually incompetent or merely so frugal that they only buy paint that's on deep discount because no one else will buy it? The correct answer can be quite different from either assumption. Some people are color blind and such a person may simply have hired a designer who has the same limitation.

It takes a long time for an organization to overcome such misleading sources of mistrust. A man who had not been trained as a plumber was often called on to do simple plumbing tasks for lawn sprinkling systems. There were two convenient stores where he could buy his supplies. Both stores offered free advice. One store was modern and fresh looking. The other store was a shambles and it was hard to find things in the store. You always had to ask someone to find what you needed. Because the employees spent a lot of time helping each customer, the wait could be an extra 20 minutes. In the messy store, staffers would always recommend the most expensive product or solution. Pretty soon, the man didn't go to the messy store any more.

The differences between plumbing supplies that last and plumbing supplies that don't last are often very subtle. As time passes, the differences eventually become obvious as certain products fail more often and sooner than others. After about 10 years, the man learned that the solutions the modern, fresh-looking store proposed and its merchandise were not good enough. The messy store, however, always gave good advice for lasting solutions and their stock held up. After being asked to redo many plumbing projects for no extra pay, the man learned to only buy from the messy store. The modern store later went out of business.

Here are some sources of mistrust that you need to be skeptical about as a buyer:

- Appearances (they can be misleading)
- Wait times (some things are worth waiting for)
- Danger (it may all be in your head)
- Difficult communications (they may be for your benefit)
- Unfriendliness (people may just be having a bad day)
- Secrecy (Coca-Cola isn't going to tell you their formula for a good reason)
- Rigid payment terms (they may have had a lot of deadbeats)
- Unprofessional behavior (they may have great integrity and poor manners)
- Over eagerness (they may just love helping people)
- Not many customers (FedEx had a hard time attracting customers at first)
- Being pushy (they may just be busy and have lots of demand for the offering)
- Lack of a guaranteed offer (some people just assume you know you can get your money back)

Here are questions designed to help you understand more about the trust people have in your organization and its offerings:

- Who do beneficiaries, customers, and potential customers trust the most in your industry?
- How far do they trust the most trusted?
- If beneficiaries, customers, and potential customers trust some other organization and its offerings more than your organization and its offerings, how do your actions, inactions, and appearances help create mistrust?
- How could you become more trustworthy in the view of beneficiaries, customers, and potential customers?
- What are the least expensive ways for you to gain trust?

Conduct Research to Find Your Biggest Barriers
to Adding Profitable Volume

We are always reluctant to suggest that you conduct formal, rather than informal, research with beneficiaries, potential customers, and customers. One of the reasons for that reluctance is that you may not know much about designing and conducting research and you may not want to learn how. Other reasons include the potential high cost of buying research and the difficulty of finding market research firms that can design custom studies of the sort you need. Also, many business people and organizational owners don't know what to do with the results of such research.

Keeping those issues in mind, we encourage you to bear with us and try a kind of research that overcomes those limitations. If the thought of conducting any research seems like too much for you, feel free to skip on to the beginning of the next chapter. We don't want to waste your time by insisting.

If you think you might like to find out more about your biggest barriers, we have created a simple, valuable way for you to do so. The kind of research we are recommending will improve your organization and make you vastly more successful. Read on if those benefits interest you.

Nth-Degree Tests Spot Large Obstacles

Here's the concept: We want you to run a simplified version of an nth degree test (that we described in *The Irresistible Growth Enterprise* and *The 2,000 Percent Solution Workbook*) with current and potential beneficiaries and customers to find out what changes you can make that will greatly expand your sales volume or the usage of the offerings of your nonprofit organization.

If you don't know or remember what an nth-degree test is, here's a brief description: You take factors about your offering that can vary and imagine that you increase and decrease each factor alternatively to ridiculously large and small levels. For instance, you might offer an economy size that's 100 times the largest size you have now at a very low price and a single serving that's just enough for a few seconds of use at a high profit margin. Usually, these nth-degree tests are mental experiments you run with yourself.

The lessons you learn may astound you. Here's an experience we had with a marketing test. When we were new to the consulting business, we decided to look for a way to eliminate all the time involved in attracting new clients. Our clients liked what we did. Presumably, nonclients would have the same reaction after trying our services. Having read a few marketing books, we focused on the custom that professional firms seldom offer guarantees of their work. Instead, the client is expected to pay for the results … even if those results aren't very good.

Encouraged by the idea that reversing the risk for clients might present an opportunity, we added a money-back guarantee to our most popular service, contacted most nonclients of any size, and waited for a surge of business from new clients.

We were shocked when we didn't add a single new client. In fact, we were dumbfounded when we realized that we had unintentionally scared many potential clients away. Why? These executives assumed that anyone who offered a money-back guarantee for professional services must have lots of problems with their quality … and were desperate for business. Potential clients couldn't imagine that such an offer could come from a position of quality and strength. It didn't help the perception of our offer that some of our competitors saw our letters and made up stories to suggest problems about working with our organization because we made the offer.

Had we run the experiment that we are about to describe for you, we would have avoided that well-intentioned and painful misfire and focused on some more productive opportunity. We would like to help you avoid such fiascos while identifying what people want.

Seven Simple Steps to Locate Your Obstacles

Faced with this chapter's focus on locating large obstacles, a market research purist would insist that you take every variable that you can influence (such as branding, price, promotion, offering, features, availability, packaging, and distribution method) and test each variable. While that would be nice to do, it's more than you need. We'll adopt a 2,000 percent solution approach instead to test one aspect of one area and find out whatever else you need to know in the process.

Here are the steps to follow:

First, *identify the current customers and beneficiaries who are employing your offerings for a small percentage of their total needs for that type of offering.* Many people describe these people and organizations as "light" or "occasional" users and customers.

Second, *identify former customers and beneficiaries who haven't used your offerings in at least three years but who still purchase or use what you offer from someone else.*

Third, *identify the most attractive potential customers and beneficiaries who have never employed your organization's offerings.* Typically, these are the people and organizations that will gain most and appreciate the benefits from your offerings and have large needs.

Fourth, *contact the decision makers in those three groups and ask to become the current or potential customer's or beneficiary's major provider of your offerings.*

Fifth, *thank all those who take you up on your offer and ask them why they hadn't previously selected your organization to play this role.* You'll want to make these contacts yourself so that you can hear and understand the reactions. If there is a protocol involved in your organization (such as no one contacts an account without a salesperson), by all means follow the protocol, but be sure you elicit a candid answer. Let the salesperson (or whomever you go with or have join you on the telephone) know that you will take no negative personal action towards him or her as a result of what you learn. Otherwise, the salesperson may work with the customer or beneficiary to hide the real reason from you. This result is particularly likely if the reason is unflattering to either that person or their activity in your organization. In particular, you want to find out "what's new" that caused a change in the customer's or beneficiary's behavior.

Sixth, *for those who turn down your request to become the biggest supplier, ask them a* hypothetical *question concerning how much you would have to pay their organization or them individually (if there is no organization involved) to become their lead supplier.* Note that this question should be conveyed in a way that doesn't sound like you are willing or trying to offer a bribe. Explain instead that you simply want to learn how to improve your effectiveness as a supplier.

Then comes the magic. Whether they can cite a specific amount or not, ask why it would take a payment of whatever sort to become their lead supplier. Encourage them to tell you what disadvantage that payment would overcome. Then write down everything they tell you. They will be describing some of the major obstacles to increasing the delivery of your offerings by 20 times.

Prepare yourself to receive some nasty surprises. Some people wouldn't use your offerings if you paid them a queen's or a king's ransom. They may be angry with your organization about some old problem or very committed to another supplier (who may even have them under a 10-year contract that they would have to buy out). Many of the other reasons will be based on a misunderstanding of what you offer. If you bump into such a misunderstanding, politely ask why they came to that conclusion. It may be as simple as their laboratory does a different quality test than your laboratory does, and you don't look as good on the test their laboratory runs. One company who paid a lot of attention to this kind of information found that its customers ranked suppliers on a variety of performance measures every month. If you fell down in one area, you lost business the next month. Returning telephone calls with accurate information within two minutes could garner your company a lot more business. But the telephone service people didn't know that. That ignorance was quickly eliminated and sales quickly climbed.

In particular, you should pay attention to any differences you hear between those who have recent experience with your organization and those who don't have any experience. The sources of discontent and disinterest will probably turn out to be different from the one group to the other unless you organization is tainted by a well-known bad reputation.

Seventh, *personally contact some of those who have never used your offerings or those of your competitors to find out why they don't choose to use these offerings.* Once again ask, hypothetically, how much would have to be paid to add them as a customer or beneficiary. Pay particular attention to these answers. Hidden under the surface of what you hear will be possible ways to expand your volume by 20 times without incurring a competitive reaction. Dealing with these unmet needs can allow you to turn on the turbo and speed up your progress. In many cases, you will discover that these people have substantial difficulties to overcome before they can make effective use of your offerings. In other cases, it will simply be a matter of cost. They are doing without because it seems like a better economic decision. Among those people, look for those who might be willing to run some experiments with you to find ways to overcome these obstacles.

Here are questions designed to summarize what you learned from this limited nth-degree research:

- What are the three most common reasons why those who are now willing to let you become their main supplier say they decided to make the switch?
- What are the five most common reasons why those who are unwilling to let you be their main supplier say they decided not to choose you despite your hypothetical offer of a queen's or a king's ransom?
- What are the eight most common reasons why those who don't use your kind of offering are unwilling to start doing so now, even after your hypothetical offer of a large payment?

Chapter 3

Design an Efficient Route Under, Over, and Around the Worst Obstacles
Decide on Which Usage Barriers to Minimize

Nobody in his right mind tries to cross a broad ditch in two steps.
— Carl von Clausewitz

Travel through the mountains by road or by train, and you quickly see the wisdom of adapting your organizational path to avoid obstacles. The alternatives are often to level mountains or build enormously expensive tunnels through them. Neither alternative is usually worth much consideration.

But the challenge of avoiding obstacles is more significant than it first seems. The cheapest road to build, or railroad track to lay, may also be the least efficient to operate. If cars and trucks are forced to switch back and forth endlessly over tedious ascents and descents, massive traffic jams will occur and wider roads will have to be built ... adding needless expense. Similarly, long delays on upgrades and downgrades may mean that a second track will have to be laid for a railroad. Make a mountain road too steep and people will die when their brakes fail on the descents. Put the road or track where erosion will cause lots of collapses, and you will have a repair nightmare and frequent traffic interruptions.

Choosing the route under, over, and around the worst obstacles has to be just right … or you will be trying to jump across a broad ditch in two steps.

In this chapter, we focus on eliminating the barriers to expanded usage that you uncover using the methods found in Chapter 2. First, you will brainstorm with others to accumulate as many ideas as possible. Second, you will thrash those idea grain stacks to separate out just the choicest seeds of potential improvement. Third, you will compare those best opportunities to select the most attractive barrier-avoiding methods in light of your resources.

Find More Ways to Overcome Obstacles to Expanding Consumption of Your Offerings

Many people use an approach to problem solving that emphasizes finding the best people and turning them loose on the issues. By itself, that approach is fine. But if that's all you do, you will miss most of the best opportunities.

Focusing on what the best people can offer is a common mistake. Here's one dimension of that mistake: People who are skilled in creating 2,000 percent solutions often develop such solutions by themselves and then share the results with others … hoping to persuade everyone else that the new approach is the only way to go. Sometimes such lone rangers are disappointed to find that others don't share their logic and may even point out important issues that have not been considered. Far better is to involve all those who are stakeholders in what needs to be improved. Still better is to involve as many good thinkers as possible in developing your 2,000 percent solutions.

Think of a gold mine as a good metaphor for the barriers to much greater usage. In many mines, there is easily 20 times more gold remaining than has already been extracted. Before you can obtain it, you have to locate where that gold is and how to extract it efficiently. It usually isn't practical to excavate all the rock under the acreage you own. Once that gold is turned into mined ore that can be easily processed and refined, you can assume that the gold will soon be in circulation as jewelry, coins, investments, and financial reserves of central banks.

An organization's business model usually has the same characteristics.

The current business model only produces one-twentieth or less of the usage that's possible. But you have to locate where changes in the business model can be profitably made before the usage can reach the higher and more valuable level.

Consider the Goldcorp Challenge example again from this new perspective. We note that even this excellent approach could have been improved. Goldcorp could have probably produced even better results if it had made the following changes in its process:

- *Invited external geologists to enter a prechallenge contest to design the challenge's structure, process, and prizes.* If these geologists had helped formulate the challenge, the geologists might have described better ways to make data available, selected better incentives to pursue the challenge, and increased interest and participation in the challenge.

- *Adjusted the design of the challenge to require using the 2,000 percent solution process for both suggesting where reserves might be found and exploration to verify those reserve hypotheses.* Determining that there might be $3 billion in new reserves at a level far below the main shaft wouldn't have done Goldcorp much good unless the company could afford to make the extensive investments in exploration and infrastructure to verify and extract those reserves. By combining the concept of finding reserves with the idea of extracting profits rapidly through using the 2,000 percent solution process, geologists would probably have found reserves that were smaller but easier to profit from than those that emerged from the contest. Goldcorp's profits and cash flow would probably have been much higher in the near term if that were the case. Subsequent challenges could have focused on finding larger, more difficult to extract reserves.

- *Provided for a follow-on contest to design the best exploration program to find and exploit reserves assuming that reserves are located in a variety of likely locations.* If you have ever visited a gold mine, you would be impressed by all the effort and time it takes to explore for ore. It's slow and costly. Most exploration doesn't turn up anything interesting. An optimized exploration program to take into account the likely prospects could be designed to remove years and tens of millions of dollars from the effort while locating more profitable and immediate gold ore to mine.

- *Sponsored a contest for geologists to design a challenge for finding high-potential reserves in locales Goldcorp doesn't own where no one is looking now.* One of the unintended consequences of the Goldcorp Challenge was to encourage many mining companies to hold their own similar competitions. That response meant that hidden value was less likely to be found in a developed mining property. But the potential to find hidden value in an undeveloped property is still as large as ever. Goldcorp did sponsor a follow-on contest, Global Search Challenge, to find new properties to acquire or develop, but the results were not nearly as rewarding as the Goldcorp Challenge. By letting potential participants design this new kind of challenge, it may well be that a better process with greater benefits would have emerged.

Utilize New Methods
for Finding More Potential Solutions

Smaller organizations often don't have the luxury to sponsor contests of the sort that Goldcorp and Procter & Gamble sponsor. Both of those organizations had large existing budgets that were going to be spent for something. The cost of the contest could simply be a substitute for part of those committed budgets. Any economic benefits that flowed from the contests could then be used to further other obstacle-avoiding investments.

A small organization might find its very existence is threatened if it spends hundreds of thousands of dollars to obtain and organize better information before even launching a contest. Clearly, a different strategy is needed for such resource-constrained organizations. Interestingly, strategies that help the resource-constrained organizations will often serve the larger companies better. Let's explore some possible approaches using the Goldcorp experience as a context to explain each point.

Scale Down the Search for Answers

Perhaps the most obvious alternative to a challenge contest is to scale down the search for answers. However, it's almost always a bad idea when scaling down the search means involving fewer people. When scaling down the search means looking at just the most productive elements, the results may actually leave you better off than if you looked more broadly. With more focus on the key elements, you may find better solutions. The earlier suggestion we made that Goldcorp sponsor a prior contest to design the challenge is an example of scaling down the search. Much of the benefit from the challenge occurred because Goldcorp put all of its geological information into an electronic three-dimensional database. That new resource created much of the potential to locate new reserves regardless of the search process employed. In fact, this new data resource was so powerful that many of Goldcorp's geologists were able to spot some of the best potential reserves before the contest was launched. A resource-constrained organization could have used that insight to focus first on developing data for those areas near where the richest deposits had been found in the past. Continuations of high-grade veins in the more developed parts of the mine would be more quickly and less expensively spotted with this approach.

Here is a four-step approach to scaling down the size of the search while increasing the size of the potential benefits:

1. *Identify what is the most valuable question to answer.* For Goldcorp, the answer might have been locating the most immediate profits from gold mining while spending the least for investment per dollar of profit. Starting from that perspective, Goldcorp might have found that the company would have been better served to develop contests to find underdeveloped properties to buy before launching a challenge to optimize the value of any one property. Such an approach could have added billions to Goldcorp's value by making more low-cost acquisitions available.

2. *Define what is the least amount of information that will answer the most valuable question.* Expert help can assist here, but you may not need to run a contest to get that help. You may only need to talk to a few people. For instance, to locate undervalued mining properties you probably only need four pieces of information: the operating costs per ton of adjoining mines (you will be mining the same geological formations in most cases); the operating costs per ton of the mine under consideration; how well the mine has been explored and developed compared to adjoining mines; and how well organized the geological data are for the mine under consideration. Attractive properties to purchase can be found

among those mines with high operating costs that are located next to low-cost ones, which have done less relative exploration and development, and where the geological data are more poorly organized.

3. *Find the least costly and most rapid ways of gaining the minimum information.* Again, you may not need a contest to locate the answers; other sources may serve better. For instance, many public companies and private firms that hope to go public reveal information about each of their mines. You could begin by examining those sources to see how much you can learn for only the cost of your time.

4. *Test your thinking.* Try out the approach you've identifiied a little by seeing what you turn up, how long it takes you, and what the csts are. Stop your approach if it seems to be slower, less effective, or more costly than a contest.

Get Help to Reduce the Costs of the Search

Having scaled down the search, you should also get help to reduce the costs of the search. There may be a database that already exists containing much of the information you want. There may be people who know major parts of the required answers and who can share that information with you at little cost to them. There may be a substitute piece of information that can further simplify the search. Here are some ways to get that help:

- *Find out how the biggest successes have occurred in doing what you want to accomplish.* In the Goldcorp case, you would talk to those who are familiar with the acquired mine properties that have provided the most profits and cash flow annually compared to their purchase and development costs. From this research, you might determine that the best deals were all done after gold prices had been at low levels for many years.

  If your current gold-price environment isn't like that, you may need to refine your search further to locate how those fared best who bought mine properties during a gold-price environment like the one you are currently experiencing. People who are regularly involved in financing such deals may well have learned how such properties were successfully selected. Since such financiers will be interested in assisting others who succeed with financing, valuable insights may be gained at no cost.

- *Look for ways to create new combinations of cost-reduction methods in answering your question.* From your interviews with those who know about the biggest successes, you will have discovered a number of different effective approaches to supplement free public data. Chances are, however, that no organization has combined several of these approaches.

  Consider how you might combine those approaches sequentially to reduce the cost of your investigation. Let's assume in the Goldcorp case that some companies used tips from former employees, while others relied on talking to mining equipment suppliers, and still others got their insights from taking aerial photographs of the sites. The easiest and cheapest of these resources are probably going to be the mining equipment suppliers. Talking to them first might reduce the number of acquisition prospects from every mine in the world down to as few as five mines. The next easiest to accomplish is probably an aerial photograph. Combining those two resources, you may determine that you are interested in three mines. At that point, you could begin to look for former employees of those three mines to provide further insights and to validate what you think you know. If you only find the former employee information for one or two of the mines, that may be enough to locate a valuable investment opportunity.

Consider Unconventional Resources

Until Robert McEwen, Goldcorp's CEO, attended a conference at MIT about the free software movement, no one had probably ever thought about accessing experts inexpensively to help find more gold. Mr. McEwen took that powerful software example and applied it in a new way to his own industry. In the process, an important business model innovation was born. But that success doesn't mean that all important business model innovations have already been developed and applied. Here are some other examples of value-adding innovations that you could apply:

- *Outsource the key development and value-adding tasks.* People are outsourcing more and more. The usual approach is to outsource what isn't very important or takes up too much time. But you could stand that idea on its head and let outsourcers bid to take on your most important activities with compensation tied to results. For Goldcorp this could have meant selling off the right to explore and develop the mine while still owning the mine and retaining an important part of the cash flow. Because each such deal would have freed up or generated substantial capital for Goldcorp, the firm would have been able to purchase and develop many more mines — and more rapidly — with this approach.

Many reject this concept of outsourcing key tasks because they appreciate the value of having an organization become superb at these tasks. That view can be shortsighted. Many organizations couldn't begin to develop a capability to do key tasks that's nearly as good as what's available immediately from another existing organization. Many entrepreneurs who understand this concept simply sell their company or assets to the organization that can add the most value. That price, however, will be lower than putting the more effective organization in harness and gaining from whatever they learn to do better.

- *Shift your focus from the main goal to finding out about the best use for the leftovers.* We all try to get more of what we understand best. A gold miner tries to find more gold and make more money from it. A writer tries to find more people to buy and read writing. In the process, there are a lot of surplus resources and materials created.

If you think of those leftovers as your main source of profits, better solutions will occur to you and to those who think about these questions. In gold mining, there is a lot of effort put into digging holes in the ground and carting out rubble. What else can you do with those holes and that rubble? In the backup electronic and paper storage businesses, underground facilities in hard rock environments are considered to be very valuable. Can some areas be inexpensively converted into these uses? Rubble may also contain other valuable minerals. Have the tailings been processed to take advantage of that? Many mines have piles of tailings from decades of mining when prices were less than 5 percent of today's prices. It often becomes reasonable to reprocess those tailings to extract different minerals. The remaining rubble with the proper treatment may help make good road beds and foundations. A Japanese railway ran into seemingly unlimited springs of mineral water in a tunnel it dug. Does your mine contain mineral water that could be profitably bottled and sold for its superior taste and health characteristics as the Japanese produced from their tunnel? See *Corporate Creativity* by Alan G. Robinson and Sam Stern (Berrett-Koehler, 1997) for more information on the Japanese example.

- *Determine if you can access free resources in new ways.* The world is full of people who would like to learn new skills that will enable them to pursue their personal interests and careers. Many of Habitat for Humanity's more experienced volunteers are involved for this reason. If you offer those who are going to help you more chances to learn that are valuable to them, you can staff many more of your efforts with volunteers. A gold mine might do this by offering internships for geologists, training for apprentice miners, workshops for those who want to learn how to maintain equipment, and applied business courses for those who want to work in higher administrative roles. Many of your existing employees and volunteers would probably relish playing these leadership and educational roles so the added cost may be slight.

    Another for-profit organizational approach could be to donate a portion of improved results to a charitable purpose. The for-profit organization could then coordinate with a charitable organization to find talented volunteers who would like to spend some time improving the for-profit organization in order to increase charitable contributions.

Here are questions designed to summarize what you learned from examining ways to avoid significant obstacles to expanded consumption or usage of your offerings:

- What are the three most expensive obstacles to avoid?
- How do the costs of avoiding those obstacles compare to the costs of eliminating the obstacles instead?
- Why are those obstacles more costly to eliminate than to avoid?

Chapter 4

Remove Some
Road-Building Obstacles
Design Away Usage Barriers

A part, a large part, of travelling is an engagement of the ego v. the world....
The world is hydra headed, as old as the rocks and as changing as the sea,
enmeshed inextricably in its ways. The ego wants to arrive at places safely and
on time.
— Sybille Bedford

Sometimes it's simply better to remove an obstacle than to avoid it. Some areas, for example, are so mountainous that the only way to avoid barriers entirely is to drive hundreds of miles out of your way around the mountains. Clearly a better choice is to travel through the mountains following a more direct route from which obstacles can be removed at reasonable cost.

If you follow roads and rail lines in such areas, you will usually find your route winds along through valleys cut by streams and rivers. Rushing water and ice have combined over the years to remove many of the rocky obstacles from the valleys. Seasonal water and ice often remain among the most significant obstacles within valleys. For instance, if you travel at the bottom of such a valley, you run the risk of being flooded out during the spring thaws and heavy rains. Because of those temporary obstacles, most valley roads and rail lines are elevated with bridges and fill above the level of potential flood waters and away from potential rock and land slides. In other cases where the cost is reasonable, water channels are redirected by dams and levees so that the water and ice obstacles are eliminated. In similar fashion, you will find that it sometimes makes more sense to eliminate an organizational obstacle than to avoid it.

In human interactions, the same observation can be made about removing obstacles. For instance, everyone who has ever encountered a bully knows that avoiding a bully only defers, at best, unpleasant occurrences. If you confront and defeat the bully's intent, chances are that you will have fewer problems in the future. Human attitudes can be tougher obstacles than rock in this sense. But by using the right tools, you can chip away at some of these human obstacles with reasonable efforts until no barrier to progress remains.

Identify Obstacles That Are Better Eliminated Than Avoided

One of the great tragedies of our time is the scourge of AIDS. In some places, most of the parents have died, leaving legions of orphans with few to care for them. Because the disease is often undetected until the later stages, many infected people unwittingly infect others. In too many countries, the cost of medicine to delay or treat symptoms is beyond what most people can afford. People die in many cases wondering why their fellow humans place so little value on their lives and contributions. Those who don't contract the disease feel overwhelmed by the enormous social costs that the survivors are bearing.

Yet the disease is relatively easy to prevent if you are well informed and committed to remaining uninfected: Avoid intravenous needles that have already been used by others. Either be sexually chaste or have sexual contacts only with people who have been repeatedly shown not to have the infection. If in doubt about a sexual partner, abstain or use condoms.

Despite the relative ease of taking such precautions, the disease continues to infect millions more. What's the barrier? In most cases, it's primarily ignorance. Here are some of the forms of ignorance that help spread this epidemic:

- Not knowing how the infection is transmitted from one person to another
- Believing that you can always tell an infected person by looking at him or her
- Not knowing about dangerous practices followed by your sex

partner
• Acting on false beliefs about what causes AIDS

Avoiding the removal of ignorance as an obstacle doesn't make sense. If you let ignorance continue, many more people will be infected, suffer, and die. If that occurs, you also somewhat increase the risk for those who are not ignorant because the knowledgeable will come into more frequent contact with infected people.

But knowing that you should obliterate an obstacle doesn't mean that you have the awareness of how to do so using the available resources. Here is where creating a 2,000 percent solution can help.

One of our students in a poor country considered in some detail how to overcome ignorance about AIDS. He determined that the obstacle could best be removed by overcoming the communications stall. Millions are knowledgeable about the causes of AIDS. If those in the know simply shared that information with a few people every month, it would not take long before everyone would have the information. Problems, however, remain.

For some of the ignorant, the news would not be credible. Some people in this country believe that AIDS is the result of a witch's incantations. Perhaps the people who believe that would be convinced if the witches they feared the most shared the correct information with them, and the witches promised not to inflict AIDS on the people if they followed the appropriate precautions.

For others, part of the precaution message is a conflict with their religious beliefs. For some religious people, condoms are an abomination and their use encourages people to sin in a variety of ways. But religious people would usually be glad to speak openly about the benefits of chastity, fidelity, and care with intravenous needles in preventing AIDS. Since those choices are all effective preventions, that message should be encouraged.

For the young, some don't have the knowledge about biology to understand a medical explanation. Like the person who wants to use electricity, but doesn't understand what electricity is, these people need to simply have faith that taking the right actions will generate the results they want. For such young people, role models among sports stars, celebrities, and moral leaders can credibly share the prevention message by drawing on the trust the young people have in their heroes and heroines.

While this example may seem far from the business interests of many readers, the lesson is profound. Even when life itself is at stake for our families and loved ones, people can be poor communicators. Imagine how much more so the communications stall blocks progress in commercial enterprises where so much less is personally at stake.

Find Obstacle-Eliminating Solutions

Knowing that obstacles exist is one thing. Eliminating those obstacles is a more difficult activity. Let's look at some simple steps you can take to identify superior ways to eliminate the most important obstacles.

Discover One Solution to Overcome All the Obstacles That Need to Be Removed

Answering the questions at the end of Chapter 3 should have identified for you the three most expensive obstacles to avoid. How should you look at the alternative of removing those obstacles? The traditional approach would be to study removing each obstacle separately and find the optimal solution for that obstacle. Then you would compare the cost of avoidance to removal and implement the solutions that provided the most benefits compared to the costs and whatever resources are available.

We advise that you pursue that traditional approach only as a last resort. Piecemeal solutions to expanding usage and markets usually work less well than more comprehensive solutions that remove all the obstacles through a single approach.

Going back to the example of building roads through mountains, a dam might eliminate all flooding and landslide dangers for hundreds of square miles. Without looking for that optimal dam site, road builders would be facing hundreds of places where bridges and elevated road and track beds would have to be erected. Each adjustment in the route would require a lot of expense to create a specific solution.

Similarly, persuading the one hundred most admired people in a small community to educate others about how to prevent AIDS and to present positive role models in their own behavior might well eliminate the need to put in place hundreds of other programs that probably wouldn't be as successful in combination.

We have learned a great deal from watching our clients and students produce wonderful 2,000 percent solutions. One of the most important lessons is that the bigger the challenge, the better people seem to do in creating 2,000 percent solutions. The lesson for you here is to frame the need for the solution as broadly and as large as possible.

As a result, we encourage you now to reframe your challenge in this part of the book to consider if there is a 2,000 percent solution that will remove *all* of your significant obstacles to expanded usage, whether or not these obstacles can be inexpensively avoided. If that idea takes your breath away, it should.

Let's look at a historic example. Hannibal wanted to invade Rome's northern territory in Italy with his Carthaginian forces. But Carthage didn't have the naval power to launch an invasion of the sort that allies used during World War II to take the land battle from North Africa to Italy. Hannibal conceived instead of invading northern Italy by traversing the Alps with elephants. In battle, the elephants initially provided a powerful strategic advantage over riders on horseback and foot soldiers. While the elephants lasted, Hannibal's forces did well. What he didn't take into account is that the Romans would learn to disable and kill his elephants. Eventually, Hannibal had no more elephants and his forces were marooned away from their base of supplies and reinforcements. The end was inevitable.

Had Hannibal anticipated a long campaign, he could instead have established an ongoing supply route to bring regular reinforcements of elephants, soldiers, weapons, armor, and food for his exposed troops. As more territory was conquered, Hannibal could have shortened his supply lines to permit friendly ships from Carthage to drop off supplies in northern Italy. With that ever shortening supply line in place, world history might well have turned out differently to favor of the Carthaginians.

Focus on <u>N</u>th-Degree Thinking to Develop Superior Obstacle-Eliminating Solutions

A good place to start <u>n</u>th degree thinking is by imagining that the 20 times expansion of consumption, practices, or usage of your offerings has already occurred because obstacles have been eliminated. Imagine also that everyone is very pleased that this expansion has taken place. Here are eight questions to help you gain insights from this musing:

1. Why is everyone pleased that the expansion has occurred?
2. How could people be even more pleased?
3. What changed from before the expansion to after?
4. Why didn't those helpful changes occur sooner?
5. How could the pace of progress have been accelerated?

6. What one approach could have eliminated more of the early obstacles?
7. What could have accelerated the best obstacle-obliterating approach?
8. What can be done in the next hour to start implementing that approach?

Let's take an example and answer the questions to make this mental process seem more real. Since we have been looking in this chapter at changing behaviors in relationship to AIDS, we continue with that subject as our example.

1. Everyone is pleased after almost everyone uses AIDS infection-avoiding behaviors because:
   - New infections virtually stop.
   - People have less reason to fear being infected and feel less stressed in their personal relationships.
   - People will lose fewer loved ones than would otherwise occur.
   - The strain on health care resources and families will stop growing at some point.

2. People could be more pleased if:
   - The number of new infections dropped sooner.
   - No one had reason to fear becoming infected.
   - People lost no more loved ones.
   - The strain on health care resources and families was already declining.

3. Here are the factors that changed from before the expansion of the improved behavior to after:
   - Everyone learned how to avoid contracting AIDS.
   - People became careful not to use drugs and alcohol to excess so their judgment did not become impaired.
   - People who are infected with HIV or AIDS always shared that information with others.
   - People who are going to use intravenous needles and have sexual relations with multiple partners always have access to unused needles and condoms.

- Important social advantages are gained by volunteers who help AIDS patients.
- Health-care technology improves so that health care workers are seldom infected through contact with HIV or AIDS patients.

4. Here are some reasons why this changed behavior didn't occur sooner:
    - There was an incorrect belief that only homosexuals were at risk.
    - Ignorance existed about the enormous social costs of an AIDS infection.
    - There was no social consensus to eliminate AIDS.
    - Discussing AIDS carried a social stigma.
    - People had few incentives to be tested for AIDS.
    - AIDS tests were unaffordable for many people.
    - Using excessive amounts of drugs and alcohol was socially acceptable for some.
    - Being known as someone who was infected with AIDS could cost your job, your health insurance, access to health care, and sexual contacts.
    - Clean needles and unused condoms were not readily available for all.
    - Caring for AIDS patients was considered undesirable and dangerous by most people.
    - Safe health-care technologies were affordable only for some.

5. Here are some possible ways that progress could have been accelerated:
    - Mandatory, universal testing.
    - Universal disclosure of AIDS infection status — perhaps through a card with a record of past test results.
    - Mandatory testing of knowledge about AIDS, such as in connection with driver's licensing and renewals.
    - Free distribution of new intravenous needles and condoms.
    - Economic and social incentives to care for AIDS patients who had followed good practices to minimize the chances of others being infected.

- Economic benefits for AIDS patients who followed good practices to minimize infecting others.

6. Reasonable people will differ on this point, but a few of these potential approaches could have made a large difference in eliminating more early obstacles. Mandatory testing of knowledge about AIDS is probably the least costly, fastest route to cutting off the spread of infections. In many countries, you are required to take blood tests before you marry, have your car inspected for safety before you drive it, use seat belts when you drive, and pass a test before you can become a citizen. It would not be too far-fetched to require that you to know how to live a normal lifespan by avoiding a deadly plague. From this reasonably universal knowledge could come a social consensus to take the other inexpensive, helpful steps such as mandatory testing, universal disclosure of AIDS infection status, and free distribution of new needles and condoms.

7. The best obstacle-obliterating approach regarding relationship behaviors concerning AIDS is communication. The challenge is to emphasize obstacle obliterating with communications about changing behaviors that affect AIDS infections. This analysis suggests that our student's focus on overcoming the communications stall about AIDS was a potentially potent approach to eliminating obstacles. The likely best approach is to enroll the most admired and persuasive community member to head up the effort of enrolling other leaders into a combined effort. Ideally, this person should be someone who has played a similar role before. In the United States, a widely admired former president of the country could play such a role. Since there are two major political parties in the United States, a team of widely admired former presidents from each party would probably be even more successful. Former president Clinton already has a foundation dedicated to this issue, and he has partnered with former president George H. W. Bush on tsunami relief. Perhaps that partnership could be extended to this problem, as well. The two men would be highly effective both in recruiting other leaders in the United States as well as visible leaders in communities around the world. A cadre of visible leaders from various celebrity fields could each donate a million dollars to

fund the recruitment effort to put the right leaders together. If you made the social cachet of joining the group strong enough, there are few limits to how much could be accomplished. Each country and community has its equivalent potential core of support for such an effort. If you like this possible approach, feel free to share this idea with those who can play that role in your community.

By lining up the most esteemed members of a community or society to espouse learning about AIDS-avoiding practices, you should soon create a situation where universal testing of that knowledge would be deemed acceptable. Governmental and nonprofit-led initiatives would soon fill in the gaps in knowledge.

8. As for what can be done in the next hour to start accelerating that approach, someone who knows the leaders who are the best candidates to spearhead the approach can call on those leaders. Be sure that follow-up is frequent.

Test Your Concept for One Obstacle-Eliminating Effort with the Benefits of Using Two Such Approaches

Most cars operate with two front windshield wipers. Those devices are designed to overlap in the middle and alternate in cleaning up water flung off by the power of the other wiper. A single wiper blade, by comparison, is usually not as efficient because the blade has to travel at higher speed to wipe the same surface area. Unless you keep a fresh wiper blade, you will also have a streaky wipe much sooner with one blade versus two.

In similar fashion, the best individual solution will not work nearly as well in some cases as two complementary solutions will. Here's an example: from the beginning, Southwest Airlines had a valid business model for dramatically lowering the cost of commercial aviation on popular, short flights. Having that model in place meant that Southwest could weather whatever the competition wanted to throw at it in the early days. Most other low-fare carriers have not been so lucky. They had low fares … but didn't always have low costs to match. Ryanair was such an airline in lacking the right business model in the beginning. It racked up lots of losses as it built a passenger base and tried to become low cost. Fortunately, Ryanair eventually adopted its improved version of the Southwest business model to also achieve cost leadership before Ryanair got so big that making the switch became too difficult.

The airlines that have profitably expanded their passenger volume by 20 times on a sustained basis have always used two methods to create that enviable success:

1. Prices far below what competitors have been charging.
2. Costs so much lower than competitors that added customer benefits become profitable to deliver even at the lower prices.

If we look at the latest such innovator in U.S. low-fare aviation, the point becomes even more obvious. The air carrier jetBlue saw a parallel opportunity to that pursued by Southwest through providing long-haul flights between popular destinations at low prices and low costs. Knowing that Southwest was probably going to be its most effective future competitor for popular, long-haul routes, jetBlue was designed to be able to withstand entry into those routes by that excellent competitor. The newer carrier chose a more fuel-efficient aircraft and larger plane than many of the older Southwest Boeing 737s, the latest version of the Airbus A320. The blue-named airline also adopted a folksy quality, with humorous blue-themed snacks and beverages and quirky blue names for its aircraft. Realizing that its long flights might lead to tedium, jetBlue installed onboard individual television screens tied to satellite television. This feature allows passengers to wile away the hours watching their favorite soap operas, stock market channels, or prime-time shows. With great on-time service, efficiency in baggage handling, and frequent flights, jetBlue was soaring on a rapid growth path based on what appeared to be lasting advantages over competitors at the time this book was written.

In the future, we can expect that astute entrepreneurs and strategists will eventually realize that there will be occasions when a complementary tripartite set of competitive advantages will work even better than lower prices and costs for growing volume by 20 times. We believe that such an approach will be essential before long in the highly competitive U.S. airline industry. For such airlines, the third obstacle-eliminating element will probably involve erasing needless ground costs and time wasters for passengers. For instance, it often costs more now to park at an airport for the duration of a trip than it does to fly. Smart airlines will eventually put in their own low-priced parking lots, great luggage handling capabilities at the parking lots, and comfortable transportation to and from the terminal. The result will be to provide a more pleasant, faster, and less expensive experience between arriving at the airport and sitting in an airline seat, and leaving the other terminal and making the reverse trip. Today, you often spend three to four miserable hours in and around two airports to take a one-hour flight.

Airlines need to look to the ground first if they want to take off to 20 times greater volume.

To test out this alternative of a two- or three-part combined approach, you repeat the same eight questions as before but based on expecting that you've reached your result after having used the two or more complementary approaches.

Take the New Approach Out for a Spin

It doesn't matter how many road obstacles are removed in your mind by such mental exercises. If your vehicle isn't up to providing a comfortable, safe, and efficient journey, you won't arrive at where you want to go. Most astute car buyers know that a test drive helps them avoid buyer's remorse. Now that rental car companies offer more types of cars, minivans, SUVs, and trucks, you can replace the traditional round-the-block test drive with a long trip. For those who are concerned about avoiding a lemon (a vehicle that just never seems to work right regardless of the repairs that are made), you can cautiously take out a lease on the vehicle with an option to buy if things work out.

Thought experiments, like those we have been describing so far in this chapter, are great ways to begin developing business models and advantaged strategies for adding 20 times more sales. But thought experiments are like the research that you do to narrow down your possible vehicle choices to two or three models. After that point, you have to shift from imagination to physically testing what can really be done. Why? It's simple. Experience has shown that two out of three strategies that organizations dream up to establish great volume increases cannot be effectively implemented.

The thinking route you've been following has probably improved your odds of success. Why? First, your surviving ideas at this point probably have the potential to gain you more than 20 times increased volume. If your implementation is somewhat faulty, you may still enjoy 20-times improvements. In addition, your execution will improve over time. The smooth operations that we all respect at Southwest Airlines and Ryanair didn't happen overnight. Second, you've been forced to look at a variety of ways that volume can be greatly increased. In the course of that thinking, you've ruled out a lot more alternatives than most executives who make faulty strategy choices ever consider. Some of those alternatives that you have ruled out are among the two out of three strategies that cannot be implemented. Third, we've kept you focusing your thinking on simpler ways to accomplish big results. Simple approaches are more likely to be implemented successfully.

But there's no way to insure against overoptimism about implementation … except to test out your thinking before you make a major commitment.

Look for a Stealthy Way to Take a Test Drive

When the major automobile companies come up with an exciting concept vehicle, they keep it under wraps for as long as possible. For this purpose, they have many indoor facilities where various aspects of the vehicle can be tested in private. As an example, you can tell a lot about the aerodynamics and potential fuel efficiency of a vehicle by putting it in a wind tunnel. You can also stage test crashes with robotic dummies filled with sensors. But when you think you've got all the flaws worked out, you still need to take the vehicle out for a challenging test drive. All automobile companies have secure facilities where they can conduct these performance tests. They find out how the vehicle feels when it takes a difficult turn, how fast it actually accelerates, what the fuel efficiency really is, how well the brakes work, and so forth. To keep these tests secret, the vehicles are wrapped in shrouds while being transported to and from the test tracks. The tracks are placed in remote areas that cannot be observed from nearby locations.

You need to take the same kinds of precautions with your implementation test. Your objective is to make the test as invisible as possible to competitors. Otherwise, you are simply running a clinic for competitors to take your thinking profitably to market.

How can you conduct stealth testing? Starting small is usually a good idea. Let's assume that Southwest Airlines wants to test methods for adding discount parking for its customers. Most airports are owned by government entities and have limited ability to transfer their resources to private ownership. But if we move just a few feet away from the airport, it's a whole new ball game. Many airports are ringed by privately owned parking facilities that charge a little bit less than the airport operations do for parking. Using various anonymous-sounding trusts and corporations, Southwest could buy one such lot next to an airport where parking is overpriced and the local airport management is open to innovations in passenger service. A new parking manager could be installed who is asked to try out new pricing schemes for parkers, new services for those with luggage, and better ways of linking parkers to their airlines. The local head of Southwest operations could be instructed to be friendlier about making adjustments and easing the testing process without letting anyone know that the two entities are owned by the same company. Then, Southwest could experiment to its heart's content until all the bugs are worked out … or the approach turns out to be wholly impractical. What is the worst that could happen if this test drive failed? Southwest would have lost some money during the experiment but could go back to profitably operating the parking lot at the end. At some point, the parking lot could probably be sold for a gain that would exceed any losses incurred during the experiment. If the first site worked okay, Southwest could secretly expand the experiment to a few more airports. Once convinced that it had a winner, Southwest could either buy a public off-airport parking chain and sell the nonairport lots or accelerate its practice of buying up individual owners at different airports. When enough lots were in place, the new program could be made public and receive all the fanfare it deserved.

What are the principles you should follow in designing your test drive? Here are our ideas. Feel free to add to them.

- Make the initial efforts as small as you can without compromising what you will learn.
- Reduce the cost of ineffective results.
- Keep your findings from being observed and understood by a competitor.
- Give yourself lots of flexibility to try different implementation approaches if the first one turns out to be flawed.
- Use the experiment to get more feedback from current and potential customers about what they like and don't like about your concept and execution of that concept.
- Expand the experiment while remaining stealthy.
- Give those who believe in the concept a chance to react to its execution during the experiment.

Speed Up Your Trip by Testing Every Promising Idea Simultaneously in Stealth Mode

Leaders are often proud of their ability to make tough decisions and drive forward despite difficulties. However, that courage is usually a dangerous attribute when it comes to taking test drives of new ways to expand volume by 20 times. Why? Many great improvements emerge from trial-and-error experimentation. The priorities that any leader establishes for expanding to twenty times volume will, however, almost always turn out to be inferior to the priorities that emerge from simply picking the best performing alternative after running lots of experiments.

We are reminded of that observation by the early days of Grey Poupon® mustard's rapid expansion in the United States. Excellent brand thinkers had developed a set of assumptions then about the brand that they ruled could not be violated. Those assumptions included some of the following:

- No package could be priced at retail over $1.00.
- The package had to be made of clear glass with painted letters and images on it.
- Only one flavor, the original version, could be offered.
- The formulation had to include white wine.
- The package's appearance had to evoke the product's French origins as a Dijon mustard.

Rapid growth followed when these assumptions were loosened to allow single serving packets that were sold to airline caterers for use with onboard sandwiches. People discovered that they liked Grey Poupon® and began looking for it in their supermarkets.

Today, the brand sells 200 times more volume than when the brand assumptions were made. If we look at how the brand has evolved, a trip to our refrigerator shows that:

- A popular size continues to be the "new" 8 ounce glass jar introduced in the early 1970s. But you can also buy the mustard in 10 ounce squeeze bottles and larger-size glass jars.
- The retail price for 8 to 10 ounces continues to be less than $1.00 a package if we take inflation increases out of the current price. But the larger-size glass jars sell for much more than that amount in constant dollars. Clearly, the convenience of not running out of the mustard as often and a reduced price per serving made the package's price point less important to purchasers and consumers.
- The squeeze bottles are made out of flexible plastic with plastic lids. The 8 ounce jars still have metal lids. The lettering is now printed on plastic sheets that are glued to the packages rather than being painted onto the glass jars and plastic bottles.
- You can buy the original Dijon flavor, a "Deli" mustard that features horseradish, and a "Country Dijon" version that is milder.
- All versions include white wine.
- The current packages all contain a blue and white emblem on

their fronts that indicate that these products are recommended on the South Beach Diet™ in all three phases.

A trip beyond our refrigerator to the Grey Poupon® Web site tells us that Grey Poupon® also comes in the following branded flavors: honey (Dijon mustard with honey added) and spicy brown (with an "extra-spicy burst of flavor").

While we can only speculate about what opportunities were missed in the early 1970s, one of the lessons this examination provides is that people want milder, but good tasting, spicy mustards in more convenient containers. Testing with such other flavor formulations in the 1970s might have helped launch this brand onto a higher growth trajectory. By becoming an "everyday" mustard sooner, the switch into squeeze bottles and larger glass containers could also have come sooner.

In retrospect, we can see that the brand thinkers were making a classic leadership mistake in the beginning: The brand thinkers were projecting their own perceptions of Grey Poupon® onto all other potential consumers. Since the product was only selling $100,000 a year at the time, most people didn't know what Grey Poupon® mustard was, what it tasted like, what it should cost, how you should use it, or what benefits it could bring them.

Had the brand thinkers instead looked at the opportunity to sell more mustard (of any kind), they might have chosen to develop a new brand name, a different formulation, and a lower price point. Had this more fundamental testing occurred, we believe that a larger and more profitable mustard brand would probably have emerged. But that inexpensive testing was precluded by the marketing assumptions, and the testing didn't occur when the market opportunity was hot to spice up growth (puns intended).

Here are questions designed to summarize what you learned from examining ways to remove obstacles to expanded consumption or usage of your offerings:

- What obstacles are better removed than avoided?
- What actions can eliminate the most substantial obstacles?
- What combinations of actions are most likely to be effective in eliminating obstacles?
- How do the costs of best avoiding obstacles compare to optimal methods of eliminating those obstacles?
- What are the costs and risks of doing more obstacle-removal testing rather than less?
- How can you run the most tests for obstacle removing in stealth mode on a time and effort budget you can afford?

Chapter 5

Publish a New Route Map and Erect New Road Signs
Let Everyone Know and Help Them Understand the Improved Choices

I keep finding myself getting off the freeway at familiar landmarks that turn out to be unfamiliar. On the way to appointments. Wandering down streets I thought I recognized that turn out to be replicas of streets I remember. Streets I disremember. Streets I can't tell if I've lived on or saw in a postcard.
— Sam Shepard

Boston has long had a well-deserved reputation as one of the most difficult cities in the United States in which to drive. Out-of-towners sometimes hire cabs to lead their cars through the city. Since most of the roads were originally cow paths during colonial times, it's not surprising to find that it's challenging to drive Hummers down these often crooked and narrow roads.

For many years beginning in the 1990s, Boston underwent what was called locally The Big Dig. A better name would have been The Big Fiasco. Someone originally had the bright idea that you could clear up a lot of traffic congestion and make the waterfront nicer. So far, so good. But how? The plan was to depress the main north-south road through town to an underground level and add a new tunnel from the turnpike's end directly to the airport. As the plan was put into action, no one could know what they would find when they began to dig, and the challenges proved to be greater than expected. The project went on for many more years than expected and exceeded its original cost estimates by several hundred percent. For a decade, Boston resembled a war zone.

A key drawback of this decade-long activity was that the route you had to use to drive to any location in Boston changed almost every day … and sometimes several times during the same day! If you stopped traffic officers and asked for directions, they often wished you good luck as they shrugged their shoulders. They had no clue either!

Near the time of this writing, many of the completed tunnels had sprung leaks. That meant that contractors shut down the tunnels at night to make extensive inspections and repairs. More recently, a part of a tunnel's ceiling fell on a motorist and killed her, requiring more extensive closures and repairs. Where did these problems leave motorists?

Here's a story to give you a sense of the difficulties. One night, a suburbanite left her home to pick up her husband at the airport. Under normal conditions, this trip would have taken 20 minutes. Fifteen minutes into her trip, she found that the road to the airport was closed and she was directed by temporary signs that said "Airport" to exit into the city streets of Boston. For a few twists and turns, there were more "Airport" signs. But then she couldn't find any more signs, and there were no traffic officers in sight.

She decided to cross Boston from south to north to reach the Charles River and take Storrow Drive east to the airport. After a half hour of this self-made detour, she found that the entrance from Storrow towards the airport was also closed. She was again on unfamiliar Boston streets with no signs to the airport. Assuming that she would eventually locate a sign to send her towards the old tunnel to the airport, she headed to the waterfront. No such airport or tunnel signs could she find. After two hours of this Odyssey, her husband reached her by cell phone. She was so lost now that she wasn't sure she could find her way back to the suburbs. The good news was that she was in front of a hotel. Perhaps the doorman could direct her back home. Her husband then stood in a taxi line behind 400 people who also hadn't been picked up while she struggled west as best as she could. They arrived home almost simultaneously. The total of the taxi fare and tip, tolls, and gasoline for the "trip home" of 12 miles cost almost double what the air fare had been for the flight and took as long as a 1,500 mile air journey. Even the taxi driver thought that was ironic.

Before you dismiss that story too quickly as an unusual case, remember that organizations often spend millions on design, development, and facilities for new offerings … while forgetting that people need help to use these new choices. Have you ever bought a toy, a piece of furniture, or a tool that needed extensive assembly? Did you ever have a smooth and easy time making such an assembly?

What's the source of the problem? Letting people know how to use a new offering is often the furthest thing from the minds of most people in the organization, including the leaders. Instead, everyone is focusing on getting the offering ready on time, meeting budgets, and ironing out recently detected flaws. There's no time and attention left for anything else.

Imagine if a bride-to-be planned her wedding this way. She would be racing around fussing with the caterers, arguing with the photographer, cajoling the clergy, pinning ribbons in the hair of the flower girl, and trying to keep her makeup from smearing. Would that distracted bride-to-be remember to tell the clergy, musicians, and wedding party about a needed, last minute change in the order of the service to adjust for a flaw in the printed program? Probably not. Confusion could easily follow as the ceremony ignored the printed program while the guests stared around in puzzled fashion.

A road designer once shared a shocking secret with us that explains why easing new use is so difficult. Many drivers cannot read road signs well enough to know what they should be doing before they need to take action. Here's why. Some drivers don't read the language the signs are in very well. Others don't read well in any language. Still others see the letters and numbers in jumbled order. Even the symbolic signage can confuse quite a few people … such as those with poor eyesight and almost everyone who is driving through a downpour or a winter blizzard.

Make Communicating Clearly About the New Route Your Top Priority

A major U.S. television network decided to run local celebrity events to encourage viewing of its flagging soap operas (daytime serial dramas). Normally, hundreds of people will show up at such free events. Fans will meet new actors and actresses in the series. Based on these personal contacts, fans will watch a given soap opera more often and encourage their friends to do the same. Since most people would like to meet such celebrities, it's a no brainer to gather a crowd. The challenge is to handle the crowd. Each actor and actress needs to have people nearby to keep the crowd friendly and under control.

Imagine the surprise of the network executives when only 30 people attended the first event ... and the second ... and the third. Red-faced managers postponed the remaining events after realizing that no one had publicized the events except for a few casual remarks made by performers at earlier events. Why? No one was in charge of publicity for these upcoming events!

The persistence of bad information can make this challenge of communicating well even greater. A season ticket holder for the Miami Dolphins routinely sat in traffic for hours to get into the stadium parking lot. Only after three years did he learn that there was a direct exit off the Florida Turnpike that would put him into a parking spot in just a few minutes. He had just been following the parking signs, of which there were quite a few, but none that indicated what the best route was.

By comparison, travel across the Hudson River on the two-level George Washington Bridge in or out of New York City and you should be able to do better. When you near the bridge's on ramps, you will see adjustable, lit signs that describe the traffic conditions on both the upper and lower roadways. If there is construction underway on one level and not on the other, you'll know that too. During those times when your choice makes a difference in your crossing time, you should almost always be able to make the right decision ... if someone in your car can read English reasonably well.

Leaving the bridge in New Jersey, though, that clarity is soon lost. Each sign beyond the bridge contains references to at least four route numbers along with various place names. Unless you know New Jersey well, you will soon be scratching your head to figure out how to get onto the right road. The roads also wind unexpectedly and have quickly looming off-ramps that are hard to see in advance. Faced with this overabundance of information, many travelers coming from New York are totally perplexed and end up where they don't want to go.

What's the problem? There's no one in charge of making your trip from Manhattan onto the road of your choice in New Jersey a simple process. Putting signs on the bridge that included diagrams of the road choices ahead would help greatly. But is New York likely to take on that responsibility once its citizens and visitors are on their way to leave the Empire State? Clearly, no.

Similar hand-off problems involving multiple departments in an organization create the same kinds of unnecessary confusion. Anyone who has ever wanted an exception to their company's human resources policies knows this. You find yourself talking to your boss, your unit's human resources manager, bookkeepers, lawyers, and insurance managers, and they all tell you the same thing: Go see someone else. Eventually, your request goes to the head of human resources who tells you firmly that no exceptions will be made. Naturally, your blood boils when you learn three years later that the company has put in a new policy that would have accommodated your earlier request … with no intention of going back and fixing the prior problem for you. This lack of responsiveness shows the tendency of group functioning to alternate between the unappealing dimensions of apathy and inertia. Pity the poor person who needs some help!

Start Sooner on Developing Your Communications

By now you are sure to realize that planning your communications for the new route is a critical priority. Otherwise, all the hard work you did on developing a route to expand your business by 20 times will be wasted. But deciding something is a top priority won't make that much difference by itself. You also have to employ a different approach to develop your communications sooner.

Here's what we mean: Assuming that you focus the whole organization on helping those who need it, you can still have delays from the sequencing of one task to follow another. Designing an offering comes before working on how to produce the offering. Packaging may have to be redone after manufacturing has been completed. Until the packaging is finalized, no one spends much time on the advertising copy. When the logos are done, someone may begin to write up some instructions for using the offering. At that point, everyone will most likely be in a great rush. There will probably be pressure to begin shipping the product or providing the new service before the end of the quarter so the revenues and profits can be recorded sooner. Chances are very slim that instructions for making the new route an easy one for beneficiaries and customers will receive much attention.

Naturally, it's tough to write directions for something you don't have. But there are important steps that can be taken in advance that will speed and smooth the passage.

First, assume that you need to learn how to best convey the message. In addition, any given approach is, at best, only going to be a partial solution. You can begin by seeing how well potential beneficiaries, users, and customers respond to simulated messages delivered in a variety of ways.

Let's imagine that you are creating communications for something that is a socially delicate subject such as education about avoiding an AIDS infection. Clearly, written directions with a few pictures aren't going to get the idea across powerfully enough to change behavior. We know that some people have unscientific ideas about what causes AIDS, and those false beliefs have to be addressed by credible people. We also know that people have differing views about what's an acceptable avoidance method. You risk insulting or upsetting people if you suggest that their sexual partners should be assumed not to be trustworthy. People who are insulted or upset aren't going to pay much attention to your message.

Realize that any one approach won't be best for everyone. Think about people facing a fire. For some, any sign of flames will trigger an immediate reaction. For others, smelling smoke will not trigger any changed behavior. Some people will respond strongly to hearing a fire alarm and others will ignore the alarm. But if you put people in a room where they feel the heat from flames, smell smoke, hear a fire alarm, and see flashing emergency exit signs, it's likely that everyone will quickly exit. From that example, it becomes obvious that the right combination of multiple approaches can make quite a difference.

A good second step is to ask people how they prefer to learn about the subject. Although they may not be aware of all the communications methods they like, they certainly will know some that they prefer. This probing should be done as discreetly and pleasantly as possible. For very delicate subjects, sensitive people may only be comfortable with a limited number of learning methods. Pay attention if that's the case.

A valuable third step is to employ a variety of methods singly and in combination to see which methods affect behavior in the most positive ways. This is an essential step that many miss. Back when your authors were learning to drive, schools favored showing new drivers gruesome pictures of automobile accidents. The schools hoped that seeing such carnage would make the teenagers more careful. Often the approach backfired. The students saw this experience as being like watching a horror film staged for their benefit and didn't take what they saw seriously. The message was too strong for them. Anyone who only thought about the potential to harm others wouldn't ever drive. A better approach is to have teenagers assist in emergency services for road accidents. After the first time the teens see an accident in which a young person is injured as a result of drunken or reckless driving, they get the message: They are careful drivers for life!

An essential fourth step involves simulating the final communications. You are using a simulation because you don't yet have either the final offering or your messages to share. To do this work may require creating a mock-up of the offering, an experience of using an offering, or demonstrating the process of using the offering.

Returning to the AIDS prevention subject, such simulated communications can help avoid lots of wasted time and effort. Imagine that the message you are working on is designed to encourage those who are unmarried to be sure that those whom they marry are free of the disease. What you want these people to do is to be tested regularly for the infection, routinely share the results of their tests with those they might marry, and expect their potential spouses to do the same. Most people would agree that such a practice makes a lot of sense ... but wouldn't feel comfortable initiating or conducting the first conversation with a fiancé or fiancée. Since it's a delicate subject, it seems like a natural for being a private conversation between the two individuals. But if one of the pair doesn't understand about AIDS, the conversation may not work well. The simulation probably needs to test a variety of ways of getting the basic facts across to young people while preparing them for the idea of adopting this testing and communications practice ... and helping them develop skill in securing agreement to do so. Given strong feelings among people of different religions, one site for simulating such communications would be as part of religious training. For those who don't practice a religion, the simulations would have to be held in some other context that has credibility — perhaps as part of the activities of a social club, during an annual examination by a physician, or by the person presiding at the funeral of an AIDS victim.

A powerful fifth step is to see how simulating the actual problem that the offering attempts to overcome can be helpful. One reason that the teens who help at accidents are so affected by seeing teens who have been injured by careless or drunken driving is that the teens can easily imagine themselves in the same circumstances. Airline pilots train in electronic simulators that look and feel like a real cockpit. The instructors create mechanical and weather-related emergencies, and the pilots emotionally experience crashing their planes and probably dying in the process. The pilots return to the simulations with greater concentration and commitment after each such crash in the simulation. That unpleasant experience becomes one they will do a great deal to avoid.

If you cannot afford something expensive like a simulator, you can always use role playing. That could be powerful with AIDS prevention as you feel strong emotions during the simulated experience of saying good-bye to your loved ones, knowing that you have infected them and that they will die too.

Embed the Essential Messages into the Offering

Wise designers of offerings will go to great lengths to make it hard for people to do the wrong thing. Most vehicles with automatic transmissions won't start if they are not in Park or Neutral. That design helps avoid having the vehicle take off unexpectedly.

But even the wisest designer can be outfoxed by people who are confused. A crucial piece of a lawn mower that had to be assembled was made in a peculiar shape so that it could only be attached in the correct way. But an impatient assembler ignored the directions and tried to put the piece on in the wrong way. When that didn't seem to work, the assembler got out his tools and bent the piece to fit the way he wanted to attach it. Fortunately, someone later noticed the error ... and the impatient assembler, now red faced, rebent the piece back into some semblance of its correct and peculiar shape and attached the part properly.

While attending events at the home stadium of the New England Patriots football team, many people park in small lots behind businesses that are up to 2 miles from the stadium. Others come by train and have to walk across a large parking area from the station to reach the stadium. Realizing that people at football games occasionally imbibe an alcoholic beverage or two, the stadium's designers must have wondered how they could keep these people from getting lost after the game and wandering around in roadways where they might be injured or cause automobile accidents.

Many people would have dealt with this situation by having an army of police on hand. But the Patriots play in a small town. You couldn't hope to round up enough police to do this in the way that a metropolitan police force might.

You could also build underground walkways for the entire routes, but that's pretty expensive.

What would you do?

The Patriots hit on a simple solution. All the remote parking sites on the north and the train station are connected by painted lines on the adjacent sidewalks that lead from those sites to the corner of the stadium that's next to the pro shop. After the game, you go to the pro shop, find your colored line and follow it until you reach your vehicle or train. There's the same system from the south part of the stadium to the off-site parking lots in that direction. If you are too dazed to find the start of your colored line, there are parking lot attendants everywhere who can easily direct you to your colored line. In a few key places, there are short pedestrian tunnels so the cars can whiz by overhead. In a few other places where people may be tempted to jaywalk, one or two police officers are stationed on large horses so they can quickly intercept people before they make a dangerous mistake. Rarely do you see anyone walking where they shouldn't be … but there are bound to be a few foolish people in any crowd. You could only restrain those few people by assigning personal guards.

How might a similar approach be applied to AIDS prevention? It takes two to pass on an AIDS infection. As we mentioned before, providing social and economic incentives to people to communicate their AIDS-infected status could be a big help. In some communities, a few of those who have such infections have chosen to add tattoos on intimate parts of their bodies that indicate that they are infected. Such tattoos help others realize the risk involved in transmitting bodily fluids during sexual relations with these infected people, and also help the infected people find partners who are also infected. So rather than being increasingly isolated from other people, for some this self-identification has brought more closeness.

If it were more socially acceptable to be seen as an infected person, such tattoos or other emblems could be located where they were more visible. That adjustment would also serve as a reminder to uninfected people that perfectly healthy looking people can have AIDS. Seeing such indications could then not only serve as a reminder of what behaviors are helpful and harmful, but could also provide opportunities for couples and families to bring up the subject of how to avoid infection.

This idea of advertising your infection status gets to be a problem, of course, if the use of the tattoo or emblem becomes compulsory. That raises all sorts of legitimate concerns about privacy and individual rights. If that point isn't clear to you, think about how you would feel if you had any kind of infection (including the flu) and you were required to wear an ugly hat until the infection had passed. You probably wouldn't like that very much, would you? But if you were honored as being a good and loving person because you wore the ugly hat and the choice was yours, you might wear the hat. Who knows what benefits might follow?

Observe, Correct, Observe, Correct …
and Keep Repeating

Like Sam Shepard in the chapter's opening quote, your new route will seem simultaneously familiar and unfamiliar, confusing and disorienting to some. It will only be after beneficiaries, users, and customers are totally befuddled that they will think to ask for help. Unless that help is at hand, they may end up like the suburbanite trying fruitlessly to drive to Boston's Logan airport.

Even after you take all the steps just described, things can go wrong. Be prepared for that. Have a method that lets you observe what's happening to beneficiaries, users, and customers. When things go wrong, use that opportunity to identify helpful changes through amending your route, improving your signs and adding more ways to communicate.

Then check out your corrections by continuing to observe behavior, asking questions, and trying new approaches. And on it goes.

If you don't keep observing and correcting, you'll set up a permanent obstacle to progress. Here's an example of that problem: On the Cambridge side of the Charles River in Massachusetts, Memorial Drive takes you past MIT as you drive east towards the Charles River dam. You see the Harvard Bridge to the right leading over to Boston … and Boston is still further on the right across the water. The road suddenly splits. The split to the left says "Boston" just before you reach it and unless you have recently taken that split, you may be in the wrong lane and your instinct will be to take the right split towards Boston — which, of course, doesn't go to Boston at all. Conversely, if you really want to stay in Cambridge, you may also be in the wrong lane and your instinct will be to take the left fork that seems headed for Lechmere Square in Cambridge. The left fork takes you across the Harvard Bridge into the Boston congestion. Like poor Charley on the MTA in the Kingston Trio version of the old Boston campaign song, you may never return. Befuddled motorists have been making those wrong choices for more than half a century. If no one starts to watch and ask motorists about their problems — and then make corrections — motorists on that section of Memorial Drive in Cambridge will still be headed off on unexpected side trips a half century from now. Don't let that happen to your new route to creating 20 times as much activity for your enterprise.

Here are questions designed to summarize what you learned about communicating improved choices:

- How can you make encouraging more beneficial behavior your top priority?
- How will you get an earlier start on developing and testing your communications?
- How could the communications be embedded into the offerings?
- How can you use observation to identify communications that need to be improved?
- How can the frequency of your testing and observation be increased?

Part Two

Follow the High-Speed Road Inexpensively to Enjoy Increased Benefits for 96 Percent Less Cost

It's like driving a car at night.
You never see further than your headlights,
but you can make the whole trip that way.
— E.L. Doctorow

A motorist's first trip after dark on a rural French highway was an experience the driver will never forget. During the day, the motorist had enjoyed a delightful jaunt from the country home where he was staying to a famous chateau located about 50 miles away. While at the chateau, the visitor bought tickets for the son et lumière show that night and planned to return after dinner at the country home.

Following a lovely meal, the man hopped into his rented car and started off. But he noticed that the headlights seemed awfully dim. Getting out of the car, he was surprised to find that only the parking lights seemed to be functioning. Since those lamps didn't cast much illumination, he wasn't sure what to do. He fiddled with everything on the dash that looked like it might affect the headlights. Nothing seemed to help. And there was no instruction manual for the car in the glove compartment. Naturally, he was concerned about trying to travel such a distance with poor visibility. The moon wasn't up yet either, which didn't help matters. But the motorist really wanted to see the show … and he thought, "How bad can it be?"

Assuming that it wouldn't be much worse than driving in fog, he started off slowly. As it became darker, he went even slower. The road was curvy and there weren't many cars on it to illuminate the route. Naturally, there were no street lights. At intersections, he would stop to check the road signs to see if he had taken the correct turn. Hours passed and eventually the chateau was reached just in time for the show. The driver was exhausted and a little apprehensive about the return trip.

Just then, the moon came out which cast a lot of light on the scene and the show started. He relaxed.

The performance was great, but now it was quite late and a drive of another 50 miles lay ahead. The car park was full of people, unlike the home where he was staying. The motorist approached other drivers and told them in sketchy French about his problem with the headlights. Shaking his head, one of the other visitors strode to the rental car and pulled the directional signal back towards the driver. On popped the headlights! There was no sign on the directional signal to indicate that this was the proper method. You just had to know what to do. Before leaving the motorist, the Good Samaritan also demonstrated how to put the high beam lights on. In places where there was no oncoming traffic this greater illumination would speed progress further. The motorist gratefully thanked the man who helped him, hopped in the car, and made the return journey in less than one-third of the time for the latest trip to the chateau. The motorist will always remember that little things do make a big difference in our ability to take high-speed routes!

There's one more point to make about that experience. Gasoline is extremely expensive in France compared to the United States. Cars are designed to operate on less gasoline at higher speeds than at the lowest ones. Because of this, the gasoline on the return trip also cost less than it did on the outbound journey. This is a simple demonstration that you can make faster progress less expensively.

Years later, the motorist returned to France and covered much the same route on the high-speed TGV (Train à Grande Vitesse). The TGV passed speeding cars as if they were standing still. The view was spectacular, the seats were comfortable, and the snacks and beverages were delightful. Ironically, the TGV was priced the same as the conventional, low-speed train.

The only difference in cost was that you had to pay a few francs to reserve a seat on the TGV. Even more ironically, the TGV was a small percentage of the cost of renting and driving a car or taking an airplane on the same route. Why? The French government wanted to encourage TGV travel so that the technology would develop into an important export. To stimulate demand, travel on the TGV was subsidized.

When they are asked to reduce the costs of using their offerings by more than 95 percent while increasing beneficiary and user benefits, some people feel as though they have been placed on a long winding road in a foreign land at night with only parking lights. But unlike the motorist who had no instruction manual for his rental car, you will go through a careful briefing to give you step-by-step directions for how to achieve this desirable, but challenging, accomplishment.

Let's consider an activity where user costs can be high in terms of time and money such as becoming fluent in a new language. At the extreme, the student could make a mistake and choose methods that are expensive and not terribly effective. An example might be traveling once a year to a country where that language is spoken and picking up a few words each time through casual interactions with native speakers there. With that approach alone, fluency might never be achieved.

We'll give the student credit for more intelligence and commitment than that. Let's now assume that the student selects a two week language immersion program that's provided in a developed country. Such programs often cost thousands of dollars for the instruction plus thousands more for meals, hotels, and transportation. If the student isn't being paid by an employer to attend, there may also be lost income … or at least vacation time lost for recreational pursuits. Many students will emerge from such immersion programs tired, but with an active, if fractured, facility with a few hundred words. That's progress. But without practice, the expensively gained facility can fade. Maintenance may require trips several times a year to a country with native speakers.

That solution works well for the wealthy leisure class, but what can a person with limited resources do instead? Assuming that the 10-year out-of-pocket cost for the just-described approach is over $70,000, reducing the financial cost by more than 95 percent allows a budget of less than $3,500 to cover all 10 years. While that much of a cost reduction may seem to be quite a trick, if you open your mind, you can quickly locate a high-profit entrepreneurial opportunity.

People do need to see and hear native speakers. But these days, they don't have to travel somewhere for that opportunity. All learners need is to have a computer with a high-speed connection and speakers.

Most daily conversations in any language employ fewer than 1,500 words. As soon as you have a working knowledge and comfort with the right 1,500 words, you can communicate pretty effectively with just about anyone. When you start thinking about 1,500 words, it sounds like a lot. Right? We agree. If, however, you break 1,500 words into 15 words a day for 100 days, it doesn't sound like so much. And it isn't. Most people can learn 15 new words a day in another language with less than 30 minutes of effort.

But on that first day, which words do you start with? Here's where an entrepreneur could help. A native speaker of that language could pick a base vocabulary of 1,000 words that almost everyone needs and supplement that base vocabulary with several different sets of 100 to 200 words that people with specialized interests and needs could use (physicians, lawyers, engineers, tourists, etc.). Then the native speaker could experiment with teaching the words and supplementary modules in different orders, employing different methods, and with fewer and more words per lesson. For instance, it might be that 15 words could be packed into one sentence. Anyone can learn one sentence, especially if the sentence is funny or otherwise memorable.

From this approach, the entrepreneur is likely to learn that people have many different language learning styles. That's an opportunity. A brief diagnostic test can be designed to select the right teaching method for an individual student. Within say 10 different teaching styles, most people will probably be accommodated better than in an immersion program conducted abroad. The new student could then begin on the first day with just those easiest and most helpful words provided in the most learner-friendly style to make the process more inviting.

But what about review? If you don't practice, you will soon forget what you learned. The entrepreneur could provide brief daily online review sessions with links to more study aids for those words that prove hard to remember and speak correctly.

Accents are important too. Arrangements can be made for students to record their voices from time to time for review by native speakers. If this is done over a Web-enabled telephone line, there may be no additional cost for the telephone call.

But ultimately, all this speaking practice isn't going to do much good unless you have a reason to speak and listen. The entrepreneur can play a helpful role here, too, by matching native speakers in one country with other native speakers in another country who want to learn each other's language. That means that someone who speaks American English could learn Portuguese Brazilian from someone who wants to learn American English. Properly done, the two native speakers should be matched based on backgrounds and interests so that they will find plenty to speak about that will be interesting to both of them. If two speakers tire of practicing with one another, they can help each other find another partner or the entrepreneur can reappear to make another match.

Let's look first at this offering from the learner's point of view. The service is a better one than what the wealthy person can afford. You spend the same amount of time as the immersion course provides, but you can schedule the experience at any time you want. That scheduling makes learning more convenient. You can also skip going to a foreign country until it suits your needs or plans. You're getting all the practice you require and enjoy the experience more in the meantime. Because it's easier to learn when you do more frequent exercises, reviews, and conversations, facility should become better over the first few years than with the more intensive approach. Ten years from now, assuming equal language learning skills, whoever is more interested in learning the language will have done best. That ultimate result is pretty much independent of which method is used.

From the entrepreneur's perspective, the offering is a dream. There's some up-front work in course development, but the courses can be reused by millions with no additional development or instructional cost. That approach eliminates a big chunk of the costs that the immersion course owner has to absorb. For example, if the instructional development costs are $1,000,000 and the entrepreneur teaches one million students, the development cost per student is only $1.00. With low delivery costs based on computer technology, the cost to assist a student in gaining 1,500 words of vocabulary may be less than $5.00 each. Let's assume that the accent work takes a total time of five hours of someone whose full cost is $50 per hour. That would mean that the basic educational delivery cost is $256.00 before considering marketing and administrative costs. Let's look at the native speaker matching program. That could be done with computer software at low cost. Let's assume that all costs of finding the speakers and matching them with one another total $100 per student over 10 years. Could such a service be offered profitably for less than $3,500 over 10 years? You bet.

Advances in transportation and communications mean that you can quickly access help and resources from unusually remote locations. Rapidly declining electronics costs further aid the replacement of expensive methods for delivering your offerings. Customers, users, and beneficiaries are also learning how to do more for themselves, which permits even faster elimination of unnecessary costs. Effective outsourcers can increasingly do your most challenging tasks for pennies compared to your costs. What you cannot do today, you may be able to do tomorrow. There are high rewards in such an environment for continuing business model innovation aimed at reducing costs.

Let's think about scale for a moment. As we pointed out in the introduction to Part One, the average business serving individuals has fewer than 1,000 customers. The average business addressing the needs of companies has fewer than 30 customers. If you compare those numbers to the world's population (more than 6 billion) and the number of businesses (many millions), you quickly appreciate that there is much untapped potential for the average business to expand. By comparison, many schools, hospitals, local charities, and town government departments directly serve no more than a few hundred people a week. At those scale sizes, overhead costs are an enormous part of total costs. Simply by adding 20 times more volume, that portion of costs should also decline by a large percentage. If more than a 20 times increase in volume occurs, even more remarkable reductions in overhead costs can occur.

Here is what you'll find in Part Two: In Chapter 6 you take your new performance focus from Part One and locate what aspects of what you do today can be eliminated because they are no longer necessary. For instance, if you are able to stop making all but an occasional minor error, a lot of your quality control activities can also be eliminated.

Chapter 7 helps you design a better process for efficiently performing the remaining tasks for providing your offerings.

Chapter 8 looks at how to shrink the delay between when your offering is needed and when it is delivered. Most of the current elapsed time in your process simply adds unnecessary costs while conveying no benefits.

In Chapter 9 you can learn to shrink the number of steps involved in providing your offerings, plus make the offerings themselves simpler to use. For instance, many people don't maintain their cars properly because they don't understand — and don't want to learn — what to do. A vehicle manufacturer might put sensors in the car that send alerts when the car needs routine maintenance. These alerts could be transmitted to the nearest dealer who automatically calls to arrange to pick up the vehicle and leave a loaner.

If the cost of maintenance for five years is included in the purchase price, these cars will receive all the maintenance they need … and the owner or lessee will have a better performing vehicle with a higher resale or trade-in value. The car will also need less maintenance, further reducing costs.

Chapter 10 examines better ways to avoid expensive mistakes by employees, partners, suppliers, distributors, dealers, customers, users, and beneficiaries. In fields such as implantable medical devices, the cost of a mistake can be someone's life and emotional trauma for those who loved and depended on the deceased. In most offerings, errors cost more than properly providing the offerings. Most of these errors occur far away from the premises of the organization that initiates the offering, so the scope of error elimination has to be expanded.

In Chapter 11 you explore the best ways to automate whatever offering processes remain. You see such automation every day with those who offer electronic information products and services over the Internet. Once the process is programmed, no human being comes near the process again until it is time to improve the process again.

Everyone loves something that's made just for them. A custom item can even make you look and feel better. However, most organizations provide offerings that are essentially one-size-fits-all. Chapter 12 explores ways to customize offerings to make them more desirable … and at a much lower cost to provide. The best way to provide such custom delight is to put the customers or beneficiaries in charge of making the offering fit their needs.

Chapter 13 takes the processes that remain and reexamines how those activities can be further outsourced. New outsourcing choices are constantly being added, and others can be quickly developed if you just decide what you want. In this chapter, you can learn how to gain productivity by spending more for outsourcing than what your internal costs are now.

In Chapter 14, we look at just the opposite situation: reducing outsourcing. Where does your outsourcing cost you effectiveness? For instance, an organization may spend so much time and effort checking on an outsourcing supplier that the net effect is to simply add a new form of bureaucracy. In many organizations, such outsourcing choices haven't been reconsidered in many years.

Many times, organizations are convinced that they have close to the lowest possible costs. In Chapter 15, you learn to question such certainty. Few organizations have checked out even 1 percent of their best choices for more effectiveness with lower costs. We help you develop the technique of employing special incentives to help better solutions find their way to you.

In Chapter 16, you find an explanation of why you need to be continually repeating the steps spelled out in Part Two. Otherwise, you will fall behind the potential to gain through cost innovations. And that is a strategic mistake that few will survive during the coming years as most organizations will find for the first time that their most effective competition comes from an organization based in a different country.

Chapter 6

Sell Your Gas Guzzler
Eliminate the Unnecessary

He's the best physician who knows the worthlessness of the most medicines.
— Benjamin Franklin

Three times since the 1960s, gasoline prices have unexpectedly spiked and held at substantially higher levels. The first occasion was during the Arab oil embargo. The second instance was during the aftermath of the Iranian revolution. The third spike began around 2000 and coincided with increased political instability in oil-rich countries and rapidly rising global demand.

On all three occasions, people began to see expensive liabilities in their garages where just a few months before they had perceived large, powerful vehicles. The newly discovered gas guzzlers soon glutted the market, causing prices to plunge for manufacturers and owners of the mighty steel assemblages who wanted to sell. We were reminded of what it must have been like for large dinosaurs after the climate changed and habitats could no longer support such enormous reptiles.

When using the nth-degree test (described in Chapter 2) to imagine that gasoline prices are high, large gas-guzzling vehicles would always be seen for what they are — inefficient users of resources. The next time you are considering the purchase or lease of another vehicle, simply imagine how you would feel about a particular choice if gasoline prices reached four times their current levels. Chances are that you will choose a more fuel-efficient vehicle after pursuing that thought process.

A simpler test can help us expose inefficiencies in nonprofit and business organizations. You should ask this question: Does a given activity, attribute, or step need to be done under any circumstances? With your new focus on activities that lead to expanding usage and beneficiaries by 20 times, you will find that much of what you used to think was important no longer is. As a double check on your answer, look into why the activity, attribute, or step was done in the first place. If you cannot find a good reason then or now, you have a great candidate for elimination.

Here's an example. Many people commute long distances. We recently heard of a man who travels more than 110 miles each way daily in southern California to reach his work. Assuming that his car uses around 8 gallons of gasoline each day, that trip costs him $16.00 a day when gasoline costs $2.00 a gallon and four hours of his time. The depreciation and maintenance costs for his car are also significant. How much would you have to earn to make that worthwhile? Reasonable people will differ on that point. But this man only earns $8.00 an hour. Jobs in local fast food restaurants pay $6.75 an hour in the town where he lives, and these positions frequently go begging. If the man worked an extra two hours a day at such a local job, his time away from home wouldn't be any longer and his pretax income minus expenses would be larger.

Here's the math. His gross pay now is $64.00 a day. From that he has to subtract $16.00 for gasoline before looking at depreciation and other expenses. The local jobs (he might have to get two of them) would pay him $67.50 gross for a 10 hour day if he earned $6.75 an hour. His gasoline expense would probably drop to $1.00 a day. The first job gives him $48.00 after gasoline expenses ($64.00 minus $16.00). The local jobs provide him with $66.50 after expenses ($67.50 minus $1.00). Naturally, when gasoline prices are even higher, his opportunity cost (lost cash flow and time) can be substantial.

Why does he do it? We don't know, but the choice is likely based on some sort of noneconomic reasoning. It can't be the weather or the neighborhood because he lives in a smog-ridden area with an enormously high rate of criminal activity. Alternatively, he could find an equally inexpensive place to live closer to his place of employment. He would have a one-time moving cost, but that cost would rapidly be recouped through the reduction in driving expenses.

Ask Your Customers, Users, and Beneficiaries What's Needed and What's Unnecessary

Most organizations that provide charitable help to the poor like to check to be sure that those who receive the benefits are really poor. Arrive at such a charitable organization, and you find long lines of people being checked in, checked up on, and checked out. That checking process may involve as many people as those who are actually providing aid. The delays that the paperwork creates may also mean that recipients stand in lines for hours. Without the paperwork, the time needed for a pickup could be just a few minutes.

If you ask those who receive this aid, they find the whole process frustrating. On many occasions, people will tell you that after standing in line to receive such contributions they are turned away because the supplies run out before it is their turn. Such problems become a bigger source of wasted time because recipients sometimes spend the night in line for morning aid distributions in climates where that's reasonably comfortable to do. Do you think that any aid recipient who goes through such a bureaucratic process favors the approach? We haven't met one yet.

Who else is inconvenienced by this approach? Young children may have to go through the same process because a single parent doesn't want to leave them at home unattended. If one adult in a household spends time going through these processes, that's one adult who has less time to provide other benefits for the family or to look for a job.

Each recipient has to be checked through each time. If the families were qualified once a year based on some simple process, the checking in and checking out process might be eliminated for the other 51 weeks of the year. Better yet, some organizations have found that they could help more poor people by simply not checking on whether people are poor. If someone asks for help, the organizations just give the help. After all, there's only a modest resale value for what is given away.

You may be thinking that charities are a special case because they have responsibilities to those who contribute to be careful. That may be so, but how would donors feel if they understood the implications of such continual surveillance?

More puzzling is why so many businesses require extensive information before accepting a new customer. It's not unusual to have to fill out pages of forms, supply references, and provide access to credit record information to be able to buy small quantities of business supplies on credit. The cost of that approach has to be an enormous percentage of revenues for customers who buy very little. It was a great relief to many such customers when suppliers began to ask instead for company credit card numbers. These numbers are kept on file, and the charges can be processed and the cash received in seconds after an order is requested. The horribly inefficient credit department of a supplier in such a case has been replaced by the efficiency of an automated credit card network.

Yet until the 1990s, many suppliers to small enterprises in the United States simply wouldn't accept credit cards. One of the last to do so was that venerable U.S. government monopoly, the U.S. Postal Service. Would any customer have said that they didn't want to be able to pay with credit cards for their small business orders and postage? We doubt it.

Experience Your Own Process
and Challenge Those Who Operate It to Improve

When more speed is required, people are often shocked by how rapidly a process can be accomplished. Consider Dell Computer. The company will manufacture a single personal computer customized to order. The customer goes online or calls a toll-free long distance number, places an order, and pays by credit card. As soon as the credit card charge is authorized, the order goes electronically into a Dell factory that has the appropriate parts in stock, and the work order is almost instantly placed in the work station queue that has the right parts and the shortest backlog. At the same time, Dell's computers are alerting suppliers that those parts are going to be used soon and requests rapid replenishments. Assuming that no errors are made in assembly, a finished machine can be ready to go in its shipping container within two hours. A logistics partner will arrange to pick up any other items (such as a monitor) the customer ordered from other Dell or Dell supplier locations and consolidate delivery to the customer on the same truck. In some cases, the computer and related gear arrive the following morning.

Most processes, unfortunately, don't operate like that. The step-by-step time to accomplish a task may be the same or less than Dell's process, but there are long delays between steps.

Here is a process that we heard about recently for making vehicle repairs in an aid organization operating in an underdeveloped country with rugged terrain. When a vehicle developed a problem, it sat in a garage until a mechanic had time to evaluate what might be needed. If that diagnosis identified that a new part was required, an order was placed and a long wait began. By the time the part arrived (often weeks later), the mechanic may have forgotten that the vehicle needed that part … or no one may have let the mechanic know that the part had arrived. Once the repair began, it might turn out that yet another part was needed. Such a discovery caused the whole process to begin again. The organization found itself with a continual shortage of vehicles due to so many being gone for lengthy repair visits to the mechanic's garage.

Someone who didn't know the repair process decided that this was an opportunity to create a 2,000 percent solution for reducing the start-to-finish time required for these repairs. The new person met with those who worked with the process and spent a few hours with them walking through how the process was implemented. The outsider could soon see that most of the delay was in idle time when no repairs were occurring because a part was missing.

The outsider convened a meeting of those involved in the process and challenged them to cut the elapsed time for each repair by at least 96 percent. Within another few hours of mutual consultations, a few simple changes accomplished that improvement. Who were the geniuses who figured out those helpful changes? Why, all those advances were suggested by those who worked with the ineffective process.

Here are some of the key adjustments:

- An analysis of past repairs showed that over 80 percent of repairs requiring long delays were on the highest mileage vehicles. By replacing vehicles before they reached that mileage, those repairs could be avoided and fleet availability could be 50 percent higher. Greater availability, in turn, meant that fewer vehicles would need to be purchased. With continuing economic analysis, an optimal trade-off could be made between earlier replacement of vehicles and making more repairs on higher mileage units.

- Recording what parts were on hand revealed that few parts needed to be ordered. The problem was that the person who ordered parts wasn't aware of what was on hand because there had been no physical organization of the inventory. Instead, parts were stacked up randomly. By analyzing the frequency of parts usage, it became possible to stock the parts needed for 90 percent of all repairs. This adjustment reduced the delays for

needed repairs on newer vehicles.
- Most of the internal misunderstandings were caused by lack of communication among four individuals located in different parts of the compound. Putting in telephone links and computer records helped eliminate many of those problems. A clever card system used on the windshields of vehicles further aided in communicating and understanding what needed to be done to a particular vehicle.
- A preventive maintenance program also reduced delays by alerting the mechanic to the need for parts in many cases before the parts failed.

The successful improvements were well received by those in the process and those who relied on these repairs being made. The enthusiasm generated by the improvements led other operating areas to do similar reviews aiming to shrink time durations. The repair people also committed to regular upgrades of their process by reusing the meeting techniques that led to these large changes.

Why hadn't the repair organization improved sooner? No one had raised the question before of eliminating unnecessary delays. The potential solutions were there all of the time.

Create a Bias for Eliminating the Unnecessary

Visit any information technology (IT) organization, and you will find a group overwhelmed with writing custom software to create special reports that often number in the thousands. Each time a database package from a new vendor is installed, chances are that new software has to be written to accommodate the existing reports while the request for new reports continues unabated. And what are all of these reports used for? No one knows. Chances are that many of the reports aren't being used at all.

Having suspected that the proliferation of reports represented one-time curiosity more often than continuing needs or usage, one IT professional decided that each time his company upgraded its software or hardware they wouldn't continue to offer any of the old reports that required new custom software unless someone asked for the report. What was the track record of this policy? He reported that in more than 10 years, no one had ever asked for one of the old reports. The savings from this policy were worth tens of millions to his company.

What's the lesson? Regularly simplify your internal and external processes and offerings to eliminate what's expensive on a test basis, and measure the results to see what happens. Then, just restore the parts of what you eliminated during the test where a real need is demonstrated.

Pass Along the Cost Information

Many organizations operate in functionally isolated units that don't talk to or understand one another very well. In a manufacturing company, these functionally focused units will often include R&D, production, service, quality marketing, sales, human resources, and finance. Most such organizations keep financial records mainly for regulatory requirements. When that type of accounting occurs, each function will probably not understand its cost impact on the rest of the organization. Additionally, each function speaks a different language and has a different focus. Those differences can make it as difficult to work together as for a Thai monk and a Brazilian circus performer trying to build an airplane from plans written in Russian.

Ultimately, there's a fundamental contradiction that needs to be understood and overcome: What's best for one function's low-cost effectiveness is often accomplished by harming every other function's low-cost effectiveness. As a result, the organization's results falter when functions fight it out to look good in their own eyes and to win kudos from their bosses.

Here's an example: A company decided that its focus should be on putting the customer first. That's a noble and potentially beneficial approach. The way the company pursued that focus, however, soon proved to be a problem. The product managers who worked in the marketing department were put in charge of deciding what it meant to put customers first. Most of these product managers were young people with limited business experience and no knowledge of nonmarketing functions except for what they picked up while earning their MBA degrees. At the start of each year, the finance department told the product managers what their discretionary spending budgets and costs were going to be, and the product managers took actions to maximize near-term profits from that perspective.

What the product managers didn't realize was that the choices they made influenced the costs they were incurring. For instance, it appeared to a product manager that there was no increased cost for adding a new package size. But in reality, there were substantial added costs. Production lines had to be adjusted, changeovers of tooling had to occur more often, and error rates rose in the manufacturing operations. With another package size there was an increased likelihood of being out of stock in a store, which would reduce revenues. At the same time, some stores would buy too much of an item, the product would be less fresh when purchased, and consumers would be less pleased with the brand ... which would further cut into sales and profits. To take up more space on the shelf, the company had to pay another slotting allowance to the retailer. For the accounting people, the new size was another item that had to be kept track of. The IT people had to add the item to all of the reports that were being generated. And so forth. As you can imagine, the hidden cost increases were even greater if the product manager decided to introduce a new product that failed in the market place.

At the end of the year, each product manager would complain loudly when profits were reduced at the last minute by variances in the form of cost overruns that were charged back as additional overhead to the product manager's items. But none of the product managers ever figured out that they were the cause of these variances. Instead, the product managers wondered why the manufacturing people were so incompetent.

Over time, the cumulative effect of putting the customer first in this way was to add all kinds of unnecessary choices for customers that increased the price to 25 percent higher than would have otherwise occurred. Over the years, many of the customers migrated to competitors who offered fewer choices but charged lower prices.

The problem was solved when a new information system and a new management process were established that required the product managers to ask how their decisions affected costs ... before a change was made. With that added perspective, product managers started to act more like general managers, and better decisions followed.

When changes are being considered, all organizations would do well to investigate the implications of those changes before embarking on them. Sharing potential cost impacts among functions is a good place to start. But you should also inquire about delays, mistakes, and other problems that will arise from the change.

At the same time, organizations will benefit if they look at how changes may eliminate costs that would otherwise occur. Some time ago a company had a fast growing product that had been cheap to make. Because of a shift in raw material costs, the product became much more expensive to supply. By projecting the trends in prices, costs, and volume, the company decided that it would be better to charge more for the product ... even though this price increase meant volume growth would be lower. But the corporate head of facility planning never got the message. He kept working on building a new facility to handle the projected future growth for this product based on the trend of what had formerly occurred. After the new facility was built, the plant never produced a single case of this or any other product. Tens of millions of dollars were wasted on a plant that didn't fit anyone else's needs either. No one ever used the facility for anything.

Visit Other Countries to See How People There Do What You Do

Someone once said that civilization is merely mass hypnosis to convince us to do all kinds of silly, cooperative things that make us feel connected to one another. From that perspective, much of what seems "necessary" really isn't. If you can find a country where the cultural assumptions are different, your eyes may be opened to vast opportunities to eliminate the unnecessary.

Visit Japan and you will be struck by the way that fashion plays a large role in decisions. Red cars are in when you arrive … until you begin to notice new white cars everywhere. Seemingly overnight, the vehicle hues change to match the demand for a new look. Knowing this, Japanese manufacturers realize that their vehicles in Japan will be driven off the road by fashion before mechanical obsolescence can take place. From that observation, Japanese companies became adept at estimating how long drivers will choose to let their vehicles stay on the road and setting their technical requirements for durability to match that fashion-reduced life. Designs don't have to be as robust for such shorter-term durability. As a result, lighter, cheaper materials and assemblies can be employed that will work just fine for the fashion-limited road life.

By comparison, an American engineer in Detroit planning a new SUV for the U.S. market will start out by assuming that some of the vehicles will be driven for hundreds of thousands of miles over 20 years. The design and equipment will reflect that potentially longer operating life … and be much more expensive even though few purchasers will benefit from that longer potential product life. Those who set specifications for such vehicles in the United States who want to compete with Japanese companies should visit Japan and think about what they see in terms of road life.

An equally revealing trip could be made to a country where gasoline prices are very high. Some countries impose very high taxes on petroleum and gasoline to discourage imports. When you see the vehicles in those countries, you find that they are lighter and smaller, and have engines that are marvels of fuel-burning efficiency. In a sense, such a trip gives you a time machine look into a future when gasoline prices are much higher everywhere. The resulting vehicle designs from such a country can usefully expand the perspective of the U.S. vehicle designer.

If you decide to visit another organization's operations, it's a good idea to do your homework first. From our experience with such site visits, we've learned that someone has to validate that the organization has an advanced practice that's worth examining. But without proper preparation, what you see may not make sense. Arrange for someone with experience in the subject area to coordinate with the host to design a meaningful visit and to brief you before the visit on what to watch out for. Let that person lead the group and ask probing questions during the visit. In that way, you'll also gain insights from what your leader learns. Finally, ask your host to sit down while you provide feedback on what you feel you've learned. This feedback will encourage organizations to host your visits. In addition, they'll have an opportunity to straighten out any misunderstandings that you've developed.

In many cases you can gain insights from just visiting accounts served by competitors, going to different regions of your own country, and talking to people who don't use any of the industry's offerings about why they choose to do without. The lesson is that keeping your eyes and ears open isn't enough if you don't see and hear something different along the way.

Redo Your Business Model
to Make Functions in Your Organization Obsolete

One of the most reliable ways to see what's unnecessary is simply to develop a new business model that eliminates some functions. Perhaps no area has been as profoundly influenced by this approach as has been environmental stewardship by manufacturers and those who deal with wastes.

The original social model for dealing with environmental problems was to create legislation that mandated what was required of those who could sully or impair the environment. Scientists spoke before legislators who usually were lawyers and didn't understand the science involved. Since the scientific research was limited concerning these subjects, the scientists often found it difficult to know what to recommend. Expert witnesses would differ more in their conclusions than they did in the schools they had attended and taught at, and in the awards they had received.

Those who were on the receiving end of this legislation faced large bills to make big changes in their operations. The organizations who were polluting lobbied for delays in implementation. As time passed, the organizations that didn't want to make the changes got better at advocating their positions. Regulators sometimes agreed with them, and public interest nonprofit groups began to step in to pursue litigation to stop this cooperation between polluters and government. Environmental stewardship was soon bogged down in a quagmire of disputes where the only winners were the lawyers who billed by the hour.

Gradually, polluters began to notice that their neighbors often favored solutions that had little to do with what was legally required. The polluters sometimes also found that government regulators were willing to provide variances if the neighbors were happy. Environmental groups might still have other complaints involving environmental interests that were not being considered.

The breakthrough came when polluters began to realize that they could make faster, cheaper progress by simply bringing neighbors, regulators, and environmental groups together and hammering out agreements that were acceptable to all parties. Everyone liked this approach better because pollution was eliminated sooner and less expensively. From these experiences, polluters next began to find out that eliminating pollution often meant saving money. Fewer raw materials were needed. Less equipment to deal with emissions was required. The expense of dealing with waste was reduced.

Gradually, consumers began to favor companies that had better reputations for avoiding pollution. These companies began to see their sales and profits rise because of consumer-friendly habits that were more considerate of the environment.

Beginning in the 21st century, the most advanced companies figured out that not creating any environmental harm was a more profitable way to operate. And a few began to sense that moving beyond doing no harm to improving the environment could actually be an even more profitable approach. As a result, the most effective global organizations are now in the process of installing advanced technology that does not pollute even in places where there are no regulations that require such technology. In many cases, the recycled raw materials they release from their facilities are cleaner than when they started. Why? They make more money this way. (To learn more about turning environmental problems into a cleaner environment and greater profits, see *A Strategic Approach to an Environmentally Sustainable*

Business [Dissertation.com, 2006] by Hiroshi Fukushi.)

If everyone adopted this new business model, regulation wouldn't be needed for many situations and the enormous social costs of prodding these changes would soon go away. In addition, there wouldn't need to be a cleanup crew for when a spill occurs because there wouldn't be any spills. The legal departments of all the organizations would become much smaller as well.

Eliminate Mistakes and Delays …
and See What Else You Can Eliminate

Unfortunately, the world is still beset with too many stalls based on complacency, tradition, disbelief, misconceptions, unattractiveness, miscommunications, bureaucracy, and procrastination. While those stalls persist, unnecessary delays and mistakes will continue to plague us all.

But a small organization could make the effort to learn how to bust all of these stalls using the 2,000 percent solution process. When that occurs, the organization will have a large opportunity to eliminate many other practices that were in place solely to deal with mistakes and delays. For instance, the first thing that a desk clerk who works the registration desk in a hotel or motel is usually taught is how to calm down an enraged customer. When there are no enraged customers, that bit of training can be dropped.

There are other costs that will go away with failing to enrage customers. Here's an example: We recently went to a hotel for a week's stay. Before arriving, we had spoken to the hotel staff three times to ensure that the type of room we wanted (a large nonsmoking room with a kitchenette and two double beds) was reserved for us in our price range. We were told there was no problem, and that all would be well. When we arrived after a 12-hour plane flight, we found that the hotel had no unoccupied nonsmoking rooms as we had reserved. No problem. We were flexible. We would just check out smoking rooms until we found one that didn't smell like we had a smoking roommate. Almost 2 hours later, we finally located such a room after trying what seemed like half the hotel. This chewed up our time and the time of three people on the hotel staff. The hotel probably could employ two fewer people on the front desk at that time of day if the rooms that guests had reserved were readily available. Will we ever go back to that hotel? I'm sure you know the answer. So there was a missed revenue opportunity involved entailing thousands of dollars as well. With more loyal customers, the hotel wouldn't need to advertise so much. Travel agency fees would be reduced as well. Now wouldn't it have been cheaper for them to have saved a room they promised for us? We think so.

Mistakes cost a lot of money. So do delays. Organizations with low error rates and few delays have smaller, simpler staffs that focus on what's important in serving customers, consumers, and users. When you visit a Dell computer factory, for instance, you don't see that many people who aren't actually assembling a computer or taking the completed product to a truck. With low error and delay rates, Dell can pay attention to assembling and shipping from those facilities. Because they do a good job of ordering and using inventory, you don't see many parts stockpiled outside the work stations. That means that the company doesn't have to spend a lot of time and effort accounting for and tracking down the inventory. It's a much better way to go.

Here are questions that you can use to help you apply what you learned in this chapter about how to eliminate the unnecessary:
- How can you find out from your customers, users, and beneficiaries what is unnecessary that you provide or do now?
- How can you experience your own processes and challenge those who operate these processes to improve?
- How can you create a bias for eliminating the unnecessary?
- How can you better cost information so that people will understand the implications of their decisions in advance?
- What other countries can you visit to see other ways of accomplishing what you do in simpler ways?
- What business model changes will make functions in your organization obsolete and able to be eliminated?
- How can eliminating mistakes and delays allow you to stop other costly activities?

Chapter 7

Buy the Economy Model
Employ an Efficient
Business-Model Design

The car as we know it is on the way out.
— J.G. Ballard

Start with a Global Perspective

Everyone today is excited about the opportunities to sell products to China's more than one billion people. To turn that opportunity into reality will require substantial changes in your offerings. How can you use cost reductions for beneficiaries, users, and customers to expand the size of the market for your offerings by 20 times while earning an attractive profit?

Imagine that you are a vehicle manufacturer. In most developed countries, the annual operating and depreciation costs of a fairly new vehicle total around $4,000. How can you as the vehicle manufacturer eliminate more than 95 percent of that cost for the new Chinese customer?

You quickly notice that there aren't enough roads in China for everyone to be driving around at the same time. In fact, many roads are already filled to capacity with bicycles and motor scooters, which take up much less room than cars, trucks, and SUVs. In addition, most of these prospective customers don't make much money.

People work long hours in China's factories and service businesses. When they are done, they have little time for leisure. Because most people walk or bicycle to their jobs, people have to live close to their work. That's a problem for Chinese people who recently moved to the expanding industrial cities but want to be able to see their elders, who often live far away in agricultural areas. Wouldn't a Chinese person's heart be thrilled by being able to drive home for a weekend visit?

Long before someone could afford to buy a car and take such a jaunt, many could afford to take driving lessons and rent small, but attractive, vehicles for such homecoming visits. In the countryside, the roads aren't as good … but they are less crowded. The pleasure and pride that come from being able to visit the elders more often would soon be associated with the car, creating the potential for a powerful brand that people would also want to use when they are more affluent, particularly if step-up models are later offered.

Let's look at the car first. It needs to be rugged to work well on those country roads. But it also needs to convey status and family reverence. If the car uses little gasoline, that's good. It can be hard to find gasoline in some rural areas of China. Perhaps it would be a good idea to have great fuel efficiency and a large gas tank. With many Chinese nuclear families having only two or three people in them, the car could be a four seater. That would allow room to take three rural family members for a spin while back in the ancestral village.

What you are describing is a Chinese-styled, updated version of the popular Ford Model T in the United States and the original Volkswagen beetle in Germany … with a few more amenities.

You also need a rental network that's well run. If as a vehicle manufacturer you own the network, you will be able to exclude competing cars while you are establishing brand loyalty.

To make your brand more appealing, you may also want to sponsor festivals that are associated with honoring family elders and ancestors.

To appeal to the step-up market, you will want to have another car model that's sportier looking and faster. This would be a good model to use in auto races, following on the U.S. NASCAR model of racing.

You seem to have a pretty good business model for slashing annual costs through auto rentals. What have you forgotten? People working in newly industrialized areas in other underdeveloped countries also want to visit their families and home villages by car. If you design your vehicle in the right way, the car can be inexpensively customized in appearance for each of the other large-population underdeveloped nations such as India, Indonesia, Brazil, and Nigeria. With that base, you are in a position to be the dominant vehicle manufacturer of the future as the bulk of the vehicle market shifts from the developed to the emerging market nations.

Based on creating a way for a family to take a trip home by car for less than $200, you have opened up a vast new rental market that will ultimately become an ownership-based market as affluence broadens and more roads are built.

Let's look at key elements for applying this kind of thinking to other product and geographical markets.

Determine How Potential Customers, Beneficiaries, and Users Can Be Introduced Sooner to Your Market

One of the easiest ways to expand your volume and resources is by using cost reductions to engage new customers, beneficiaries, and users around the world who have less money to spend. For many benefit programs and offerings, the population of those who have never been involved before is more than 20 times larger than the population that regularly uses such offerings and benefit programs. For example, telephone usage is mostly concentrated in the developed world. Yet the bulk of the population is in lesser developed countries.

For most benefits, services, and products consumed in the developed countries, you can expect that parallel desires to consume will eventually flower in many lesser developed countries. However, there are some differences to keep in mind. First, the lesser developed countries have populations that are much younger than in the developed countries. It makes sense to focus first on younger beneficiaries, customers, and consumers. Younger people have fewer ingrained habits for favoring one offering over another, and you have the potential of attracting their attention for more years. Second, the normal cost of providing offerings is way above what most people can afford on a regular basis. But most people have some special or occasional need for a benefit or an offering that will make them willing to divert part of their scarce time and money in your direction. A desire to visit or be in contact with one's original home for those hundreds of millions who have undergone urbanization will be a strong need to serve for many decades to come. Third, many people could earn substantially more money if they could acquire more education that's relevant to their economic opportunities. Tying in such education to a potential economic benefit can greatly expand the potential usage of your organization's offerings or benefits. For instance, English-speaking people in India could be provided with language training by schools to make the students more likely to be hired to provide remote customer services for the United States, United Kingdom, Canada, and Australia. If a call center provider offers such education, the call center benefits from both having more potential employees and from fees for providing the education.

An essential element of any such development is to measure how new consumers, beneficiaries, and users are entering the market now. In looking at these measurements, be sure to consider the effectiveness of the introductory method for stimulating trial and encouraging people to repeat the experience. A giveaway, for instance, might draw people for a one-time experience, but the money is wasted if people feel like such handouts aren't making desirable offerings available. Give away desirable offerings too often, and they become degraded by the perception that something free probably isn't the real thing or cannot be very valuable.

An introduction method that has worked well for many offerings is to provide small units of products and experiences. In some parts of the world, you can buy a single razor blade from a vendor who separates them out from five packs. Cigarettes are sold individually in other areas. In some villages, street vendors offer cell phone calling cards with small units of just a few prepaid minutes. In poorer areas, you borrow a cell phone from a street vendor to make a call like a public pay phone is used in developed countries. In Bangladesh, the Grameen Bank offers loans that are often less than $100 to entrepreneurs and farmers, many of whom use the loans to offer small units of products and experiences. A medical charity, for instance, might offer a well-baby screening to begin to wean some mothers away from exclusive reliance on traditional healers before offering other medical services to poor families.

Consider How a Global Base Can Be Used to Reduce Costs

Talk to most organizational leaders about how the global marketplace can help them reduce costs, and visions of low-wage manufacturing employees seem to fill the leaders' heads. Hiring such employees may well be an opportunity, but often that opportunity will be the least important part of your global cost-reduction business model.

The marketing opportunity can be vastly more significant than the production opportunity. Let's develop more aspects of the Wall Drug example that we introduced in Chapter 1. As you recall, Wall Drug is located in Wall, South Dakota, near the main road to Mount Rushmore, a must-see attraction in that part of the United States. Wall Drug became famous for its highway signs proclaiming how far away the emporium is. In the early days, offers of free ice water on the signs drew crowds of hot, thirsty travelers. Then the owners had the inspiration to begin offering free signs to visitors as well. On the store's Web site and in the store, you can see photographs that visitors have sent back of places where they have placed these free signs. In the pre-Internet age, these "X Miles to Wall Drug" signs were amusing sources of free publicity that helped draw more people to the store who were going to be in South Dakota anyway.

With a Web presence, these signs also began to serve the purpose of drawing Internet browsers and buyers. Having those signs be seen by anyone who ever buys on the Internet is good for Wall Drug.

As global travel increases, Wall Drug would do well to find ways to provide those free signs to poor people in places where potential customers will see them. Making the signs decorative in ways that make them a nice addition to the outside of residences could be a good solution. If the signs are produced and distributed locally, the marketing cost of providing the signs will be lower, and local people will take more interest in finding clever ways of making them ubiquitous so that Wall Drug will pay for more signs.

In our overly commercialized world, authenticity becomes scarcer and scarcer. Remote locations may provide access to original sources of designs, improved ways of preparing materials, and unique resources. Would as many people visit Australia if it didn't have wild koalas and kangaroos? People are intrigued by differences when they deepen their understanding of what interests them. We are constantly amazed, for instance, by how many different ways there are to make beer and vodka. Both were once seen as virtual commodities in the developed world. Yet now these products splinter into ever more types, segments, and brands. Most of those unusual choices have their base in someone's authentic old recipe, regionally admired ingredients, or local stories and culture. Television is going the same way. More and more choices are provided, and the most popular new choices are often not new stories … but new locations. For instance, one of the most popular cable channels is the Discovery Channel, which allows people to travel vicariously and experience vastly new places from the comfort of their homes. Network shows based on so-called reality like *Survivor* (where individuals set out in a remote location to compete against each other in survival skills) feel the need to move on to ever more exotic and remote locations that most people have never seen or heard of before. When you mix in authenticity in the right way from local sources, you greatly increase your sales and reduce your marketing costs.

Energy is one of those costs that many people don't feel as if they can do very much about. But they are wrong. The cost of energy varies enormously around the world. In some countries, energy is subsidized by the government. In other areas, plenty of direct sun and relatively few cloudy days provide low-cost opportunities for solar heating. Windy sites can use propellers to generate power. Strong tides in other areas can generate inexpensive electricity. Enormous rainfall in other regions provides the opportunity for low-cost power from hydroelectric dams without flooding a vast territory. Agricultural waste in some regions, such as bagasse from sugar cane, can be an inexpensive fuel to burn for electricity.

Similarly, raw materials are more available and less expensive in some places than others. When you are close to a low-cost source, you can expect your total costs to benefit as well. If that raw material is expensive to transport, you will often gain by doing your processing to upgrade its value closer to the source.

You can also see the globe as a living laboratory that's open to all at low cost. Benefits, rituals, methods of interacting, and experiences spread rapidly from a few places into mass offerings. One of the most curious examples of this trend involves fire walking where people walk across superheated rocks or burning coals in their bare feet. We first saw the practice in Fiji as part of a fertility ritual in 1986 that was slightly commercialized to entertain the tourists. By 1996, it was hard to avoid offers of courses that would let you directly participate in a fire walk experience. In 1986 we were intrigued to see that the people in Fiji were able to accomplish this feat (pun intended), but could find no one to explain why it's possible to us. By 1996, we were walking barefoot on red hot coals ourselves. We still can't explain the phenomenon, but we know it's real. Experts argue that burning is avoided because wood is a poor conductor of heat to our feet and that our circulating blood helps cool the bottoms of our feet. Calluses undoubtedly assist, as well.

Successful companies often develop their offerings by creating a globalized version of an authentic product or experience. In essence, that's part of what Walt Disney did in creating the original version of Disneyland. In Adventureland, you can still ride across the rivers of the world to experience the wildlife in a simulation of the real thing. In Frontierland, you live the life of a rugged American frontiersman or cowboy as depicted in more American B movies around the world than anyone can count. In Fantasyland, you walk through Sleeping Beauty's castle (based on a real French chateau), drive wildly with Mr. Toad in England (drawing from children's literature), and ride a boat through Storybook Land where *Grimm's Fairy Tales* await. In Tomorrowland, you could formerly take an imaginary, but realistic-feeling, trip to the moon and back … all in 12 minutes. And now you can experience these same adventures and more in France and Japan where the American Main Street of 1890 probably seems as exotic to people who are native to those regions as the Jungle Cruise seems to Americans in California.

And, of course, if you are going to try to tap into everyone's ideas such as Goldcorp and Procter & Gamble have done through their contests, you are wise to go global. This broadening approach expands the number of ideas you can draw on and delivers you into greater diversity of thinking. To date, a weakness of such contests has been assuming that primarily experts are the people who can help. That's an incorrect assumption. In fact, nonexperts have a big advantage in that they come to problems and opportunities with fewer preconceived ideas. In addition, many of the successful innovations for poor people have been designed by poor people with no technical expertise. Those who are interested in creating vast new markets need to engage these future consumers now.

Be Prepared to Step Up to Serve Customers as They Become More Affluent and Educated

We live in an age of galloping increases in affluence for those who already are affluent. That trend is often hidden by small changes in the average numbers. There are several causes for the booming wealth expansion among the affluent. First, in many countries the number of people with more education who can be employed in the global marketplace is rapidly growing. These people earn higher incomes and are more likely to start successful businesses and make good investments. By contrast, the number of people who do not have the skills to compete globally is also growing rapidly. These people, unfortunately, see their incomes dropping in proportion to their fellow citizens. As a result, average incomes in a country may be little changed while dynamic shifts within those averages are happening. Second, global demand has meant that those with global skills find their skills enjoying more demand due to communications technology. Your MRI scan may be read by someone in Russia, India, or a country you cannot even spell before your local radiologist even looks at it. As a result, incomes in lesser developed countries for those with education and skills are being pulled rapidly upward toward the world averages. Third, a higher percentage of people are involved in nonagricultural entrepreneurship than has occurred before. That increasing percentage is partly due to communist and socialist companies embracing some aspects of capitalism as an economic incentive system. It's also partly due to shifts in cultural norms so that it's considered more acceptable to make money from commerce today. The advent of management as a discipline after World War II (thanks to Peter Drucker) means that more people have training and skills for creating and expanding organizations than ever before. Charitable organizations are also emphasizing practical education for beneficiaries more than previously, and much effort is going into facilitating the development of entrepreneurs from among the ranks of the poor. Many are copying the success of the Grameen Bank in this regard.

This expanding affluence doesn't mean that these individuals are now dollar millionaires. More often, more affluence means that educated consumers are seeing discretionary income grow at a rapid enough rate to expand their ability to pay for higher quality services and goods. In the past a poor family might save for years to purchase a sewing machine to make some clothes that can be sold commercially. Such a family today is much more likely to have borrowed money inexpensively to buy that first sewing machine and has by now expanded into a local shop employing eight sewers each working on a separate machine to serve rapidly growing demand. Such a family may be interested in purchasing samples of higher quality fabrics and clothes than are available locally in order to create better designs and versions of their own products. Clearly, there will be a demand to surf the Internet to see pictures of new items from around the world. As a result, Internet cafes are springing up in more places so that local people can gain a global access to better knowledge, services, and products. Someone in the family may also want to take trips to fashion centers to see what the new items there look like.

The expansion of affluence can often be breathtaking. We recently heard the story of an entrepreneur in the Indian countryside who started as a street vendor of consumer products and then shifted to renting cell phones by the call. Very quickly, she turned instead to selling prepaid cell phone cards because everyone seemed to own a cell phone. From there, she opened a small store where she sold a wider variety of goods. Now she's expanding into various services that her increasingly affluent neighbors can afford to purchase for the first time. In the process, she has gone from being poor to being middle class. All of this happened within five years.

Traditionally, global companies have assumed that their developed world step-up offerings will work well for anyone anywhere. Increasingly, that's a bad assumption. The belief that goods produced in a developed country are better made is becoming increasingly suspect. Designs that are more in tune with a local culture, in particular, can make an item speak more eloquently to a newly affluent purchaser.

For entrepreneurs heading smaller enterprises, increasing affluence is a golden opportunity. They can focus on step-up products while demand is relatively small and feel confident that those with large, established branded businesses will probably ignore the local opportunity for some time to come. If the small entrepreneurs do their jobs well, they can limit the existing bargain-basement supplier to being the choice for ordinary use while establishing a classy reputation for themselves as providers of what's right for those who are getting ahead in life and want to show off a little.

Aid organizations have a similar challenge. They are used to being confronted by a mass of displaced people (whether by war, famine, or natural catastrophe) and treating these people like troubled children who need tending. More often, displaced people will include substantial numbers of those with the knowledge and skills to help organize and implement relief efforts. Rather than ferry in an army of relief workers at great expense, risk, and difficulty, aid organizations would do well to figure out how to self-organize those they want to help and can so that those in need can quickly and efficiently help themselves.

Governments with faltering educational programs are seeing local entrepreneurs increasingly taking on the key tasks of literacy, language, and numeracy training. Governments would do well to either duplicate these successful innovations or make it easier for poor families to access those resources.

Establish New Brands That Have Emerging Market Authenticity

Consider Japan after World War II. The nation's industrial base had taken a pounding. Because Japan lacks most raw materials, the country needed to export goods in those days of gold-backed currencies if the Japanese were to be able to purchase the oil, minerals, and agricultural goods needed to sustain the nation. Those first postwar exports were often made in factories on jury-rigged equipment that produced only low quality offerings. But Japanese people worked long and hard for low wages, and their goods found a market among those who wanted to pay a low price and were relatively insensitive to quality. The label "Made in Japan" by 1950 stood for something that was shoddy and wouldn't last long … unless, of course, the product was a hand embroidered silk kimono. Such a lovely item was the envy of the world, and visitors to Japan almost always returned with some.

First with consumer electronics and later with cars, Japan reformed its reputation by creating innovative designs, pioneering high quality manufacturing techniques, and adapting rapidly to changes in consumer markets. Today, in many parts of the world, "Made in Japan" means high quality backed by wonderful service — epitomized now perhaps best by Lexus, Toyota's trade-up brand.

Many Asian nations learned to do the same, but in different industries. The Asian Tigers of South Korea, Taiwan, Hong Kong, and Singapore soon benefited from following Japan's example.

What's missing from this picture? People first fell in love with the vivid, authentic designs, and wonderful workmanship of those Japanese kimonos. That love could have been transformed into substantial growth in products based on such art and apparel. It still could.

But there's a larger opportunity. Currently the global standard for many products and services is built around either an American or European model. People wear jeans that are designed to improve on those first developed by Levi Strauss and VF Corporation. Much sportswear has a European look based on Italian designs. Occasionally, fashion has come out of the lesser developed world into the developed countries such as the Nehru suit many years ago. Few are developing new international clothing designs that have authentic roots in one country, but have been adjusted to be appealing to those in a variety of countries. Such products, if based on those from Japan, might feature silk blouses and shirts with marvelous oriental designs embroidered into or hand painted onto them.

Those would be high-end products, of course. So how might a step-up apparel line be created? It would make the most sense to create apparel that would appeal to the greatest number of people. One possible route would be for an apparel maker to sign up Chinese celebrities to create their own lines of clothing that the celebrities would wear at all times. Inexpensive versions of those lines would be sold throughout China and wherever Chinese people live. Chances are that if these are good designs, the designs would soon catch on among non-Chinese people as well. Versions of the goods that employ better materials and tailoring can be offered for those who want to pay top yuan (pun intended).

Many people reading this idea will be unimpressed with that opportunity. The rag trade has long been a tough way to earn a living. But the same concepts apply to producing consumer electronics, foods, restaurant chains, and television shows with the authentic look and feel of another country with a rich artistic heritage. In that last category, the popularity of British musicals (anything by Andrew Lloyd Webber) and television shows (Masterpiece Theater rebroadcasts of BBC shows) in the United States has long shown the way for such culturally based exports.

Build Your Business Model to Expand the Market Faster

To this point, we have explained cost reduction in terms of matching an unmet need to an available capability that few have chosen to pursue. We focused on that theme to help you appreciate that traditional ways of developing markets, enterprises, and habits are working from only one business model, a model that is increasingly irrelevant. In this chapter, we are trying to help you see that there are many alternative, advantaged business models. In fact, you may well develop such an alternative business model that is better than the ones we propose. When that occurs, we will be pleased. Our purpose is to stimulate your imagination and experimentation, rather than to give you a recipe to rigidly follow.

The key element of this new way of thinking is to see the location and circumstances of the bulk of future consumers for your offerings as the base for all aspects of your new business model — from design and branding to production and service through to purchase and consumption. On the surface, that idea sounds like the developed world manufacturer who wants to sell more refrigerators to Chinese people. The goals are the same. But in the new model, that refrigerator isn't like the one that is made now in Louisville, Kentucky, doesn't have the GE brand, has different capabilities, is endorsed by Chinese celebrities, and is clearly based on a Chinese heritage. And (here's the most important difference) this new refrigerator is so terrific that people in Louisville, Kentucky, will want to buy one. Chinese food has made it to Louisville. We've often eaten it there. There's no reason why Chinese-featured refrigerators shouldn't too.

Let's conduct a thought experiment about what such a refrigerator might be like to help you see the new business model alternative we are describing. Most Chinese people live in small homes with limited space. They don't refrigerate much food because they prefer to buy and consume fresh food. They also have small nuclear families. So we're talking about a small refrigerator. Today, a refrigerator tends to have a cool compartment and a frozen compartment. Why couldn't a refrigerator have more compartments providing more preservation choices? With more compartments, it would be possible to maintain different types of foods at quite different temperatures, for instance. If an oven can vary heat, why can't part of a refrigerator vary coolness? For dishes that require marination, a higher temperature would often allow greater absorption of the marinade while just enough coolness would help retard bacterial growth. For items with high bacteria risk like chicken, there could be near-freezing compartments. In such compartments, families would avoid the flavor and appearance degradations of freezing while keeping the bacteria count lower. Some compartments might have higher humidity levels and temperatures to help keep delicate items from drying out, such as snow peas. With a little research, you could probably figure out how to adjust temperatures and humidity by compartment to allow fruit to ripen to match the schedule for its use. Each compartment could have its own door to reduce the numbers of times that other areas experience temperature fluctuations. Some compartments would have the ability to adjust humidity and temperature over a wide range as well to provide for more flexibility. Add enough features and you have a refrigerator that would also appeal to anyone in a small household who appreciates having higher quality ingredients available at home without a last-minute shopping trip.

A manufacturer could then hire authors to create new books that describe how to use such a refrigerator to produce more authentic versions of other cuisines such as Indian, Pakistani, Indonesian, and Brazilian. For the larger countries, the manufacturer could also copy the Chinese refrigerator business model to create local brands with an authentic base in each country.

Instead of stainless steel or solid color enamel finishes, the refrigerators could be produced in a variety of artistic designs and colors much like wallpaper is now. You could order a custom-made refrigerator, as you do a Dell PC, to fit the size, shape, and décor in your kitchen or bar.

And there's another opportunity. Many homes in developed countries sport consumer electronics in virtually every room. Why should refrigerators only be in the kitchen? Specialized refrigerators could be available in other rooms to keep beverages and snacks at ideal temperatures.

But why is this business model cheaper for customers, consumers, and other beneficiaries? The major cost for a refrigerator over its life is the electricity that powers it. If a consumer can buy a refrigerator that exactly fits his or her needs, the refrigerator will be smaller and more energy efficient. For instance, most refrigerators have a frozen compartment that's much larger than a family needs. Since most of the energy goes for that compartment, there's an opportunity to cut costs a lot by providing a smaller compartment. If beverages are kept at ideal temperatures, refrigerators used solely for that purpose won't need freezer compartments at all. If temperatures can be adjusted, some compartments can be kept at room temperature as dry, humidity-controlled storage rather than refrigeration. Baked goods, for instance, could be kept in humidity-controlled surroundings while not lowering their temperature. If compartments aren't going to be opened and closed as often, it will make sense to put better door seals on to keep warm air from intruding. The frozen compartment can also be placed at the center of the refrigerator so that less energy will be required to keep that section cold.

But the big problem for refrigerators in many homes is that they no longer match a planned update in kitchen décor. If you can buy replacements to update their exteriors to get a new look, most refrigerators can remain in service much longer.

Here's another big cost. How much food does a family throw out because it goes bad or is no longer satisfactory in appearance or freshness? For those who shop infrequently, this cost can be substantial. If you are able to keep foods in peak condition longer, that wastage goes down. Such savings could be hundreds of dollars a year per household.

If you provide a family with such a new concept in food storage while reducing costs for electricity and wastage — plus preserve better looking and tasting food — you are bound to see an explosion in refrigerator sales. Why? It won't make economic sense to keep the traditional models. If refrigerators are normally changed every 20 years, you might see an expansion in sales by 400 to 600 percent for a few years among those who own refrigerators. That market demand will be higher if the multiple refrigerator use in households becomes widespread. The market demand will go through the roof if those in underdeveloped countries who have no refrigerators or very inadequate ones also upgrade to an entry-level version of this product. Putting authentic designs from that country on the exterior will make it irresistibly attractive to make such upgrades for refrigerator owners.

You still have a problem among those who cannot afford a refrigerator. Why not develop a larger model that can be the base of a refrigeration rental business? In the same way that people in many countries go to laundromats to wash clothes by inserting coins in a public machine, people in a small town could rent a secure compartment or two in a large common refrigeration unit for much less than the cost of owning an entire refrigerator. If the family needed a larger space for a special meal, they could rent more space just for that purpose. Each compartment could be accessed by key and sanitized between renters. Local entrepreneurs could use this offering as a way to help attract people into a local store that's open late at nights (when most people are preparing their evening meals).

Expand 2,000 Peccent Solution Capacity Among Your Stakeholders

In all of our books, we've advocated having as many stakeholders as possible share their concerns, ideas for improvement, and reactions to experiments and other initiatives. That's because even a new business model that starts way off target will soon begin to go in the right direction as a result of continuing feedback from those who help create, deliver, purchase, employ, and consume an offering. Make each individual step in establishing the business model small enough, and any misstep is quickly and cheaply remedied.

If you don't believe that, try this experiment. Ask three people to help you, one of whom will drive the four of you to some location none of you has ever been to before. On the way, close your eyes and have someone blindfold you. You'll learn more from this experiment if you are totally in the dark.

Once at the destination, a mall for example, tell your helpers to pick a location for you to walk towards. That might be a map of the mall. It could be at the rest rooms of the mall. Or it might be a sandwich shop in the mall's food court. Explain to your helpers that their job is to give you feedback on how well you are doing in moving toward your goal and to keep you from hurting yourself.

Get out of the car and start walking carefully. Your helpers will tell you to stop, turn left or right, or whatever. You'll be impressed by how quickly they learn to give you feedback that you can use. If they prove to be good at keeping you away from potholes, racing cars, and obstacles, you'll soon relax and walk faster and more confidently. Since they may not yet know where the goal is located, they may have to gain some information, too, by looking at the mall's internal map or going to the information counter before proceeding directly to the goal. You'll find yourself arriving at your destination in most cases in little more than double the time it would take you if you could see and knew exactly where you were going.

What's the lesson? Get enough feedback and even the totally unexplored can be handled reasonably quickly and safely. How can you do better? Get feedback from people who can help you design 2,000 percent solutions for your business model and stakeholders.

Let's consider how getting such feedback might work for an aid organization. Most humanitarian groups do fine work and provide beneficial help to those who need it. What else might such an organization do? Staffers and volunteers could also teach the aid recipients to create 2,000 percent solutions so the aid provision could be greatly improved in effectiveness for the beneficiaries.

With the increased effectiveness from implementing these 2,000 percent solutions, such an organization would then have resources to provide more kinds of aid to beneficiaries. For instance, those beneficiaries who were interested in starting new enterprises could be taught how to start up new businesses using limited resources by working with those who are also aid beneficiaries. Donors to the organization could make available limited grants to help start such enterprises for those with the most appealing plans. Such a program could ease and speed the transition away from being dependent on the aid organization. That result is especially desirable when people may not be able to return to their old way of living anytime soon. If a drought continues, some may be better off finding nonagricultural ways of earning a living — or at least establishing more effective methods of affordable irrigation — than going back to replant and see crops wither.

Alternatively, a new type of aid organization could be established that would become the entrepreneurial version of Habitat for Humanity International. The organization could test a variety of business models that might be used by aid beneficiaries to recover economically from natural disasters, wars, and droughts. The best of these business models could be demonstrated and taught to the beneficiaries who might like to establish new businesses. A loan for the start-up capital would be provided and repayments would be used to fund other entrepreneurs. Some of these business models could be established around a franchised branded base so that the new entrepreneurs would have an easier time attracting customers. As the entrepreneurs began to succeed, they would lead other aid beneficiaries into the normal economy.

Here are questions that you can use to help you apply what you learned in this chapter about how to employ an efficient business-model design:

- How can potential customers, beneficiaries, and users be introduced into the market sooner?
- How could you use a global base to lower costs further?
- How should you prepare to serve new needs as customers, beneficiaries, and users step up to require more demanding preferences?
- What's the best way to create new brands with emerging market authenticity?
- What elements can you add to your business model to expand the overall market faster?
- In which ways can you inexpensively expand 2,000 percent solution capabilities among your stakeholders?

Chapter 8

Tune Up Your Engine to Avoid Stalls
Cancel Delays

Automobiles are free of egotism, passion, prejudice and stupid ideas about where to have dinner. They are, literally, selfless. A world designed for automobiles instead of people would have wider streets, larger dining rooms, fewer stairs to climb and no smelly, dangerous subway stations.
— P .J. O'Rourke

First-time car owners often have no clue as to what a tune-up is. It's the routine maintenance of cleaning out the fuel lines, replacing the spark plugs, setting the fuel injectors for better efficiency, and making sure that the combustion is occurring optimally. Fail to have tune-ups and eventually your vehicle will begin to cough, sputter, and stall. If it stalls at the wrong time and place, you may have a long wait before you can proceed on your journey. The tune-up can also help spot bigger problems such as an oil leak that can leave you without oil … and an engine that's only good for the scrap-metal market.

But there's a delay involved in having a tune-up. You usually have to drive to a dealership or garage and leave your car for the day. Or you have to wait with your car for a few hours. Neither option is desirable for most people. Dealerships and garages are rarely anyone's first choice of where to hang out. Decades ago, some car dealers would provide you with a loaner car at no charge while yours was in the shop. That option is seldom provided any more.

Some luxury brands, though, have a better idea: When your vehicle is ready for a tune-up, a technician shows up at your home or office to pick up your vehicle and then return it a few hours later. You hardly notice that your chariot is gone for a tune-up. In fact, some manufacturers go so far as to provide all scheduled maintenance as part of the vehicle's purchase, lease, or rental price. If this service model becomes popular enough, it would make sense to develop ways to provide most of the needed service at the customer's site to avoid the delays of driving to and from the dealership or garage. Replacement automobile glass companies already do something similar by bringing the glass to where your vehicle is parked and putting the new glass in while you are at work or home watching television.

And we don't know about you, but software is a big pain for us, especially when we write a book. Microsoft Word likes to "improve" what we write into formats and versions that we don't agree are improvements; our "undo" button gets a workout. Our antivirus scanning software loves to tell us that we have adware, trojans, and other undesirable programs, but can't seem to permanently rid our computer of those programs without us becoming software engineers. Each reminder wastes our time as we have to click to get rid of the warnings that do us no good.

It's not just software that wastes our time. We cannot remember the last time we saw most of our physicians within a half hour of the appointed time. We always bring reading material to help offset that expected wait. But we usually also encounter genuinely sick people who are sneezing, wheezing, and sniffling, and spreading their germs all over the place where others are waiting. Would a physician know how to avoid this dispersion of disease? Probably. Would she or he do anything about it? Probably not except to put in a glass partition to protect the office staff. So you may find your progress slowed for two weeks while you recover from a nasty cold contracted during your long, but expected, wait in the doctor's office.

The world today is full of product and service providers who like to point fingers. If you have a problem with the provider's offering, the provider will be quick to assure you that the fault lies elsewhere. That approach doesn't do the poor delayed beneficiary, user, or consumer much good. Few want to play the role of judge. Most people just want to get on with their lives without delay.

Few beneficiaries expect product and service providers to be perfect. But most people do hope that providers will step in to make life easier for beneficiaries whenever possible. When the same old problems recur, beneficiaries are naturally anxious to find some way to escape those vendors and nonprofit providers.

Sometimes the supplier cannot do much to improve things. Physicians cannot ban sick people from their offices; that would make no sense. But if the provider does as much as is reasonable, delays can be reduced and sometimes eliminated. Those who might experience such delays will be helped. For instance, someone who is wheezing and sneezing can be taken into an examining room rather than left out in the waiting room. That examining room can be doused with disinfectant after the patient leaves. If no waiting room is available, the office assistant can provide tissues so that the quantity of infected spray is reduced. If the wait is going to be long and the person appears to be sick enough, the office staff can be trained to ask the physician to take a quick look to see if the patient needs to be sent to the hospital emergency room. Larger waiting rooms can be designed to have separate "sick" and "well" waiting areas. Some thoughtful pediatricians do that now.

What about that pesky software? We'll continue to experience annoying delays until viable competitors with superior offerings come along. We can hardly wait. For an entrepreneur or professional, the value of the time spent with balky or slow software may be worth hundreds of dollars an hour. Add up those delays over a year, and you have a major opportunity cost. If vehicles performed as poorly, we would probably choose to ride in horse-drawn carriages instead.

There's clearly potential demand for buying your software with a warranty under which the vendor will fix any problems without requiring you to learn how to hire and supervise software programmers. In many cases, the vendor could probably make a one-time adjustment for a small cost, and the problem would go away. Currently, most software companies will try instead to sell you an expensive, one-time fix or send you to unending pages of message boards for incomprehensible or confusing free advice.

Offering software without those delays would make the software much more valuable to the user. Even if the price were to double, users would in most cases see their productivity rise so much that the expenses and opportunity costs would drop by over 95 percent.

Make It Simple

Many nonprofit organizations and for-profit providers get confused when a beneficiary encourages them to make it simple. The providers imagine some bare-bones offering that provides no choices.

Let's look at the problems with providing bare-bones offerings to make life simpler for beneficiaries. Among tools, a standard screwdriver is considered by many to be a simple offering. But if you need to attach or remove a Phillips-head screw (with slots in the shape of a +), a standard slotted screwdriver (which fits a screw with a single straight slot on it) won't do you any good. Even if you have a Phillips-head screwdriver, that screwdriver needs to be the right size or you still have a problem. You either cannot fit the screwdriver into the screw slots, or you tear up the screw head as you wield a too-small screwdriver.

The person who wants to screw or unscrew needs a kit that will fit virtually any kind of or size screw head. The alternative is to own lots of screwdrivers … a choice that's of limited interest to those who rarely use screwdrivers. In addition, the casual repairer often lacks the hand strength to drive in and remove screws. When you pre-drill a hole of the right size, the screw goes in more easily. For a tough-turning screw or for those with arthritis, an electric screwdriver is a much appreciated help.

As a result, a wise manufacturer interested in serving new homeowners might sell kits that include a cordless drill with drill bits that would work for 95 percent of home repairs and a cordless electric screwdriver with screw driver ends that would fit 95 percent of all screws found in the average home. But that's not enough!

What are typical uses for such screws? Hanging pictures, putting up new drapes and blinds, and working on furniture account for almost all of the applications around our house. For most of those tasks, it would be helpful to have a tape measure that a person could use with one hand and a level (whether the traditional sort or a laser-based one). For the heavier pictures, it would be great to have a stud finder so that the screw would connect into something more solid than plaster.

And if you ruin a screw, it would be a real time-saver to have some replacements in the right size.

With the right tools and materials, a home fix-up goes fast and is uninterrupted by trips to the local hardware store or the more distant home improvement center. The time savings from avoiding those trips can often be more than 95 percent of the time expended for such tasks in many homes.

As you can see, making it simple for casual home tool users means providing them with a more complete and complex offering. With enough research, the tool provider would be able to assemble different kits that work well for 95 percent of the people in various residences such as small apartments, typical condos, standard townhouses, small single-family homes, and larger single-family dwellings.

The offering provider has (or can learn) the information needed to eliminate most of the delays. When such providers take the time to put together what beneficiaries, users, and consumers really need, delays disappear. But eliminating those delays has to be on the offering provider's list of priorities or avoidable delays will continue.

Notice that there's a secondary benefit from eliminating the delays for the manufacturer. The offering provider's tool kits block competitors for many years to come from having a chance to sell those same offerings to the well-stocked customer.

Create a One-Step Solution for Providing Your Offering

Delays are created when someone or an item has to proceed through a multiple-step process. Delays are eliminated when a multiple-step process is replaced by a one-step action.

Here's an example of how batch manufacturing used to work in the steel industry: A customer placed an order. The salesperson had to write up the order in a certain way. Once the order was filled out, it had to be checked by others, including the credit department. All of this filling out and checking usually took two weeks.

At that point, the order was sent to one of the plants. Schedulers would look around to see if they had any partially processed inventory on hand that they could use. If that looked possible, someone had to check out the inventory to be sure it would work for the customer. This procedure required finding the inventory (usually sitting out in the rain or snow in a vast yard), taking samples, and testing the samples. If the results were ambiguous, a meeting would have to be set up with the sales and production people to figure out whether to produce from inventory or to make a new heat (start with raw materials in a blast furnace).

At some point a billet of steel was either selected from stock or produced that then had to be further processed. This processing might mean rolling the steel into coils or producing solid shapes like I-beams or rods.

The coils would then need further processing at the slitter to reduce them to a consistent width. If the edges weren't quite smooth enough, additional steps were required.

Some customers didn't have the facilities to make their own sheets from the coils or wire from the rods. Further processing in a distributor warehouse could make those adjustments.

From beginning to end, it could easily take six to eight weeks to produce the required steel ... assuming nothing went wrong. What could go wrong? Well, everything could go awry. The steel could become faulty at any stage in the processing and the process would have to begin all over again.

Imagine now that you are a steel customer. You require something special in your steel that's a little hard to make. That something special usually means creating high-strength alloys so you can cut down on how much steel you need to use. If a mill fails to make you a batch of steel on time and in the right quality, you may not be able to produce your product. Your kind of steel isn't sitting in inventory in any distributor's warehouse.

What do smart customers do in such circumstances? They ask a lot of questions about their orders and might request daily updates on every order. While customer-service people can certainly talk to the customer daily, these service providers don't really know what's going on either. They have to rely on computer reports that are notoriously inaccurate. Each mill usually has one person who can actually walk around and check on the steel. Each such person has a hundred service agents who want him or her to take a special look almost every day. It's an impossible situation.

The customers learn to keep a lot of inventory, order from several suppliers, favor the more reliable ones, and pray a lot. Even then, multiple disasters sometimes happen involving more than one supplier, and life becomes dicey for the customer who wants to keep a factory going.

But a fascinating alternative would occur when a customer plant was truly facing being shut down for lack of steel. Everyone involved in order processing and manufacturing would sit down to figure out if they could expedite an order through the process. This approach meant that the steel would receive high-priority handling by reducing delays from one step in the process to another. So instead of a coil sitting for eight days before the slitter was ready to work on that size coil, the slitter was adjusted to make a special run for this coil. On some occasions, steel was produced in as little as eight days for the whole process.

But it was costly to shrink the delay. No steps were eliminated; they were just compressed. In fact, extra steps were required to shrink the delays. This speedup meant that all the equipment was run inefficiently. Lots of people had to scramble around providing special expediting. And all the big bosses called endlessly.

Customers had to be fascinated by learn that their steel could be produced more rapidly. Such experiences probably made them realize that the steel-making process was designed to make life simple for managing a batch manufacturing process rather than for the customer. And steel inevitably is going to be a batch manufacturing process when plant scale is large. Few customers need so much of the same kind of steel and in the same shapes to allow you to just run the same items continually. The exception is the vehicle industry, which requires lots of standard stamping sheets for a given vehicle type.

While all this was going on, U.S. steel companies were deathly afraid of a new Japanese technology called continuous casting. In continuous casting mills, steel was produced in furnaces and the red hot metal was directly delivered onto processing mills for shaping. This method saved both time and money because the steel didn't have to be cooled, stored, and reheated. A number of finishing processes, though, still had to be done in separate steps such as applying special coatings.

How could you produce batches more efficiently and with fewer delays? Nucor realized that the Japanese manufacturers were onto something with their continuous casting method whereby heated steel was turned into finished product in many fewer steps. How could such a simple process be made viable for smaller customer quantities? Nucor hit on the idea of creating one-process steel manufacturing by melting down scrap steel instead of starting with the raw materials for steel. Furnaces for melting scrap were smaller and cheaper than big blast furnaces. Melting furnaces could also be made in different sizes without affecting efficiency. By connecting the melting furnace to the processing line, steel was produced very quickly. Gradually, Nucor learned how to do more processing steps on the same processing line. Eventually, what once took weeks was compressed into hours.

This approach was an amazing breakthrough for customers. They didn't have to plan their orders months ahead of time. Customers also had more flexibility for acquiring steel if something went wrong. A problem with one line could be offset by running another order through a different line a few hours later. This flexibility meant not only fewer sleepless nights, it also meant that customers didn't need so much steel inventory. Some customers could go from keeping 120 days of supply to less than 5 days, thus gaining a 2,000 percent inventory solution by switching to Nucor.

Create a One-Step Solution for Purchasing Your Offering

To reduce delays for beneficiaries and users, you need one-step actions for them and for your organization. Perhaps no better example of reducing delays can be seen than in the ways that some retailers are streamlining purchasing processes.

If you go to the usual mass merchandiser's store, you soon have a shopping cart full of bulky items or overloaded arms. You make rapid progress until you reach the checkout lanes. You scan the choices and notice that most registers aren't open. Of the ones that are, several people are usually standing in each line leaning on overflowing shopping carts. It would be faster for everyone if all customers waited in the same queue and then went to the next available register. You'll find that method in some banks and bookstores but not in mass merchandisers. These merchants don't want to give up any merchandising space, even if it means more customer convenience. You try to guess which clerks and customers will process transactions the fastest; often you are wrong.

Home Depot has given you another choice. You can go to a self-checkout and pay for your merchandise using automated equipment. With several such self-checkout stands, chances are good that you won't have to wait. You pass the item's bar code over the scanner or wave a laser wand at the bar code on larger items until everything is scanned in. Then you either insert a credit card or cash to pay. Bags are available to put your purchases in. Unless you have dozens of items, you can be on your way in a few seconds. During busy times, there is a Home Depot associate lingering in the background to help you with any problems. Some grocery chains also have self-checkouts available.

In the future, the items in many such stores will have radio identification tags on them. With such tags, it will be possible to tally your bill electronically without using a scanner. Some predict that credit and debit cards will also have such radio communications capability. If that occurs, you may someday have the option to simply walk out the door with your merchandise while your bill and payment are automatically processed.

When you buy items online, by comparison, an annoying drawback can be filling out endless requests for shopping cart information. Your computer's software will often ask you if you want to save the information you input. If you select that option to save, your computer may also sometimes fill in the information for you with the vendor ... and sometimes your computer may not.

Other vendors may also store your shopping cart information so that when you reorder, you don't have to reload. Amazon.com has always taken this convenience one step further by offering a "one click" option to buy goods based on prerecorded data.

Some suppliers go even further and anticipate what you want to buy. For instance, Staples.com has for many years asked you if you want to create lists of what you've just ordered. Then, you can simply select from among those lists on the home page to find the items you want without looking them up on thousands of item pages. With so many office supplies being similar, but potentially unsuitable for a given task, this time-saving choice can be a real help.

That's all fine and good for simple purchases, but what about buying something complicated? Dell has a better idea there. You can call a toll-free number and find a representative who is friendly, knowledgeable, and quick to take you through your choices for ordering a custom-made computer. Presumably these helpful people are backed up with lots of computer screens they can quickly access for frequently asked questions. While you are on the phone, they'll also let you know what the hot deal of the hour is (something Dell uses to steer customers towards parts that are in excess supply or to avoid parts that are out of stock). You'll also be asked if you want interest-free financing, and the representative can check out the availability of that option for you in a few seconds by employing a fast credit investigation. Naturally, you can also pay by credit or debit card.

So why is creating a one-step solution for purchasing so valuable? If you make it easy to purchase, people will purchase more from you. They won't feel the need to shop around or ask endless rounds of questions. If purchasers use what you offer in a business or nonprofit organization, they'll also start thinking of ways to accomplish more by employing your easy-to-access offerings.

Compare all of this ease with the problems that welfare recipients in the United States often face. Although qualified for many special kinds of assistance from the government, many people cannot read and write well enough in English to make successful applications for aid. As a result, many needed benefits are unclaimed. An alert social worker can make all the difference for such families with young children by alerting the family to its benefit choices and helping with the applications. The social worker is providing a one-step process for these beneficiaries.

Eliminate the Need for Solutions

In some businesses and nonprofit organizations, you can make one decision and receive your offerings automatically for years. Here's an example: We recently learned about a new magazine, *Make*, that caught our fancy. Ordering a subscription online, we were pleasantly surprised to be offered a discount on the first year's price if we agreed to be automatically billed for renewals. Obviously, if we decide we don't like the magazine, we'll have to remember to cancel our subscription when it expires in a year. Otherwise, *Make* will keep coming until our credit card is out of date.

Many suppliers provide similar options for those with continual needs for their offerings. But they go even further and provide services that make their offerings operate without delays. Snack food manufacturers like Frito-Lay go into retail stores frequently, check the shelves to see what's missing, restock, and tidy up the shelves while they are there. In manufacturing plants, some vendors monitor the level of inventory and continually replenish to meet a target level that the customer has established. Invoices are triggered by the use of the inventory, and payments are automatically received on a pre-agreed-upon schedule. Contract manufacturers take that system one step further. Customers tell the supplier what they want, when and where they want it, and so forth. The contract manufacturer then ensures that the products are available to the customer's customers in pre-agreed-upon ways. To accomplish part of this commitment, the contract manufacturer may partner with a logistics specialist to create the required results.

Some government agencies now simplify by allowing payments to be made by radio-controlled devices. For instance, you can skip long lines to pay tolls for bridges and roads by having a transponder that automatically withdraws money from a toll account you set up. The account is automatically replenished from your credit card or checking account. Unless you lose your transponder, don't pay your credit card bill, or have an empty checking account, that's the last you will have to do until it's time to replace your transponder in five years.

To operate this way, the offerings, methods for delivery, and support of those offerings have to be nearly perfect. When that happens, another benefit occurs. The customer's costs plummet due to eliminating activities that are now unnecessary such as incoming inspection, rework, service inspections, and repairs. To do things faster, you have to do them better. Otherwise, errors grow exponentially out of control.

 Here are questions that you can use to help you apply what you learned in this chapter about how to cancel delays:

- What adjustments can you make to simplify the use of your offerings to eliminate customer and beneficiary delays?
- What process will allow you to eliminate as many steps as possible in providing your offerings?
- How can you simplify purchasing or ordering into a one-step process?
- What relationship with beneficiaries will turn your offering into an automatic and pleasant part of beneficiaries' operations or lives?

Chapter 9

1, 2, 3, Go!
Simplify, Simplify Again,
and Simplify Some More

Very simple ideas lie within the reach only of complex minds.
— Remy de Gourmont

Imagine if you had to assemble your car, truck, or SUV before you could drive it. Even the most talented and experienced mechanic would find that a challenge without a good set of instructions and a well-equipped garage. As daunting as that task seems to us, Henry Ford realized that if he broke down the assembly process into simple steps and provided the right tools, virtually anyone could learn in a few minutes to be an expert assembler of one or two parts. From that insight, the automobile age was born as the assembly line eliminated many costs and cars were priced within reach of the average working person.

Take something complicated and make it simple, and you will find that it's much easier to attract beneficiaries, customers, and users. Do the same simplification for providing your offering, and costs will evaporate like gasoline on a hot summer day.

Most people would agree that offerings are frequently too hard to understand and use. How many people read all of the instruction manual for their new vehicle and follow the manual's dictates? Not very many. Most people who work in organizations see lots of unnecessary complexity in what they do. Yet it's comforting to some employees to know that the complexity makes it harder to replace the people and provides more work to do — a perverse sort of job security. Ironically, that tempting thought encourages stalled thinking that can lead to a lack of competitiveness ... and a loss of jobs.

The author of the opening quote, Remy de Gourmont, argues that it takes a complex mind to develop very simple ideas, and that's normally the case. But if we follow Henry Ford's insight and break down simplification itself into discrete steps, anyone can simplify well. The first step is to look at your business model.

Simplify Your New Business Model

In chapters 6, 7 and 8, we focused on eliminating what's unnecessary by employing a more efficient business model that cancels delays. From applying that thinking you should now have a new business model that emphasizes prompt, effective methods for selling and providing your offerings. Like all new business models, this one is bound to be too complex ... simply because it is new. How can you find attractive business model simplifications? We offer a simple concept to guide you: *Do the minimum to create a perfect result.*

How often do you see "minimum" and "perfect result" in the same sentence? We wager that you may not have ever seen that combination before. When most of us think about perfection, we immediately think of something exquisitely "maximum" ... like a 20-tiered wedding cake large enough to feed 600 guests. Just cutting and serving from such a cake is a complex undertaking.

There are a number of problems with such a cake. The cake probably has to be assembled on-site. If the facilities aren't adequate for such construction, the cake will suffer. Cakes like these are also very hard to carry from one room into another. A dropped cake can cause a wedding disaster. In cutting such large and complex cakes, you have to be careful or the cake will tip over. The price per slice of these cakes can be enormous as well.

What does the bridal party really want? Many want a cake that provides a nice decoration for the reception and a memorable backdrop for some of the wedding photographs. In addition, the wedding party wants to feed those 600 guests. Unless the bride and groom want to enter the book of *Guinness World Records* for their cake, the simpler alternative is to separate the function of "for show" from the function of "for feeding" to create the perfect result.

Wedding cake bakers have long understood those needs. Many such bakers will offer an alternative — a smaller wedding cake for show and many flat cakes that can be easily cut and served for most of the guests. Some bakers don't even have any cake in the for-show version. Instead, they decorate a cardboard base as the for-show cake and use precut pieces from a flat cake for the obligatory photographs of the bride and groom feeding one another.

Naturally, doing the minimum perfectly is a lot easier for those with simpler needs. If you can find enough of those customers or beneficiaries, you can simply concentrate on providing what they need. For instance, if you end up doing only wedding parties for 100 guests, your for-show cake can be sculpted from permanent materials rather than from icing and cake. We saw a clever version of that idea at the Four Seasons Hotel in Las Vegas. For a wedding anniversary, cake slices were delivered at lunch in an exquisite container made up to look like an actual anniversary cake. We never tumbled to this being a simulated cake until the server popped open the top and pulled out six precut slices. The rest of the cake we ate was out in the kitchen.

Determine the Needs of Beneficiaries, Customers, and Users

From that example, we're sure you have already figured out the first instruction for doing the minimum to create a perfect result: *Determine the needs of the beneficiaries, customers, and users.*

Organizations often skip this step. Here's a typical example: When you want to rent a function room in a nice hotel or restaurant, the establishment will have a target profit they want to earn from you for use of that space. Let's say that they want to make $1,000. But they are usually wary of quoting you that amount for the room as a line item in your proposal. You might then shop around for a lower room rental rate. So these establishments try to hide the room charge by insisting on providing food and service for a minimum number of guests at quite high catering prices. Undoubtedly feeling a little guilty about those prices, the catering managers will often deliver three times the food and beverages you need. Their objective is probably to make you feel like you got a bargain by having more than you could eat and drink.

Let's say, though, that your purpose for renting the room is to have a business discussion with your guests. While your guests are sashaying back and forth from the outsized buffet with endless piles of shrimp, not much business conversation is going on. After overeating, the guests may only want to take a nap. That food-induced semi-coma isn't too great either for the discussions you wanted to have. Here's another problem: All that surplus food makes the guests uneasy, thinking that perhaps you had a lot of people not show up at the last minute and wondering what's wrong with your organization.

Such a hotel or restaurant would be better off to ask the event's organizer what the purpose of the event is, how the setting and meals can support and not hinder that purpose, and how else the hotel or restaurant could contribute to making the event more successful. For a host organization that wants lively discussions, a special menu could be developed. The food would be light and modest, but of remarkable quality in ingredients and appearance. To avoid having people receive too little food, there could be several courses. Courses would be served at the table only during times when it would not be an interruption to have such service. Deliver the food on a schedule that allows for time to rest between courses and by dessert many people will be waving away the choices … which also helps the guests be more alert. The hotel or restaurant might also train and direct the staff to drop subtle hints that the servers are honored to be assisting such a distinguished group as an additional way to make the guests feel special.

Where offering providers go wrong is in assuming they know better than the customer, user, or beneficiary what is needed. Instead, involve the customer, user, or beneficiary in examining each important area of choice. The best way to do this is to have an expert asking key questions and providing information as the choices are pondered. If you cannot provide step-by-step guidance in person, the ideal approach is to unbundle your offerings instead so that customers, users, and beneficiaries can highly customize what they receive and experience. To that unbundling, add your expert knowledge via helpful answers to frequently asked questions that can stimulate customers, users, and beneficiaries to make better selections.

Focus on Those You Can Serve Most Effectively Using the Fewest Resources

Every organizational leader knows that you cannot be all things to all people, or you will fail to have a distinct image and competence advantage. The best business models work on that basis to move in the opposite direction: Do the fewest number of things for the most profitable customers where the organization can gain or increase a competitive advantage. A nonprofit organization can stretch its resources by focusing on beneficiaries it serves less expensively and better than anyone else.

If we revisit parallels to Pareto's Law (such as the law's restatement by Dr. Joseph M. Juran, the Quality Management pioneer, into Pareto's Principle), we usually find that 80 percent of the profits of any business come from 20 percent of the customers. When enough customers are involved, 20 percent of those most profitable customers (4 percent of the total) will provide 80 percent of the profits from the most profitable customer group (64 percent of the total). Attract more customers like these, and profits soar. Specialization can definitely help.

In a nonprofit organization, 80 percent of the people served will typically require only 20 percent of the organization's resources. If you serve a large enough population, 64 percent of the people served require only 4 percent of the organization's resources. If you can focus on serving only those beneficiaries, you can help a lot more people. If the impact of your help is similar in its benefit to all beneficiaries, specialization can be a wise move. This case for specialization is enhanced if other nonprofits specialize in inexpensively serving those you cannot serve nearly as efficiently. In this way, more people are helped … or fewer resources are required.

But don't stop there, look deeper. Start with those you don't serve at all. How do they compare to those you can serve most efficiently? If there are enough of such businesses, organizations, and people out there, you may be able to specialize further. The ideal is to find a large enough customer, beneficiary, and user base so that you can eliminate the least attractive offerings, and the inefficient aspects of your business model, and make the tasks of delivering perfect results for your remaining offerings simpler and easier.

Add Partners Who Complement You in Achieving a Perfect Result

If the chef at the Four Seasons Hotel in Las Vegas had decided to become expert in creating faux cakes, costs would have undoubtedly soared. Artists are usually better at such tasks than chefs. A similar specialization is possible for ice sculptures. Years ago, chefs would descend into the freezer wearing hats, mittens, scarves, and overcoats to carve a block of ice into a sculpture. Today, many restaurant supply houses offer molds for freezing water to create similar ice sculptures. The molded ice sculptures look a little artificial at first, but after they have been melting for a half hour or so, they are indistinguishable from many of the hand-carved sculptures. Likewise, some fine restaurants don't make their own cakes. Instead, they rely on master bakers who create custom cakes to order that arrive just before the meal. In the busy restaurant kitchen, such cakes would have to be made much earlier in the day and wouldn't be nearly as fresh.

Some people take this approach to partnering to extreme limits. During a discussion of how to create a billion dollar business with only one employee, an entrepreneur described how he felt this could be done in providing broadband Internet, cable television, and Internet telephone services for businesses and apartment buildings. Every step in providing the service, from making the initial sales call to removing the service, could be handled by very capable suppliers who could be organized and trained to achieve a perfect result for this man's business model.

If such partners don't yet exist, you may want to help launch them. Many large enterprises were founded originally to serve one specialized role for a single customer who grew to enormous size. Knowing that, intelligent entrepreneurs are often willing to create a complementary partnership that enables your business or nonprofit organization to accomplish more and become larger than would otherwise occur.

Simplify Each Business Model Step
for Customers, Users, and Beneficiaries

If you pursued the ideas for simplifying your business model well, you probably now have a business model that you haven't considered before. If you consider how you might deliver the benefits of that new business model, you will find that many activities that you or others do or have done are no longer needed.

Here's an example: Years ago, few public companies had ever hired anyone to interview their institutional investors to find out ways to improve communications. Initially, those offering such interviews had to convince skeptical executives that investors often held back some of their opinions from the executives during routine conversations. Why? The investors wanted to keep friendly and open access to the company. If an investor tells a CFO that the investor thinks that the CFO doesn't know anything about operations, that CFO may not take that investor's call the next time. If protected by anonymity, the investor would like the company to know that the CFO needs to develop more operational skills. After learning from a few such surprises gained through anonymously sponsored interviews, companies became more open to purchasing such interviews. Once the value of such interviews was understood by executives, those who provided interviews were able to simplify the sales and presentation processes to exclude explaining why new information was developed from what had been learned in routine conversations.

Consider If the Step Is Needed

Go into most banks and you need to provide identification to cash a check or to take money out of an account. That's a prudent practice. If your business model is to provide great service to wealthy people, however, you might instead want to greet these customers by name and skip the identification process. A new teller could rely on other tellers to help by discreetly signaling that this is a good customer. Skipping the manual identification process doesn't make the bank any less careful, but it makes the customer feel ever so much more appreciated and saves time for both the bank and the customer.

A more powerful business model might consider the banking customer's time as being even more valuable than the bank's time. Such customers might not always want to head to the bank to pick up certified checks and large amounts of cash. A bank solely focused on wealthy customers might provide delivery services in those instances. The customer might also welcome a secure escort to the site of a transaction where the certified check or cash is to change hands.

These days it's almost an anachronism for a legal transaction to require certified checks or cash deposits. Wiring money is usually faster and easier. For customers who don't realize that, the bank could offer to handle the wire transaction beginning with obtaining the correct wiring and account information from the other party.

In fact, if you offer these services, multiple debit cards, great electronic banking, and various bill-paying services, your wealthy customers shouldn't ever need to come to the bank to obtain cash or certified checks.

Take that time-saving one step further. Help customers learn how to arrange for incoming payments to be sent to the bank electronically, and the customers won't have to go to the bank to deposit checks. Should the odd check arrive anyway, make it easy to mail in those checks with prepaid envelopes.

But a bank wants to have happy customers. How enthralled will customers be if they never see anyone from the bank? Instead of tellers, such a bank might have personal bankers who are available at all times to their customers. Each customer would work with more than one personal banker so that not every banker will have to do overnight duty.

How will such customers open accounts, meet with their bankers, and conduct other business? The personal bankers will come to the customers. The bank would then be able to skip having so many branches and use some of the savings to pay fees to allow customers to use any ATM network.

Keep pushing like this and pretty soon you may well have eliminated many banking transaction steps. In the process, you'll be approaching the theoretical best practice in providing better offerings and performance.

Customize to Simplify: Turn Ruby Slippers into Traveling Shoes

In *The Wizard of Oz*, Dorothy flies in her family home propelled by a tornado until she arrives in the magical land of Oz. But Dorothy doesn't want to be in Oz; she wants to get back to Kansas. When Dorothy's house lands, the Wicked Witch of the East is crushed. The witch disappears, leaving only her ruby slippers. Glenda, the good witch, tells Dorothy to wear the ruby slippers and keep them safe. Near the end of the story, Glenda tells Dorothy that she can go back to Kansas anytime she wants. All Dorothy has to do is to click her ruby slippered heels together. If Glenda had customized her advice to provide Dorothy with that simple solution sooner, Dorothy would have been reunited with her family earlier in the story.

In the same way, many steps can be turned into simpler, but higher potential, operations through customization. Here's an example: Enormous numbers of entrepreneurs want to make their fortune on the Internet. Most believe that they cannot hope to succeed without developing a list of people who are interested in receiving their offerings. With great effort and skill, such entrepreneurs succeed in adding e-mail addresses to their lists. What's the result of all this solicitation? E-mail recipients' accounts are clogged with more and more solicitations, the modern version of direct mail offerings from magazine publishers whose offerings you once subscribed to.

What do most e-mail users really want? They would like to receive only offers and information that are relevant and interesting to them. Most won't send an "unsubscribe me" e-mail though; that's too much trouble. It's simpler and easier to just change e-mail addresses every so often and leave the old address's junk e-mails behind.

There's an opportunity here for some smart Internet entrepreneur: Provide a service to attract offers and information that are more relevant to people while screening out ones that are less relevant. Presumably this service would work by developing a more complete profile of what the customer is and isn't interested in and updating that information fairly frequently through interaction with the customer. This profiling has to be done, of course, in a way that limits the time and effort the customer has to make. Spam filters are used to partially fulfill this purpose now, but you usually find yourself needing to review hundreds of such junk e-mails in the file of suspected spam to be sure you don't miss one communication that you wanted to receive.

Through providing this simplifying innovation, the customer doesn't have to fill out forms to register for various things, spends less time deleting unwanted material, and gains access to more relevant and interesting material. The key will be for the customer to create a document that's somewhat like the common application that many colleges require. Fill the common college application out once, and applications for most schools are greatly expedited while the amount of work is decreased by 50 to 80 percent.

A key element for successful customizing is to provide the beneficiary, customer, or user with the outcome that's desired without needing to spell what is wanted in very much detail. This objective requires simplifying the choices. Henry Ford didn't expect his customers to pick out each part for their cars and trucks. Make it simple for people to figure out what they want and order that result, and you will sell more. You shouldn't require your beneficiaries, customers or users to get into such details either … unless, of course, they crave that choice. So be sure that you allow people to order choices that many people want. Some hotels and restaurants will tell the host or hostess considering a private function room that table service for a large party is only available in the main dining room. If the host or hostess doesn't want the meal or event to be in the main dining room but wants table service, chances are the event will be held elsewhere.

Extract the Annoyance and Add Enjoyment

Some steps are unavoidable. There may be a law requiring a particular step. For instance, banks have to report a large cash deposits in an effort to cut down on laundering of illegal drug money. Safety may require a step. You can't become immune from many dangerous diseases without either having the disease or receiving an immunization injection. Your life may depend on the step. Certain surgeries are the only known way to prolong life, yet few want to be operated on.

Rather than making these inevitable steps as simple as possible, sometimes we will do well to refocus the steps from their unpleasant aspects towards creating more enjoyable experiences.

Some hospitals are discovering such an approach can make a lot of difference to their revenues and profitability. Hospitals that attract the best surgeons often find themselves in competition with other hospitals around the world to attract the wealthiest and most reclusive patients. Sometimes these patients have special security needs because they are heads of state. In other cases, the patients simply value their privacy. Other patients may want to be surrounded by their families during such a trauma.

A number of these world-class surgical locations now have special buildings or wings that provide luxury hotel amenities for patients, their families, and entourages. (If you have to be sick, you might as well enjoy the room service!) Inside such areas, privacy is a must. Staff members are carefully trained to avoid identifying who any of the patients are or the names of those who have been treated there.

Such a shift in approach to making the unavoidable more pleasant only works, of course, if the medical treatment is first rate. Powerful, wealthy patients know how to check these things out, so you'll need to improve surgical and infection-avoiding performance as well.

Simplify Simplification

How can you reduce the time and effort it takes to create attractive simplifications? Creating a totally new process will usually work better than reforming an existing process. This approach goes counter to today's fascination with Six Sigma and other quality disciplines that wring errors out of existing processes. But if you fix an obsolete process to eliminate flaws, all you may have is a way to create error-free buggy whips. How else can you explain the paradox of Motorola's long slide in market share for mobile communications equipment and telephones during the 1990s despite the company's Six Sigma prowess?

Entrepreneurs have long understood this point. Those who have built billion-dollar businesses almost always began by creating fewer, simpler, and more effective processes for delivering high value at low cost to beneficiaries, customers, and users. This observation is equally true for those who start entrepreneurial nonprofit organizations.

Habitat for Humanity International is one of the world's largest home builders, but the organization doesn't operate like the for-profit home construction firms. Plans are simpler, offer less customization, and permit homes to be created at far less cost than for conventional construction of similar size. In addition, the land, materials, and labor are usually donated. By the time Habitat has completed a new home, the mortgage that the new owner assumes may be as little as 10 to 25 percent the size of what a comparable new private-sector home would cost. The new homeowner pays back principal, but no interest. Unlike the happy real estate flipper, the new homeowner cannot sell for several years. Habitat is building homes for families to live in, not creating houses as speculative investment vehicles. In addition, the down payment won't cost the homeowner anything, but will require lots of sweat equity working with volunteers at the home site. The Habitat construction model can also operate at astonishing speed. Annual events prove that point by constructing homes in just a few hours through careful coordination of building activities. (See www.habitat.org for details.)

Had Habitat opted instead to use the traditional building model and take the errors out of it, most of Habitat's beneficiaries would still be waiting for housing. The same lesson can be drawn from the success of the Grameen Bank, which makes low-cost, small loans to families, farmers, and entrepreneurs in Bangladesh. While a normal bank with its cumbersome lending and documentation processes would lose its shirt making $100 loans, the Grameen Bank thrives at that lending level. The difference is that Grameen relies on its owner-depositors to do most of the lending work as volunteers. These volunteers make loans only to other owner-depositors who live in the same community. As a result, the volunteers are in a good position as a lending committee to assess credit risk and apply peer pressure to encourage repayment. Borrowers also know that if they want to borrow again they had better make good on the current loan. (See www.grameen-info.org for the full story.)

Let's return to an example we briefly mentioned in the Introduction that's drawn from *The Fortune at the Bottom of the Pyramid*. Professor C. K. Prahalad describes a fascinating combination of new business model and simplified processes for eye surgery. The Aravind Eye Care System in India is dedicated to eliminating needless blindness among the millions needing surgery, particularly for cataracts, which are a leading cause of diminished sight and blindness. Dr. G. Venkataswamy, the organization's founder, was determined that such eye care could be inexpensive, mass produced, almost error free, and high quality in serving rich and poor alike. Cataract surgeries were provided in recent years at charges of $45 to $331 for those who can pay. These prices are so low that the United Kingdom's health service can afford to fly its cataract patients to India and still save money, and the medical outcomes are better at Aravind than in the United Kingdom. Here's the best part of the story: At those low prices, Aravind is so profitable that the organization can afford to treat many poor patients with the profits from the paying patients. How do they do it? Aravind created vastly superior new processes that allow eye surgeons to be more productive and accurate. As an example of the new processes, Aravind surgeons operate five times as often as comparable surgeons in India and gain more experience.

Have a More Exciting Purpose

Many effective simplifications followed casual observations and suggestions by nonexpert stakeholders. Because the humanitarian purposes of the examples we just examined are so inspiring, everyone wants to make a contribution to helping more people. The exciting purposes of the organizations also help lower the organizational barriers to accepting new ideas and using them to develop simpler processes.

Compare motivation to simplify between those who work for a typical start-up for-profit bank and the Grameen Bank's owner-depositor volunteers. Those who assist in the for-profit bank's simplifications only benefit if they are shareholders. Since most employees, customers, and other stakeholders aren't going to be shareholders, that approach eliminates a lot of potential stakeholder motivation. By contrast, everyone in the Grameen Bank is a shareholder and a depositor. In addition, almost everyone in the Grameen Bank's community who isn't a depositor-shareholder will benefit indirectly from their neighbors' prosperous use of loan funds. In the for-profit bank, stakeholders seldom see the money put to work. In a community served by the Grameen Bank, many people see the benefits on a daily basis and can contribute to producing more benefits. If a new entrepreneur is making a mistake with her new business, for example, Grameen Bank depositors will be inclined to make a helpful comment because they have a stake in the results too.

Most stakeholders of for-profit organizations are emotionally starved in this dimension of their lives because their firm lacks a compelling purpose. One way to add such purpose is to conceive of a new type of organization, one that serves both the for-profit needs of customers and the nonprofit requirements of beneficiaries and users who would not otherwise receive benefits. One of the first examples we saw of this approach was when financially stressed inner-city hospitals in the United States began raising money to put in world-class centers for special surgeries. The hospitals then used the profits from the special surgeries paid by wealthy foreign patients to subsidize medical services to the uninsured in the local community.

Another way to create such a purpose is to have an organization-wide self-examination to identify inspiring results for the enterprise to create. Such a self-examination goes well beyond the typical vision exercise that delivers to a well-rounded statement about providing helpful results for everyone. With a leader who is highly motivated to develop and pursue such a purpose, amazing concepts can emerge. If you would like to get a sense of how this can be accomplished, we recommend you read *Let My People Go Surfing* (Penguin Press, 2005) by Yvon Chouinard, founder and owner of Patagonia. That firm sponsors effective environmental activism, helps maintain wonderful wilderness environments, and provides a great place to work for the company's employees.

Challenge Your Organization to Simplify Further

Can leadership make a difference in simplifying? You bet! Here's how: An organization's leaders can establish goals that focus everyone's attention on simplification. Frank Lucier at Black & Decker did this well when he was the firm's CEO several decades ago. For each of the firm's major power tool products, goals were set each year to reduce the price and cost by about one dollar each. At first, these goals led engineers to substitute cheaper materials for more expensive ones. After awhile, the engineers began to notice that reducing the number of parts by simplifying the design was a more predictable way to cut material and assembly costs. Product defects also dropped with simpler designs. After several more years, engineers began to wonder what would happen to expensive component costs such as electric motors if more than one product could use the same component. Voila! That proved to be another breakthrough in simplification.

An unintended lesson of this experience was that Black & Decker probably could have accelerated its simplifications. How? The goals could have provided the direction. For instance, after understanding what simplification and parts commonality could do, the annual goals could have been made more challenging such as to reduce prices and costs by two dollars.

Intel learned a powerful lesson from its CEO and cofounder, Gordon Moore. The firm had been a pioneer in memory chips and followed that with microprocessors. In 1965, Dr. Moore made a prediction that the number of transistors on a semiconductor would double about every 18 to 24 months. That prediction, which came to be known as Moore's Law, proved to be astonishingly accurate for a number of years. By 1978, however, many were skeptical that silicon-based technology could continue to improve at anything resembling that pace. To test that skepticism, we visited Dr. Moore and chatted about what he expected. Our impression at the time was that Dr. Moore felt that the law wouldn't continue to hold much longer.

Fast forward to 2007: Moore's Law continues to work just fine, thank you. What's going on? Everyone knew about Moore's Law. Because of that knowledge, no one was willing to run the risk of falling behind other semiconductor companies. As a result, competitors vied to produce the next generation of chips with double the number of transistors every two years. Someone always found a way to keep the law operating more or less on schedule. Competitors would soon catch up or have to drop out of a particular product line.

How long will Moore's Law continue to work? We believe it will be in place as long as semiconductor companies set goals to match the law's predictions. We often wonder what would have happened if Dr. Moore had originally set a more aggressive prediction.

Today's chips are vastly more complex and larger compared to those in 1965. Those differences are important because more complexity and size, for instance, make it easier for engineers to design new products to use the latest chips. What do these more complex, larger chips have to do with simplification? The answer lies in looking at how semiconductors are designed and manufactured. The simplifications came in those activities, allowing greater complexity to flourish and be productive.

Here's an example: Semiconductors are produced in part by creating lines on their surfaces. Such processes originally were so crude that quite a wide line had to be made in order to ensure that the circuit would work properly. As manufacturing became better, lines could be thinner. By focusing on making finer lines that worked well, much of today's progress occurred. Most of this progress came from employing equipment that was supplied to the chip manufacturers. Simplification was important there. For instance, semiconductor chip equipment makers learned that you could produce to finer tolerances if as much equipment as possible came from the same vendor. Applied Materials' CEO Dr. James Morgan realized this point early and used a combination of internal development and acquisitions to create an unparalleled breadth of mutually tuned equipment from the same supplier.

Create a Process for Simplification

Most people have ideas for making organizational processes simpler and better at lower cost. Why? Because people become frustrated with the many foolish ways that they either receive or deliver offerings. While they are being stalled by this foolishness, stakeholders will often reflect on how an improved alternative could be created. That's the good news.

The bad news is that these potentially helpful ideas have no clear outlet. Those who come up with the ideas don't know what to do with them. What's the protocol? Who do you tell? What do you tell?

Chances are that your organization has a number of people in it who enjoy simplifying and improving things. That potential for enjoyment probably isn't being fully satisfied by their current duties. Check to see if any of these people would be interested in receiving suggestions from stakeholders. If so, you've got a starting point. Ask someone who is interested to head a study group to create a process for simplifying processes. Give the person only one direction: Involve as many people as possible to get ideas and later to evaluate the most promising suggestions and proposals.

While Tom Golisano was CEO of Paychex, the firm had an effective process for simplification. At weekly meetings of the organization's most senior officers, one agenda item was to propose new ideas for simplification, both for existing offerings and new ones. Keeping that focus, the officers reported that they were always asking people for any ideas they already had, observing what was being done to spot possible simplifications and discussing balky steps with those who might develop good ideas for better methods.

Here are questions that you can use to help you simplify, simplify again, and simplify some more:
- How can you simplify your business model?
- What business model simplifications can you make based on only delivering what stakeholders (customers, beneficiaries, partners, suppliers, employees, distributors, shareholders, lenders, and the communities in which you operate and serve) need and want?
- Which customers, users, and beneficiaries can you focus on who

need the least resources for you to supply them with what they want?
- How can you involve your stakeholders in looking for ideas that simplify your tasks?
- How can you gain help from partners to achieve near-perfect results?
- What simplifications can you apply to each remaining step in your newly simplified business model that will expand stakeholder benefits?
- In what ways can you simplify simplification through adding inspiring purposes for what you do, using better leadership methods, and creating simplification processes?

Chapter 10

Supply Driver's Education
Help the Unskilled Avoid Accidents

Education is what remains when we have forgotten all that we have been taught.
— George Savile, Marquis of Halifax

You can do unexpected damage by employing many offerings in the wrong way. We were reminded of that sad fact when one of our young colleagues offered to lead a tour of his old college so one of our offspring could learn more about the school.

On the way into town, the colleague pointed to a large scar in the bark of a tree about 15 feet off the ground. That scar, he informed us, was where his BMW's bumper hit the tree as the car tried to become an airplane during a high speed trip through the mountains. We slowed down in honor of this shrine to youthful folly and tried to think of reasons for our offspring not to apply to this school.

In various parts of the world, it's permissible to drive long before teenagers have the skill or the good sense to do it well. We are humbled to remember our driving accidents at 16 that did not recur at 17, 18, or 19. Experience must be a good teacher.

But experience has quite a price. Vehicle accidents take hundreds of thousands of lives and leave millions maimed and saddened every year. Inexperienced drivers are involved in more than their fair share of such accidents.

Having taken courses in how to drive and having arranged for our offspring to do the same, we noticed that young people are helped by such education while they are unskilled. Seat belts are fastened. The right foot reaches the brake pedal faster and is more tentative in pressing down the accelerator. The head swivels left and right before entering an intersection. There's more distance between the car and the one in front.

Vehicle manufacturers lose potential business because young drivers aren't very skillful. Families are more likely to keep old Betsy running as a teenager-driven vehicle until their children reach the safe and sane driving stage. If teenagers drove more safely, new vehicle sales would be a lot higher because teenagers love new wheels more than all but sports car buffs. Having teenagers in the house also inhibits Mom and Dad from indulging in something racy that they would enjoy. Taking a hot car out for a spin would be too tempting to the younger generation.

The same thing happens in other markets. Fearing that accidents will happen, purchases are deferred or reduced to reflect concern about those potential accidents. If teenagers can create mayhem with a vehicle, think what they could do with a racing boat!

By comparison, the commercial aviation field rarely experiences accidents. Airlines feel confident about buying new planes that cost tens of millions and trusting the planes to their crews. What's different?

Before becoming commercial pilots, all but a few aviators have logged many hours in the air in military aircraft. Since many people want to become commercial pilots, only the most talented and reliable are selected from among the experienced. But that's not enough. Pilots have to qualify to fly an aircraft. Qualifying usually involves lots of time in a simulator where ingenious controls allow the person conducting the simulation to create instant hurricanes, wind shear at landing, equipment failures of all kinds, and other disasters. Airlines have found that if you practice dealing with situations that could lead to accidents, you are more likely to avoid accidents and to know what to do to minimize the problem should an accident become unavoidable.

Unlike the education a new driver receives, a pilot is expected to keep practicing these important lessons under strict supervision. Flight hours must be maintained. Practice time in simulators needs to be logged on schedule. Regular physicals are required to catch medical problems before they impair flight performance. Show up for work with alcohol on your breath once, and someone will probably turn you in. That slip will get you permanently grounded by your employer.

But education can only go so far. Offerings have to be designed to avoid accidents. Imagine our surprise when we first backed out of the driveway in our new car … and nothing happened when we hit the brakes at the end of the driveway. Fortunately, there were no cars coming as we slewed into the street just before the brakes miraculously began to work. The next time we backed out it was more tentatively and the brakes also didn't work. After a few telephone calls to the manufacturer, we eventually learned that this car briefly disengaged its brakes a few seconds after you first drive forward or backward before allowing the brakes to function normally again. To us, that's a design flaw that will cause accidents. To the manufacturer, it was a good engineering design for some reason that's incomprehensible to us. With time and understanding of the design, we learned to go very slowly until we have permanently effective brakes. Perhaps this quirk is disclosed somewhere, but we have never seen a written warning about it. Even with a dangerous design, educating people about what's going on and what to do can cut down on accidents.

What's it worth to avoid an accident? The savings can be enormous. If a new pharmaceutical turns active people who mix drugs inadvertently into shut-ins who need constant care, the cost can be millions for each affected person. If a vehicle has a flaw that causes it to roll over when drivers take turns too fast, thousands of unsuspecting families may be destroyed by death, paralysis, and recriminations aimed at the surviving purchaser or driver. The economic costs alone will be measured in billions of dollars.

Accidents from using offerings are often one of the biggest emotional and financial costs for beneficiaries, customers, and users. Help these stakeholders avoid accidents that come from a lack of skill in using the offerings, and you'll expand the use of the offerings and slash costs for everyone.

Simulate Accidents to Create Self-Education in Avoiding Accidents

Most testing of offerings assumes that the offerings will be used in the so-called intended way. But everyone knows that many offerings will not be used that way. Figure out what those dangerous misuses are, and you've got a great head start on figuring out what education is needed to avoid or minimize those possible accidents.

Many will do some sort of in-lab testing to see what can go wrong. Unfortunately, that testing usually occurs after an offering has been designed and finalized. We suggest that you begin looking for possible accidents during the prototype stage … and keep looking as you move forward.

A good place to start your early testing is exposing your offering with careful supervision to those who should never be near the offering. Babies, for instance, shouldn't be taking adult pharmaceuticals or driving vehicles. But as anyone knows who has been around babies, they are remarkably good at getting their hands on things that are put away in supposedly safe places.

Naturally, you don't want any babies to be hurt in the process. You set up your observations so that no actual harm can occur while potential harm is uncovered. Don't stop at babies. Let people of all ages, sizes, backgrounds, and degrees of education tinker around with the offering to see what they do with it. As with the babies, encourage this trial and error in a way that safeguards people from harm.

But people aren't the only ones who can be harmed. Check out pets, wildlife, and the environments that are connected to the production, use, or disposal of your offerings.

After they've all done their worst, ask the people involved what other potential accidents they thought of as they played with the offering. For instance, many misuses occur when products are acquired without directions or warnings. Imagine if someone mistakenly tossed your item onto the trash pile in front of their house and someone stopped and took the item along … unaware of potential dangers.

Limited test markets can also be helpful for this purpose. The sales of many items suddenly take off for unexpected reasons. There can be a dangerous usage involved when that occurs. For instance, how many times have hot sales to teens meant that the item could be used to get "high" or get into mischief in some obscure way?

You can also learn from those who have made the most similar offerings in the past. What complaints did they receive? What lawsuits ensued?

This next piece of advice will seem like a bad idea to many, but we recommend it. Let various watchdog groups that monitor your industry, activity, or function take a look at your new offering before it's finalized to see what problems they spot. That approach may seem like asking for trouble, but if you identify a problem before it becomes an accident, everyone is ahead of the game. Many watchdog groups have their own testing facilities and experts who may spot things that you would otherwise miss in the beginning.

When you start early enough, there's an unexpected benefit from such accident testing: You may find such a fundamental problem that you need to redesign your offering. When that happens, be happy. You may have substantially improved your chances for success while eliminating an enormous future financial burden.

Consider closures for medicine containers. Before the tampering incidents a number of years ago, medicines usually came in containers that anyone could open. Undoubtedly, that led to people taking medicines that weren't intended for them. How hard would it have been to anticipate misuse if anyone could get into an item? Children got their hands on adult medications that way and were poisoned. You have to assume that manufacturers weren't looking very hard to identify potential accidents in those earlier days.

When the first "childproof" and "tamper-proof" closures came along, there was an almost audible sigh of relief. That relief lasted for only a few days until people began to realize that children could open many of these new containers better than senior citizens could. Gradually, new forms of safer closure systems were introduced that were easier to use for the intended consumers and kept some children out.

Now, if someone could redesign containers to ease the difficulties of opening jars of preserves, pickles, and other hard-to-enter items, we could get away from banging containers on their lids to loosen the seals until the glass containers break in our hands.

Serious accidents are inevitable with the way that most offerings are designed. It's as though no one wanted to think about the consequences. Take intravenous needles. Nurses and certain technicians have to handle so many of those needles that these health workers are bound to be stuck from time to time by the typical needle. Get stuck with a just-used needle and who knows what disease might enter your body. Until after AIDS was identified, needle manufacturers and health-care facilities left health-care workers vulnerable to such infections. Safer systems have been introduced now.

If the health-care industry was so careless, imagine what other organizations were doing. Images come to mind of the U.S. government testing the effect of radiation on unshielded soldiers by having them stand a few miles away from atomic tests. Clearly, new attitudes towards avoiding harm are necessary.

Part of the challenge is to introduce an accident-free culture to your organization. If you put safety first, you'll see some amazing reductions in accidents ... and your costs for insurance, litigation, and damages will evaporate. Many organizations mistakenly put current budget promises ahead of creating current and future safety. That's near-term penny wise, and long-term pound foolish. To ignore safety rigor can lead to more accidents and eventually cause budget-busting events. To avoid this myopic focus on near-term budgets, make inducing simulated accidents a continuing part of your effort to avoid real accidents.

Ask Beneficiaries, Customers, Users, and Other Stakeholders How to Avoid Accidents

Those who have experienced simulated or real accidents can usually give you chapter and verse on what they were thinking, how they were confused, and what misled them into taking a dangerous action. But after a simulated, real, or potential accident most organizations see their job more as calming down the beneficiary, customer, or user rather than learning from their perception of what went or could go wrong. This instinct is partly well intentioned … wanting to make the person feel better. But part of the reaction can be inappropriate calculation … wanting to avoid lawsuits and bad word-of-mouth comments about the offering.

Naturally, you should be sympathetic and helpful to people who've just had a bad experience. But you shouldn't stop there. Try to sort out what went wrong. A good model to consider is what happens after a fatal airplane crash. Expert investigators look for the plane's flight recorders to see what the conditions were, what was said, what the pilot and crew did, and how the plane functioned. Like crime scene investigators, these experts also pick up the pieces and examine them for clues as to what failures contributed to the crash. Investigators will interview eye witnesses and review computer-based maintenance records. From these investigations, patterns emerge that lead to inspections of other planes, reviews of maintenance procedures and reconsiderations of appropriate pilot training.

In some cases, carefully staged and measured simulations may be run to find out what might have gone wrong. Here's another example from the commercial airline industry: When new commercial planes are being certified, tests are run to see how long it takes to evacuate the passengers and crew from the cabin under various less-than-ideal conditions. These simulations might include having the lights go out and simulating a cabin filled with smoke. Occasionally a plane is so poorly designed for rapid exit that many are injured during the initial simulations. By filming the actions that each participant takes, the airframe manufacturer can see some of what misled people or hindered smooth and rapid safe exits. After an accident, such a simulation can be used to detect the apparent sources of unexpected problems.

But that's not enough. From talking to those who had been in accidents and participated in safety experiments, designers learned that panicky passengers are likely to look to exit towards the door through which they entered the aircraft … and overlook a closer safety exit located behind them in the plane. Those who had been involved described how being seated facing towards the flight deck focused their attention on what they could see without turning around. Safety demonstrations now feature showing those in the cabin where the nearest exits are for them. Undoubtedly, these instructions have saved lives following accidents.

Parents will sometimes have to be proxies for explaining what babies do. That necessity is observably true since every year new products are designed and distributed that babies can take apart and swallow. Check the latest reports of recalls and you'll soon see what the problem is. Many offerings are designed by people who don't know very much about babies, and never think to ask parents about what might go wrong.

Pet owners will often be required to translate the psychology of their animals for offering designers. Many offerings intended for pets are primarily designed to appeal to their owners. But that appealing design may contain potentially harmful flaws for Fido or Kitty. Pets are inclined to turn any item into little bits and pieces that they may consume, for instance. Although that's not the intended use, that likelihood needs to be taken into account in designing safe offerings for pets.

Sometimes the dangers aren't well understood by the beneficiaries, customers, and users. Such lack of understanding is often the case with plants. We are constantly astonished to see plants with brightly-colored poisonous berries planted near a home's front door. Presumably, the person who planted the shrub either didn't have any children or was unaware of the danger. At the same time, we are struck that labels in plant nurseries often fail to describe the poisonous nature of berries, leaves, roots and other seemingly edible parts of plants. In such cases, it makes sense for offering providers to seek advice from experts about how these potentially deadly ornaments can be made safer. One obvious choice is to be sure that Christmas wreathes and other seasonal decorations eliminate such poisonous substances as holly berries, mistletoe and yew branches. If you use natural items in your offerings, be sure that you check with experts about how those lovely items can lead to harm.

Observe Beneficiaries, Customers, and Users
Employ Your Finished Offering
to Uncover Potential Accidents Before They Happen

After an offering has been finalized and delivered to the beneficiaries, customers, and users, flaws may remain. In the worst cases, offerings will have to be recalled to remedy the dangers. In other cases, user warnings will suffice. In some cases, it will be simple to make adjustments in other ways to eliminate danger.

Long before complaints begin piling up in your offices, accident reports roll in, and lawsuits are filed, accidents and near-accidents will be occurring. A wise offering provider assumes that such problems will ensue and plans for them. A possible model to consider can be found in the software industry. Developers know that internal testing will only reveal some of the many flaws. Rather than expose people to dangers from flawed software, developers make beta test software versions available to people who test the software in various practical ways that can identify some unanticipated dangers. These testers may be paid to try out the new versions or given other benefits that make the effort worthwhile. Have enough of these tests by savvy users, and the remaining flaws will be greatly reduced.

Software designers have learned to prepare for their designs' flaws. As a result, the software is written so that it can easily be repaired by sending out "patches" to fix various issues. With the advent of the Internet, such patches can be distributed automatically to those who subscribe.

While safety is our focus in this chapter, avoiding harm has an unexpected benefit for many organizations: Acting with care to fix faults makes customers, beneficiaries, and users more likely to do business with you. This positive response to your care increases sales while decreasing the need for marketing expenditures, providing another important cost saving.

Here's an example: When Saturn first shipped its sedans, the company realized that a batch of its cars had been filled with faulty radiator coolant. While most companies would have alerted the owners to the problem, replaced the radiators and the coolant, and felt satisfied, Saturn went further. Saturn wanted to have the reputation of being a different kind of car company, one you could trust to look out for you. Saturn decided that the right thing to do was to replace those cars with damaged radiators … with new cars! And you didn't have to go to the dealership to make the swap. The dealer would come to you with the new car. Talk about word-of-mouth advertising buzz. One man reported that neighbors and relatives bought over 40 Saturns after hearing about his replacement experience.

Provide Hands-On Experiences
Before Offerings Are Purchased or Used

Hands-on experiences benefit stakeholders and organizations. The experiences allow potential beneficiaries, customers, and users to see if the offering is right for them. While such experiences may drive away some who are mismatched, those for whom the offering is a good fit will be encouraged to act. In addition, during the hands-on experiences, you can observe any habits or misunderstandings that could lead to later accidents. You can alert the person to the risk before they use the offering on their own. Further, you can simulate accident conditions, as the airlines do for their pilots, to help prepare the beneficiary, customer, or user to avoid accidents. Finally, you can discuss with people what their reactions to the experiences are and help them to adopt better ways of preparing for future risks.

Many people who provide inexpensive or free offerings will shudder at this suggestion. How can they possibly afford to provide such hands-on experiences? There's always a way. You just have to look for it.

Start by considering the roles that volunteers can play. Many organizations with public purposes are interested in promoting greater health and safety. If your offering normally has a positive purpose that is undermined only through misunderstandings or misuse, you may well find that existing organizations are interested in adding relevant training for your beneficiaries, customers, and users. Here's an example: A new type of defibrillator may make it possible for those with limited medical knowledge to save lives. Automated external defibrillators (AEDs) determine what level of electric shock is required to help the struggling heart beat normally. No longer do you have to know how to interpret the heart's patterns before using such a defibrillator. Since AEDs were developed, the Red Cross stepped in to provide training programs for AEDs on the job and other public places. Such training helps the manufacturers to sell these items, and we can probably assume that the manufacturers assisted the Red Cross in designing its training.

From there, think about having beneficiaries, customers, and users receive some of this training at public expense. If the purpose is one that benefits all of society, the community may pick up some or all of the tab. In some communities, for instance, part of the driver's education training is provided as part of the high school program. Typically, families are expected to pay for at least the behind-the-wheel training.

Driver's education courses taken in high schools also provide another model: Ask beneficiaries, customers, and users to pay some of the cost of providing the experience. Although this may seem like a way to drive your audience away, the result can instead be an accelerator that makes these prior experiences more valuable and enjoyable. Here's an example: Everyone who buys a sports car wants to take it out for a spin before purchasing. Provide enough test drives, and you've given away more value in free joyrides than you gained in selling expensive cars. Rent a local race track and provide racing instruction for those who want to pay for the experience, and you'll soon have lots more people who know how to safely travel at high speeds in your sports cars. Once they've gotten the bug and know how to do it, these drivers are more likely to buy … and be safer drivers.

Don't forget to consider if beneficiaries, customers, and users want to help each other gain the relevant experience. How can you provide incentives for that to occur? For instance, many people learn subjects better if they teach someone else. But someone who is a new learner will be reluctant to take on the teaching role without materials that provide easy-to-follow steps for instructors and learners. What if you don't have the resources to create such materials? You can lower the cost dramatically by sponsoring a Goldcorp-type competition. By substituting recognition for compensation in appealing to developers, you will probably end up with better materials and plenty of positive publicity that will encourage people to use the materials.

Provide Safety Solutions
for All Levels of Skill and Experience

It's good to help people to be well prepared before their first experience, but complacency and developing bad habits can turn even the most careful people into risky operators of offerings. For instance, industrial accidents occur among those who aren't adequately trained and those who are so experienced that they decide to ignore safe methods. A dangerous piece of machinery may have a safety guard on it that keeps fingers out of harm's way. Such guards are wonderful safety features. Many guards have a drawback:

They slow down the work process. When that's the case, those who earn piecework payments are likely to remove the guards or ignore them in order to produce more.

What's missing? The kind of safety device that a novice needs may be different from what will seem right to an experienced operator. The offering maker should continue to study how its offering is employed and find ways to adjust for those with more experience. Since an item may have an expert using it for part of the day and a novice at another time, safety features need to be very flexible — in the same way that seat belts in vehicles adjust to adapt to the body size of the driver or passenger.

A similar issue arises among offerings for children. Even age-appropriate items will be used differently over time. A model rocket may initially be used as an educational experiment to learn about physics. But some youngsters may instead become fascinated with firing the rockets at objects to see what damage occurs. In both cases, model rockets have lots of potential dangers. But with different uses, the dangers vary. The methods required to offset those dangers are different, too. Being sure that the rocket cannot fire without a parachute decreases the chances of someone being harmed as the rocket returns to Earth. But that parachute doesn't do much good if the rocket is fired horizontally at someone. Perhaps a design that doesn't allow for firing except vertically would alleviate that risk.

Offer Ongoing Education and Refresher Experiences

Pilots have to return to the simulators on a regular basis. Why? Well, their knowledge starts to degrade into less and less "education" as George Savile pointed out in this chapter's quote. You don't face accidents every day. But you need to be ready for such accidents as though you did. Simulations can be part of the solution.

Those who provide offerings would do well to provide opportunities like commercial airlines do for refreshers and new learning. Chances are that ideas about the best way to handle dangerous situations from five years ago are now considered hopelessly inappropriate. Knowledge progresses ever faster, and it's not uncommon to find advanced practitioners of important subjects sticking to the old, inappropriate ways.

If you build such continuing education and refreshers into your business model, you'll find it natural to have beneficiaries, customers, and users looking for these experiences. As an offering provider, you can also use these interactions to learn more about unmet needs than you could by revising your offering or providing new offerings. Fail to satisfy the most advanced users of your offering, and you will soon have created an opportunity for a new and difficult competitor. If you are in an underserved social-service field, it may be highly desirable to attract competing providers. But if you are in a commercially competitive industry, such a market reaction may be harmful to your future success.

Here are questions to remind you of how to help the unskilled avoid accidents:

- How can you create simulated accidents to learn what risks need to be eliminated?
- What will encourage beneficiaries, customers, and users to tell you how accidents can be avoided?
- Which forms of observation will be most helpful in uncovering potential accidents?
- Who should receive hands-on experience before the offering is made available?
- How can you adjust safety solutions to apply differently for those with various safety needs?
- What will convince beneficiaries, customers, and users to pursue updated safety education and training?

Chapter 11

Use Cruise Control
Automate Important Tasks That Remain

Automate success, not failure.
— Paul A. Strassmann

Cruise control can be a good thing or a bad thing. What makes the difference? On a fairly straight road with little traffic during good weather, letting the car operate at a constant speed frees you up to pay more attention to the road and enjoy the driving more. Pick an optimal speed and you'll also get better gas mileage. But keep the cruise control on when traffic thickens, and you increase the chances of an accident by driving too fast and following other vehicles too closely.

Similarly, we have to be sure that we automate actions that are perfectly helpful when we use them and avoid automating anything that would lead us astray. That's why we haven't spoken about automation before this chapter. We wanted to be sure that you'd first replaced bad business models, poor processes, unnecessary steps, and harmful approaches.

Like the cruise control example, *always* automating will be a bad idea. General Motors proved that by investing in robots whenever possible during the early 1980s while Toyota went in the opposite direction and created less automated, but more highly productive work teams for car assembly.

The flexibility of the human team allowed Toyota to develop lean manufacturing methods that deliver low costs, high quality, and the ability to build customized cars shortly after they are ordered. General Motors found that the robots reinforced its commitment to the assembly line approach and left the company with less flexibility to adjust to consumer demand. It's not that Toyota didn't use robots. The difference is that Toyota's robots reinforced a more productive and effective process that fit the market. In some circumstances, General Motors was automating failure.

We always tell procrastinators that they should "hesitate to procrastinate." We feel the same way about automation. Hesitation over automation will often save you expensive mistakes.

Recheck the Process Before Automating It

Despite admonitions to automate the best of what's possible, most automation simply reduces costs somewhat for yesterday's obsolete practices. You only avoid that stalled approach by rechecking the steps in this part of the book as you consider the possibilities for automation:

- Eliminate the unnecessary (Chapter 6).
- Employ an efficient business-model design (Chapter 7).
- Cancel delays (Chapter 8).
- Simplify, simplify again, and simplify some more (Chapter 9).
- Help the unskilled avoid accidents (Chapter 10).

Such a recheck will often locate additional business model, process, and implementation improvement opportunities. Consider Kroger's use of information technology in this regard. When the company first began looking at automation possibilities in the 1990s, the venerable retail grocery chain realized that it had a large cost disadvantage versus Wal-Mart, its ever more important competitor.

Rather than consider how automation could reduce the cost of what the company was already doing, Kroger looked at how automation might be a bridge to better processes that would eliminate the unnecessary for its stakeholders. Here's an example: The accounts payable process had become an albatross. Invoices reflected initial shipments, and credits for returned goods lagged. Until everything matched up, Kroger didn't pay. Vendors were annoyed, and bookkeeping time soared.

Kroger decided to replace that system with one that paid automatically against bar code scans of received and returned goods. After educating vendors about the benefits of this system, a new accounts payable process was installed. The new process eliminated almost all of the accounts payable processing costs while allowing vendors to reduce their costs and prices, too. The result was a double saving for Kroger and its customers. Suppliers were thrilled to be paid sooner, which improved their willingness to provide

Kroger with better merchandising programs.

What can a more efficient business model design do if enabled by automation? Prior to considering automation, Kroger had operated like a traditional retailer. Many tons of goods were piled up in warehouses and even more goods were stockpiled in the backs of stores. But the shelves were often missing the frequently purchased items that experienced seasonal demand. Those goods were sitting back in a vendor's warehouse somewhere else. Such a system had high costs, required large working capital investments, and was even more expensive in terms of lost sales and profits due to popular items being out of stock.

Kroger changed to a process that reordered goods from most suppliers based on checkout scanner purchase records of what was being bought minute by minute from each of its stores. Instead of sending piles of identical goods through each stage of the process, shipments from vendors were consolidated into just what each store needed for the next day or two (JITL — just in-time logistics). Many of these shipments went directly from the manufacturer to the Kroger store. A store-specific shipment could then move directly from the truck onto the shelves in a few minutes, knowing that there would be just the right amount of space to receive these recently purchased and received items. Almost all of the volume that used to go through Kroger warehouses and be held at the back of stores was now eliminated as was the handling involved.

Eliminating long, slow steps in the distribution process also served to reduce delays. Kroger was able to pay vendors based on bar code scans. These processes also turned up shipment errors sooner so that the appropriate items could be received where they were needed most.

Kroger decided that one way to simplify further was to put its automated processes in place a bit at a time, rather than waiting to install a large, integrated package. The strategists believed that such an incremental approach would permit time for Kroger to observe what else could be done to simplify and improve a process before linking that process to another newly automated system. That decision proved to be wise when many processes turned out to offer additional simplification opportunities.

Kroger also discovered that even its best operators didn't always get the message. During a tour of a store offering the latest processes, executives were chagrined to find that store management didn't realize that it could stop performing many of the old processes. The store managers were doing double the work and wanted to know why. After spending more time letting store managers know that the old processes should have been dropped months earlier, the company installed new methods for ensuring that the conversion from old to new processes was better timed.

Create Flexible Automation

The General Motors approach to automation was inflexible. It did optimize costs if you made tremendous numbers of exactly the same vehicle. If you needed to change over to offer vehicle variations, the robots needed a lot of tending. Toyota countered that challenge by automating relatively stable processes such as the link between a customer's order in a dealer showroom and the parts order process, while not automating that which would be desirable to change quickly such as providing any extra features a customer wanted.

Flexibility is an important point for two reasons. First, customer satisfaction soars when customers can have just the features they want without waiting. The traditional assembly line produces lots of standard cars that the manufacturer and dealers then try to sell at the best price. Only a small number of customers want exactly the features a particular vehicle has. You can order a custom-made car or truck with just the features you want, but there's a long delay in many cases. In some automotive companies, these custom cars cost a fortune to produce. You take the standard car and rebuild it into a custom car. This method of customizing also means that the car is more likely to have faults.

Second, those who assemble cars hate assembly lines. They find it hard to stay focused. As a result, more errors creep into the cars they produce. The Toyota assembly teams, by contrast, enjoy the variety of tasks they do and like being part of a team. This team-based assembly process means that the Toyota teams make fewer errors due to higher morale and having more eyes looking out for errors at each stage of the vehicle's assembly.

Similarly, the Dell processes are both highly automated … and not. If you go to Dell's Web site, you can find information to help you select the features you want and order your custom-made computer. That's great if you've owned quite a few computers and want to use a new one for a similar purpose. It's even better if you simply need a machine to use at work. Dell will probably have established a customer account profile that will ensure your order is compatible with your firm's network, hardware, and software.

But what if you're clueless and need someone to talk to? That's no problem. You just contact a Dell representative via a toll-free call. We have ordered equipment from Dell this way. The knowledge and helpfulness of the people we've talked to are most impressive. You get the impression that Dell has rounded up thousands of experts with great personalities.

But wait. Are there really so many technophiles who love talking on the telephone? Dell didn't find that to be the case. Instead, they found people who enjoyed talking on the telephone and who knew something about computers. Dell made it easy to help by providing automated help screens written in plain-vanilla English that the representatives could use to deliver the latest technical information. Dell also provides classes and additional information to make its representatives more knowledgeable. That's important because Dell also provides many other kinds of electronic equipment.

Once that order leaves the Web site or the telephone representative, automation takes over again. Supplies by plant are checked against the customer's location to see where the custom machine should be made. The assembly is then automatically scheduled for where the inventory is in place and shipping distance is shortest. That scheduling triggers orders for more parts and accessories from the appropriate suppliers. If a needed part isn't yet at a work station but is in a plant's inventory, an automatic order goes out to move the part from the inventory to the work station before the computer is due to be assembled.

At the work station, however, things were not so automated when we visited a Dell factory in Texas. It was more like Toyota's approach to assembly. There was a work order that listed all the parts that were needed. Those parts were pulled by someone from the work station inventory into an assembly kit. The kits were picked up by a two-person team who then assembled the computer, checked it for simple faults, and sent the computer on for automated upgrades.

One of those next steps was to load the software that was ordered with the computer. Automated testing turned up flaws in some computers. The ones with minor errors went to a nearby repair specialist. Those with major errors were not repaired. Instead, another computer was produced in the following few hours.

From there, packing and shipping looked pretty much like any other factory except that the labels were automatically printed for each order to facilitate fast, accurate deliveries. These labels notified the shipper how to combine shipment of the computer with the monitor, printer, and whatever else had been ordered so that although these components shipped from different sites, the customer received a complete order in one combined delivery.

But the automation doesn't end there. Your new computer's software will direct you to register with vendors to receive automatic updates. Dell will also send you updates from time to time about subjects that affect the computer you purchased. Your order information will be stored so that the next time you call about ordering a computer, the choices you are presented with reflect your prior purchasing habits.

As you can see, Toyota and Dell are using automation to make the customer and the employee experiences better by creating a flexible process for rapid customization. Whenever automation doesn't create a better experience, they avoid automation.

Let's look at a contrasting experience. The first time we ate in an automat in the 1960s, it was a new experience. You went to a wall covered with glass doors. You opened one of those doors to remove the item you wanted, took your tray, and headed for the cash register. But after one time, the experience paled. It's more pleasant to go to a coffee shop, diner, or fast-food emporium and order something prepared the way you like it and receive some personal attention. It's no wonder that automats faded from the landscape. They automated the wrong part of the process and didn't enhance the customer experience. Avoid that mistake.

Make Automation Easy to Turn Off …
Rather Than a Customer Turnoff

An assembly line moves a vehicle along at a steady pace. The speed is set to reflect a trade-off between having enough or not enough time to add each part. But naturally, things can go wrong. A tool can break. Parts may be defective. The inventory bin may be empty. What do you do then?

Well, it is possible to stop the assembly line, but the manufacturer doesn't want that to happen very often. To avoid that stoppage, hundreds of supervisors and "expeditors" try to anticipate and quickly correct those problems. A 5-minute delay in the assembly line could cost thousands of dollars in reduced production. Awareness of those economics can lead to letting flaws go through rather than incur the obvious, immediate cost of halting the line.

Contrast assembly lines with processes where a momentary delay doesn't affect any other aspect of the process. In these other systems you can take an extra moment to get another tool or a missing part, or to ask a question. Naturally, such processes make it easier to produce an item that has fewer flaws.

When you produce items that won't require as many repairs after they are purchased, you decrease customer service and warranty costs. If customers are more pleased because they have fewer problems, sales increase and profits are higher.

Ordering online often presents some of the same challenges as an assembly line does for a worker who has a problem. Here's a typical problem: As a customer, you can't find what you're looking for. You've checked the site map. You've gone to the help list and queried. You've read the FAQs (frequently asked questions). And still nothing makes sense. Just before you give up, you fondly wish you could talk to a kind and knowledgeable person. At some Web sites, however, the motto for the customer seems to be "Type or Perish" (an uninspiring contrast to New Hampshire's motto, "Live Free or Die").

At other Web sites, you will find a toll-free number you can call. Taking that choice, however, can bog you down in an endless list of menus. In frustration, many will give up before finding what they are seeking. But if that toll-free number lets you easily reach a helpful person, you feel a sense of relief and your desire to purchase strengthens.

Such an approach to helping you is still highly automated, but a customer feels happier because it's possible to cut through the automatic response logjam of unhelpful information. A new thought enters your mind: Perhaps the offering provider really does want to help! Ah, wouldn't that be nice?

Lines aren't just for assembly. They are also for people waiting to be served. As you well know, many processes require unnecessary waiting. Each person is directed to follow exactly behind a specific other person. You then move in a fixed sequence from one station to another. At some point, you are finally done.

It doesn't seem to matter to anyone running the operation that some stations are underutilized while other stations are swamped. Eventually, everyone moves at the pace of the slowest station in the process that's still ahead of him or her. Relief organizations and military groups are famous for adopting these approaches.

Leaders who view resources as scarce and worth using well take another approach. These leaders offer more immediate service by being flexible.

Golf course pros have long understood this principle. Traditionally, everyone has started on the first hole and proceeded around the course through all 18 holes in numerical order. But if you start every golfer at the first hole in the morning, that means that the remaining 17 holes are unused until someone reaches each hole after starting at hole one, going on to hole two, then to three, and so forth. Since many people take four or five hours to play a round, that leaves too much empty space on busy weekend mornings. For instance, that approach means that the 18th hole is empty until the afternoon.

To overcome that undesirable slack, members are encouraged to come early on weekends for "shotgun" starts after the grounds crew has finished its morning chores. Foursomes of golfers are simultaneously sent to all 18 holes and directed to start at the same time. Years ago, shotgun blasts were used to alert players on distant holes when to begin. Today, most courses rely instead on sirens or the members' watches.

Even this helpful idea can be improved. Groups tend to back up at par three holes. That often means an empty playing space on the next par five. Astute pros will start the fastest foursomes on the par threes and put one fast and one slow group to follow one another on each of the par fives. This arrangement will allow 22 foursomes on the course operating at about the same speed as 18 random foursomes.

Try to add more foursomes than 22 or have too many slow groups, and the round's length will soon stretch well beyond five hours with lots of griping from the players. Course utilization over the course of the day also drops.

Golf pros also figured out that they could further speed up play and add more fun by changing the rules. Rather than having every golfer play every shot, some contest formats call for a golfer stopping on a hole after a given number of shots (usually one over par, the number of strokes a good golfer would normally shoot on a hole, after adding on a player's handicap, the amount the golfer normally shoots over par) in points-based competitions. In such contests you don't record your individual score, but, rather, earn points depending on how you do versus par, after adjusting for your handicap. A handicap-adjusted par might earn you two points, an adjusted bogey one point, and an adjusted birdie four points.

This approach keeps hackers and slashers (poorly performing golfers) from having to take 16 swipes at the ball on a given hole, while delaying everyone on the course. The golfers also like this change in the rules because it makes their scores seem better than they actually are with those occasional disaster holes taken out.

An even faster format is best ball where each player on the team proceeds from the best shot that any player made on the team's immediately preceding shots. The players on the team with less good shots pick up their balls and move on to take their next shots from the most advantaged position. This format can be made still faster if you mix talented and untalented players onto the same team. The less talented players are usually playing from the best player's ball.

Wise organizations could follow the same principle: Only require a beneficiary, customer, or user to make a limited effort to use an automated way of doing things before a helpful person intervenes to simplify matters. Wouldn't that be great?

Consider how so-called customer service usually works online. A Web site decides to become more secure by requiring you to select a more complex log-in name and password. If you try to make this new selection on a Web site and make a mistake, you are usually advised to try again. Make too many unsuccessful attempts, and the site shuts you out. You gnash your teeth in annoyance, but to no avail. You are being treated like a potential criminal trying to hack into the site rather than a confused person seeking a service.

Many such sites, especially for security brokerage firms, then make it very difficult to find someone who can help you. You can reach a human being by telephone, but that human being usually has no clue what the problem is. But before they can confess their ignorance, you have to answer several kinds of identification questions such as when was your last deposit, what was your last trade, and so forth.

Naturally, you cannot answer those questions in your paperless account without being able to open your account. Eventually, you establish that you are a real customer. The clueless service representative then passes you along to someone who may have a clue. You start the whole identification process all over again with different questions that are all but impossible to answer.

It would be pretty funny if you weren't the one being treated like a new army recruit. Every time this happens to us, we find ourselves looking for a new online broker.

Use Adjustable Automation

Here's a better idea: Encourage beneficiaries, customers, and users to decide how much automation they want to use … and when they want to use that automation. Customize your automation to uniquely fit each beneficiary, customer, and user in the same way that Dell customizes its computers for each customer.

Let's consider how this principle might work for credit card customers. Some customers would like to be able to look up details of their account on the Internet. Others would like to receive a standard oral report customized to their interests by making a toll-free telephone call. Some would like to be able to call someone who can answer their questions. A few might want to receive e-mails that provide updated account information every time there was a transaction, while others might simply want a daily e-mail update.

Whatever those individual preferences are, the customer's desires are bound to change. The process to go from one set to another set of solutions needs to be very fast and simple.

But information isn't the only thing that's automated about a credit card: The basic offer is also automated. A customer signs up for certain benefits and agrees to pay certain charges for those benefits. Credit card companies treat customers as though their needs never change. Customers only find out about more relevant choices when yet another unsolicited offer arrives in the mail from a competing credit card company. Wouldn't it make much more sense to just allow customers to shift benefits and charges at will on an existing account?

For instance, a company that uses its credit card very heavily to make purchases at certain times of the year might want the maximum percentage of cash back during those periods of time. When the same company's cash flow is temporarily lean, the company may find itself carrying an unpaid balance and may wish instead to receive the lowest interest rate rather than a high cash-back percentage of purchases.

Payments for credit cards are usually required to be monthly. That schedule is fine for those with a steady cash flow, but many small enterprises have greatly variable cash flows. Such firms may be strongly profitable over the course of a whole year, yet struggle for many months to make minimum payments.

Credit card companies take advantage of such variability. Carry a balance due and miss making a minimum payment, and the credit card company begins to charge penalties and interest like a loan shark. Clearly such customers would prefer a payment schedule that required regularity as measured over a multiple-month period of time. Credit card companies might argue that regulators don't allow such flexibility. But if the cards were issued by offshore financial institutions, few regulations would limit more flexible offerings.

In fact, companies involved in global commerce might find it attractive to be able to select the currency in which charges occur and a different currency for payments. Select depreciating currencies for making payments and that's an additional discount for the company using the credit card. The credit card issuer wouldn't be harmed because the overall currency position could be inexpensively hedged and the expense passed along to those who wanted this flexibility. Such a program would allow small companies to have the kind of inexpensive currency hedging choices that are only available now to larger firms.

Governments could do a better job as well by offering flexible automation. In a spirit of fairness, many benefits for citizens are doled out equally — regardless of need. It would be better if citizens could automatically adjust those benefits.

Here's an example: In the United States, a major retirement benefit is to receive pension payments based on the taxes paid into your Social Security account during your working years. The pension's size is also partially based on the age at which you retire.

But many people find their needs are changing. Some may retire and later decide that they've made a mistake and want to go back to work. But they cannot stop their Social Security checks from arriving and delivering taxable income. If they could suspend those payments until they permanently retire, the pension could be a lot higher when they permanently retire while taxes would be reduced in the meantime.

Others aren't very good at investing money and don't want to learn how. Some of these people would probably like to have an opportunity to put extra money into their Social Security accounts to increase their pensions.

And some people are from long-lived families and don't need pension money at the maximum retirement age. If such people are still healthy and working at the maximum retirement age, they might want to defer receiving their pension in order to increase its size after they aren't able to keep working.

Other retirees may be more concerned about avoiding long-term health care costs than having a certain sized pension. These people might want to swap part of their pension benefit for more coverage against nursing home care should they need it.

Allow everyone at their will to move benefits from what they get automatically to what they want to receive automatically, and you can probably deliver much more benefit to citizens at a lower cost. Perhaps if politicians continue to be insensitive to individual needs, entrepreneurs will find ways to allow retirees to swap for better bundles of government benefits.

Here are questions to remind you of what to focus on to properly auto-mate your offerings and the ways you deliver them:

- What process steps should be improved before the steps are automated?
- How can automation allow you to provide even simpler, more effective offerings through improved processes?
- When and where would it make sense to encourage beneficiaries, customers, and users to avoid automation?
- What aspects of automation should you let beneficiaries, customers, and users adjust to meet their preferences?

Chapter 12

Write a Great Owner's Manual
Add Do-It-Yourself Features

I acted and my action made me wise.
— Thom Gunn

If beneficiaries, customers, and users can help themselves, costs can fall while satisfaction rises. For instance, some stores now offer the experience of being a potter. Everything you need to make and decorate a pot is there, and your artistic creation can be carried away to use after it has been fired and cooled by the store's staff. Selling you a decorated pot simply wouldn't be the same. This experiential approach is also a lot cheaper and less time-consuming than taking a pottery course. With plenty of written directions at the work stations and people you can ask for help, customers find it easy and pleasant to create pots.

But many organizations start with the idea of people helping them-selves to reduce costs and fail to execute well. Why? Setting up workable do-it-yourself conditions is hard to do. Here's an example: Promises are sometimes easier made than kept. That's a lesson we learned the hard way when we founded The Billionaire Entrepreneurs' Master Mind. Members were promised that they would receive recordings of all the group's teleconferences in MP3 format. Why did we promise that? Because the teleseminar-based courses we have taken provide replays in MP3 format. We liked listening to those replays and thought that such recordings must be the best way to go.

After touring more store shelves than we would have liked, we picked up a few boxes from a section that said "MP3 recorders" and bought the version that a wandering teenage clerk told us would serve this application. Since the first teleconference was now less than 14 hours away, we opened up the box and began to read the directions. Good news! There was a separate owner's manual to make a "fast start" and we soon had the item charged up and running.

But after the fourth "fast start" step, we could never get the control screen to change to the one shown in the manual. We each tried to follow the "fast start" directions, but to no avail. Frustration was setting in. More buttons were pushed and different batteries were tried. A flashlight was used to inspect the minute buttons but revealed nothing helpful.

Then one of us eventually noticed that the "screen" was actually a piece of protective plastic with a printed imitation of a real screen on it. Peel off that plastic, and you could see that the actual screen was showing just what it was supposed to … as the owner's manual promised. But there was no mention anywhere of an opaque printed plastic strip pretending to be a real screen that needed to be removed. That item of missing information was strike one against that manual.

In baseball, a batter is out if three strikes are recorded against him or her. Americans often accept three failures from organizations and directions before concluding that there has been unacceptable performance.

Feeling more confident, we decided to test the player to be sure it was recording. We read the manual from cover to cover and learned how to record voices. We next did the "testing, 1, 2, 3" routine as a voice check. But we could find no place where the operating manual told us how to play back and listen to voice recordings. We could see that something was happening when we recorded our voices, but without hearing a playback we could not figure out how the sound quality needed to be adjusted. That lack of information about voice playback was strike two against that manual.

Feeling less confident, we decided to also use a regular tape recorder for the teleconference in case the MP3 recorder wasn't working properly. With both recorders appearing to function, the first teleconference took place and was recorded. A great sense of relief set in. Now all we had to do was to send out the MP3 recording.

We reread the manual a few more times and couldn't find any description of how to send an MP3 voice recording to someone else over the Internet. Thinking that we had just reached strike three, which would mean pitching the recorder out or going back for a refund, we noticed a 5-inch by 5-inch piece of orange paper that said in large letters: "STOP! Having

Trouble? Before you return it … Contact our Web site. We Can Help."

Okay, now perhaps we were getting somewhere. We visited the Web site and felt pretty good until we realized that all of the information there was a PDF version of the owner's manual we had already read more often than the Bible. Strike three was clearly headed for the plate when we noticed in tiny type on the orange sheet a toll-free number to call.

Picking up the telephone with shaky fingers, we soon reached someone who calmly asked what the problem was. We told him, and without pausing he told us the eight required steps. He double checked to be sure the steps worked, and we were off the phone in less than two minutes.

Wow! We were about to score. The MP3 file was quickly loaded onto the computer and we could listen to its lovely quality. Ah! Relief was setting in.

Quickly opening an e-mail program, we began attaching the file to e-mail for the members. After grinding and grinding through the attachment loading process, nothing happened. After six false starts, we noticed that the file seemed to be too big for our service. No problem. We would just compress the file. After finding out how to do that, we tried to attach and send the file again. The same problem occurred. Feeling a little panicked, we bought the upgraded e-mail service that allows e-mailers to send huge files. You guessed it. The file was still too big.

Here's what we began to understand. The reason that MP3 files sound so good is because they record vast amounts of sound details. But within 15 minutes, you've got more data than most e-mail accounts will send or accept. No wonder those course replay MP3 recordings we had been listening to always divided the material into 20 to 25 minute segments. Also, the courses never sent us the files by e-mail. The courses always directed us to sites where we could download the files.

Did the MP3 recorder manual mention this issue? No, of course not. So we had a file we couldn't share electronically unless we posted it to a Web site (not a very secure solution) or burned the file onto CDs and physically shipped those all over the world.

And so we needed a plan B for electronically sending this recording. Thank goodness for that tape recording. We played the recorded tape back in 15-minute segments and recorded each segment as a separate MP3 file. Then we e-mailed five times to the members to send them all the segments as attachments. Naturally, we overloaded many of their accounts with data, too. One poor fellow had his segments sent to three different addresses before he received a complete set.

But we did succeed in keeping our promise. Fortunately, this story has a happy ending ... if you overlook the nine hours dedicated to buying the player, learning how to make it work, and sending the eventual files to our members.

Thom Gunn was right. We acted and that action made us wise. But that wisdom came from an unexpected direction. Mainly our actions made us wise about how to write this chapter to help you avoid the mistakes that many make in adding do-it-yourself features to their offerings.

Make Doing-It-Yourself Faster Than Getting Help in the Usual Way

What benefits can come from having beneficiaries, customers, and users doing more for themselves? In our harried lives, most people favor doing things themselves when that action saves their time. That observation seems like a paradox. How can do-it-yourself be faster than having a service fully provided?

Part of the answer is that many offerings with full service are provided inefficiently. Here's an example: Half the gas stations and vehicle repair shops near our home prominently advertise low-priced oil changes. Go for one of those oil changes, and you'll probably end up waiting two hours, even if you have an appointment. Be sure to bring a book or pick a location near where you can do some useful shopping.

Every 5 miles or so we drive, however, we'll pass another choice — a quick oil-change emporium. If no one is waiting at the quick place, you can drive right into a bay designed to make oil changes fast. Unless you decide you want some other service, you'll drive out of the bay again in about 10 minutes and be on your way.

What are the do-it-yourself elements? First, the quick emporium makes the timing of oil changes an impulse buy through allowing passing drivers to see when fast service is available because no customers are waiting. That aspect of the business model is like being a mass merchandiser. The customer helps himself or herself to an offering based on noticing the offering, rather than having a prior intent to purchase.

Second, the drivers never leave their cars. In essence, it's like an improved version of a drive-through lane at a fast food restaurant. We are often reminded of that comparison when we end up waiting in line longer for fast food in a drive-through lane than for an oil change. In part that's because quick change places usually have at least three bays while fast food drive-through lanes usually have only one line served by a single window.

For the customer whose time has an economic value to herself or himself, the quick oil change emporiums offer a good value. You save almost two hours over standard "full service" by spending an extra $10 to $15.

Do-it-yourself time savings can be even greater for accessing a physician to help you solve a medical problem. Let's look at an inefficient method first. In the United States, seeking most such health solutions begins by visiting your primary care physician who is usually a general practitioner, an internist, or a pediatrician (for children). Primary care physicians are busy people, so you won't get to see them for at least two weeks unless you are experiencing a near-emergency. Once there, you are sent out for tests.

Depending on the test results, you either come back to the primary care physician or are sent on to a specialist. If it's still not a near-emergency, you will wait one to six months to see the specialist. The specialist will then examine you and order more tests. Once the second round of tests is done, you'll have another chance to make an appointment and see the specialist again in one to six months. At this point, you've been pursuing this health issue for more than two months, and no one has started to treat what's wrong with you.

When you return for your second specialist visit, you can expect in some cases to be referred to one or two other specialists. Of course, unless it's a near emergency, you cannot get into see them either for another one to six months. After those visits and tests are over, you make an appointment to see the first specialist again. Once again, you wait one to six months. Chances are, too, that each time you visit one of these physicians, you wait to be seen.

Between travel, tests, waiting time, and more travel, you may have invested four days of your time by now. Hopefully, your medical problem has gone away on its own. Otherwise, you're on a three-month to two-year treadmill that may or may not lead to a solution.

What's the alternative? One choice that many people favor is to visit one of the famous diagnostic clinics. You'll be poked and prodded continually for two to three days, and you'll pay quite a lot out of your own pocket for the visit. But you won't leave until all of your physicians have received strict marching orders from the clinic for how to treat you. If you really need medical treatment, you're now way ahead of the game.

What's the problem? You may have to wait six months to a year to get an appointment at the diagnostic clinic. But that can be a big improvement over two years that may lead to inconclusive results. Some people gain an access advantage by simply scheduling annual checkups at such clinics.

What's a faster, less time-consuming alternative? Conjure up a scary symptom, and you can simply head for the emergency room of the best hospital in your area. If your problem is serious, you'll be admitted to the hospital within hours and you'll have specialists checking you out within 24 hours. Tests will also be accelerated. Two years of waiting may be compressed into a few days in the hospital.

As you can imagine, this do-it-yourself approach to health care is increasingly popular in the United States. Emergency rooms are overwhelmed with people, most of whom don't need to be seen there. But the appeal of fast service brings patients in, much like the quick lube place with no lines.

Recently, more hospitals are getting smarter about this back door into accelerated care and now locate general-purpose outpatient clinics next to their emergency rooms. As you enter the emergency room area, a triage nurse figures out if you are well enough to go to the outpatient clinic and wait to be seen on a first-come, first-served basis.

This choice does speed things up for the patient by eliminating the need to wait to see your primary care physician when she or he next has an appointment opening. If such clinics can learn to affordably help people track down their health-care solutions faster and by spending less time, many patients will flock to these clinics.

Lay Out Low-Cost, Do-It-Yourself Paths That Are Easy, Valuable, and Engaging

As you can see from these examples, a key advantage to providing do-it-yourself solutions is to engage the beneficiary, customer, or user in picking a choice that better fits his or her needs. If you can make it more obvious to the beneficiary, customer, or user what the delays will be, how much time and effort they will have to expend, and what the total costs are, those who will be advantaged by your solution will wear out a pathway heading to your offering.

But a lot can go wrong in trying to make things obvious. The most usual problem lies in confusing the choice maker with too many complications.

Let's take that MP3 recorder. The main use the manufacturer appears to have had in mind was to record and play music. But if you can record and play music, you can also record and play voices. It didn't cost the manufacturer much extra to offer voice recording. Presumably, if you know how to record, play, and send music, the same process applies to voices. The manufacturer probably imagined that we were buying the equipment for music, knew all about that application, and had an occasional need for voice features. If that's what the manufacturer was thinking, it was an incorrect assumption in our case.

How could employing the voice option have been made simple for us? Instead of a manual and a PDF file of the manual online, the manufacturer could have provided a demonstration via DVD or streaming video online. The operating manual could have just included the fast start information and referred you to the demonstrations for everything else. Creating such a demonstration wouldn't normally cost more than $5,000. If you saved lots of returns and calls to customer service, you as the manufacturer would be way ahead. If you had the demo playing in the store so people could see how easy it is to do-it-yourself with this equipment, more equipment would be sold.

What's the lesson? Whenever possible, demonstrate rather than describe the do-it-yourself features and choices.

What's an even better lesson? Demonstrate in more than one way. For instance, there are probably terrific ways to use this MP3 recorder to create better recordings than we are doing now. If someone demonstrates, for instance, how much better it sounds to mix music and voices, we'll probably want to do that. Then another demonstration can show how to create that more exciting version of our recording.

What's a still better lesson? Make demonstrations that are fun to watch. For instance, you can demonstrate mistakes in humorous ways.

What's a better solution than that? Make the demonstrations portable. Many people have a cellular telephone. If you can access the demonstration on a cell phone with a pause feature, you've made it as convenient as possible to explore the choices. When you are stuck with one of those inevitable waits somewhere, you can be checking out demonstrations of how to use the items you've recently purchased.

As you develop these demonstrations, you'll notice that some ways of using your current or proposed offerings aren't so easy, valuable, and engaging. Go back and see if there's another do-it-yourself method that will be easier to understand and more compelling.

Design Your Offering to Be Friendlier to Do-It-Yourselfers

The people who design offerings are often the worst people to design do-it-yourself directions for beneficiaries, customers, and users. Why? Designers know too much! They can help themselves very easily. But do-it-yourself features aren't going to do much good unless they are easy for everyone to use.

What's a good way to make offerings more do-it-yourself friendly? Prompt the person with what they need to do next.

If you've ever stood behind the lectern at a large event, you may have noticed that the two big sheets of glass at either side of the lectern are actually screens to run the text of a speech. To the audience, these look like slightly unattractive decorations. To the speakers, there are prompters. If you lose your place in your speech or cannot remember enough to approximate the text, you can glance at the prompter and get back on track. In the same way, you can post prompts for using your offering from beginning to end. If no one needs the prompts, the prompts will be ignored. If prompts are helpful, they will be eagerly sought out and appreciated when needed.

If possible, make your prompts simple. For example, "yes" or "no" choices help. A computer screen might ask, "Do you want to save the changes you made?" Or for our MP3 player, it might ask, "Do you want to save this recording on your computer?" If we hit "yes" that would take us into a step-by-step demonstration of what to do next. Each screen would then give us the choice of whether to continue or not. A more advanced set of prompts might allow us the choice not to be asked a particular question again the next time we come through a screen.

A better approach is to make your offering self-sufficient for do-it-yourselfers by designing for simpler use. That may sound like an obvious point, but few organizations put any emphasis on simple use. Why? Those who work on the project have different objectives. Designers frequently want the offering to appear to be "cool" while the engineers want an elegant design that other engineers will admire. The operating executives want an offering that's easy for them to provide. The accountants want the offering provider's costs to be low. Pursuing such objectives will normally lead to an offering that's unnecessarily complex and time-consuming for beneficiaries, customers, and users to employ.

What's the difference you should seek? Designed-in prompts can take you through a complex process. Make the process simpler to begin with, and you may not need to use any prompts. For instance, those who want to make voice recordings as their primary use could be offered a different MP3 recorder designed solely for voice recordings that will be e-mailed. This recorder could have buttons resembling those on a tape recorder. The player's software could then automatically segment the recordings into 15-minute sections for easier handling of the files as e-mail attachments. With the right design a beneficiary, customer, or user would be taking the right steps within a few seconds of popping in the battery. Few would miss going through hours of advance preparation for a recording.

Here's another idea: Have someone who wears reading glasses help design your offering. In the race to miniaturize almost everything, the symbols and words on some devices are becoming microscopic to those who wear reading glasses. All 16-year-olds will do well with the miniaturization, but few people over 50 will be able to make out what's being communicated.

Finally, make your offering more mistake-proof. Have you ever looked at those plug-in sockets at the back of your computer? If not, take a look. Sometime when your system is off, take out the various wires and inspect how the sockets vary for different devices that are attached to your computer. It looks like someone with a weird taste for modern art has been at work. Actually, the reason is far more practical. If you make the sockets unique enough, no one will plug a device into a socket that will cause harm to your computer. To speed finding that unique receptacle, you'll usually find that the plugs and sockets are color-coded to aid those who aren't color blind.

In other words, the computer makers realized that most people would be putting their computer systems together on their own. You need to make such a do-it-yourself step foolproof. Otherwise, manufacturers know that they will simply be receiving back a lot of computers that have been destroyed during the installation process.

Follow the Rules of the Road
for Helpful Do-It-Yourself Owners' Manuals

Because of potential lawsuits related to harm caused by misusing an offering, few will decide to avoid providing directions. For elaborate offerings, owners' manuals will be required. In addition, some of your beneficiaries, customers, and users will want to refer to these directions and manuals whether or not they need the help. Rather than providing directions and manuals that become the butt of comedians' jokes, how can you turn on people to using do-it-yourself features?

Many newer vehicles now have global positioning satellite (GPS) systems that provide driving directions. You input your destination and the system spells out a route for you and displays a map. Those systems do something even more helpful. When you miss a turn, you can quickly get revised directions. This capability can help overcome a problem that most people have experienced. With preset directions, you may find yourself driving extra miles simply to arrive back at where you missed a turn. After not following a direction, a GPS system may locate a new route that will eliminate most of the looping back to where you made a mistake. That iterative quality of GPS directions relieves a lot of frustration as well as saving needless backtracking.

Directions and manuals can be designed to operate in a similar way. As soon as you're stuck or seem to have made a mistake, your directions could be quickly adjusted to tell you what to do next. That interaction would be a great help. Many people don't realize they've made a mistake until after doing a lot of work that then needs to be undone. The best way to provide these error-recovery messages would be to have the directions or the manual actively monitor the offering and what you are doing with it.

Not everyone prefers the same format for directions and instructions. Naturally, some people will want to have a written manual. They are used to that approach. What are the lessons? Make that manual's index as complete as possible. Few people other than your proofreaders will examine the manual from cover to cover. Most people will have a question or a problem with your offering at some point. When that happens, people want to turn immediately to the most helpful page. One nice feature of some manuals is to have more than one indexing system. For instance, sections may be color coded at the edge of the page for their subject matters. Die cuts may help you find the first page of a section like the ones you use to put your thumb into a physical dictionary to find the first page for a letter of the alphabet. Other manuals also employ symbols to identify locations. These symbols often match icons on the offering itself such as a stylized image of windshield wipers. Of course, the page that most people latch onto is the index where all of the most common problems are listed along with a cross-reference to where the relevant do-it-yourself details can be found.

With more and more offerings, it's also possible to include an electronic directory inside the offering that can be queried in a manner similar to employing an online search engine. That approach is of great value when you are using the offering in a different location from where you normally keep your directions and manuals.

Many times, it's just not convenient to carry around all of the relevant information because it's so bulky. How many people, for instance, carry around telephone directories in their vehicles? Think of how many times you've been traveling and needed to contact a certain type of local business for which you don't have any names or telephone numbers. If there's a classified directory near a pay phone, you're all set. But if someone has torn out the page you need or there's no directory in sight, you have a lot of potential frustration and wasted time ahead of you as you work with directory assistance and begin making calls.

Another advantage of electronic directories is that you can inexpensively update and bookmark them. When you become aware of new issues or locate better information for ordinary problems and tasks, you can adjust your directory. Make those updates automatic (such as anti-virus programs do) to bookmarked pages, and you're making do-it-yourself more and more desirable.

But there are times when reading just doesn't make sense. For instance, it's a good idea to stop your vehicle before you read anything other than a road sign. But you may not be able to safely stop when you need immediate information. That's when voice-based information systems can be a great resource. A helpful version of such a resource works just like an electronic directory except that you speak to the resource and listen to the answers. Many credit card information lines now have this technology.

General Motors provides this kind of help in another way through its OnStar services. At the push of a button, OnStar allows you to be in voice communication with operators who can assist you with a variety of driving needs. Operators can remotely unlock your vehicle when you've left the keys inside or provide emergency advice and assistance after you've had an accident.

However you provide your information, connect together everything the do-it-yourselfer will need. Switching back and forth among six different information sources or sections in a manual isn't going to do the trick when your vehicle is broken down after dark in a scary location while your eight children in the back noisily demand their dinners.

Here are questions to make it easier for people to succeed in helping themselves with your offerings:

- How can you help beneficiaries, customers, and users save time by doing things for themselves rather than getting help in the usual ways?
- What features will make do-it-yourself solutions easier and more engaging?
- Who can help you design do-it-yourself features for offerings that are very simple to use?
- How many simple ways can you provide helpful directions, manuals, and assistance that fit the needs of a do-it-yourself moment?

Chapter 13

Take Out Insurance
Check Your Solutions with Outsourcing

What can't be cured must be insured.
— Oliver Herford

When a vehicle strikes another vehicle, an object, or a person, the consequences can be grave. Part of the price paid for mobility is the cost of such accidents. The human toll is often much greater than the economic one. Although one can never hope to compensate for the human costs, insurance can certainly help soften the economic blows.

In most places, laws require you to purchase insurance for operating your vehicle. That's a prudent way to ensure that individuals and families have some buffer against the harm from vehicle accidents. Otherwise, people would be at greater risk of suffering personal or property damage with no compensation to cushion the blow. But you may still be hit by an uninsured driver. To help alleviate that problem, many vehicle owners purchase insurance against that uninsured-driver risk.

Receive benefits from your insurance policy after you've had a serious collision with an uninsured driver, and your economic health has a chance to recover. The funds you receive can be a vast multiple of all the vehicle insurance payments you'll make in a lifetime. Now, that's a big cost saving!

What are the low-risk alternatives to purchasing insurance? Well, you can walk. You can also ride with others. In some areas buses and subways are helpful choices.

Companies often have another opportunity. They can self-insure by keeping a pot of funds available to pay for accidents. If a company is large enough, self-insurance may be a good choice. If the company's drivers are cautious and the vehicles well maintained, it may be that safer driving will add up to fewer accident expenses than the average experience. Employ a simple way to administer the accident payments to those who are harmed, and you've saved some administrative overhead that insurance companies add to their rates. If there's a profit on such insurance, you keep that profit for the company as well.

Obviously this option has some drawbacks for those who operate small companies. One accident costing millions can wipe out the company. The small company may also find it more costly to administer its own insurance than what a well-run insurer would charge. A small company also may not know how its driving compares to others; there simply isn't enough information. Even the worst drivers don't get into accidents every day. Or a good driver may suddenly take to drinking and become a hazard to everyone. But most importantly, people in small companies are usually doing many different jobs. Burden them with one more time-consuming activity, and something important that has to be done goes undone.

This analysis of how insurance works also applies to when an organization should outsource an internal activity. It's good to start thinking about what could go wrong. If you haven't done much designing of new offerings, hiring another organization to help you test out the safety of your design may eliminate many potential accidents. Isn't that a form of insurance? It's also helpful to think about how large the cost of something going wrong could be. Then consider how much it would cost to outsource and how often such expensive accidents could occur.

Insurance companies also use this thought process to consider if they have too much exposure to potentially expensive risks. If insurers sell too many home owners' policies in areas subject to hurricanes, they will resell some of that risk to another kind of insurance company called a reinsurer. Even reinsurers sometimes find that they need to buy policies from other reinsurers to keep their balance of risk at an affordable level should claims soar due to a natural catastrophe.

Notice that this is a kind of contingent thinking based on "what-if?" examinations. A normal business analysis tends to focus on what is likely to go right and then optimizes the various choices for pursuing the opportunity to create the largest result. Many people draw these conclusions from spreadsheet analyses derived from simple financial models. In this chapter, we're suggesting that the opposite kind of thinking also be pursued. We're recommending that you also look at what could go wrong that would take away most of the benefit from pursuing a given opportunity. Then explore ways that outsourcing could increase your chances of success and reduce the risk of large negative events.

Avoid Incorrect Methods of Identifying Outsourcing Choices

Most people pursue outsourcing choices in an incorrect way. When you spend time on alternatives that don't make sense for your organization, you've missed an opportunity to outsource something that will put you ahead of competitors. Here are the typical approaches that can draw your attention away from your best outsourcing opportunities:

- Examining only choices that potential outsourcing vendors propose.
- Looking at outsourcing methods that competitors use.
- Pursuing opportunities that journalists have favorably described.
- Considering only choices that may offer large cost savings.
- Trying to clean up poorly run operations by putting a new person in charge.

Relying on vendors to determine your outsourcing agenda means that you'll spend most of your time looking at large outsourcing alternatives such as those for contract manufacturing. You will be seeing these choices because the vendors can make so much money from a sale that they can afford to continually engage your attention. Such a decision may or may not be in your best interest. Your agenda is probably being controlled more by the self-interest of vendors rather than your own self-interest.

Competitors may have made bad choices in outsourcing that they have taken pains to hide. If so, you're wasting your time looking at their outsourcing methods. Competitors' circumstances may also be substantially different from your own. For example, a smaller competitor may not be able to efficiently engage in a level of value added activity that makes your organization much more profitable. In the early days of 5¼-inch floppy disks, only a few vendors could afford to coat their own magnetic media. Everyone else had to buy such media from 3M or another supplier. Despite being a small company, market leader Verbatim was large enough to run a coating line and enjoyed much higher profit margins than those who purchased coated media.

Much as most people like to extol a free press, you'd be surprised to learn how *many articles in leading publications closely follow vendors' press releases.* These reported ideas are more likely to describe the marketing pitches of those who make the most money from a new customer. As a result, it's rare that such stories capture important information that anyone should apply. Much like focusing on outsourcing options brought to you by salespeople, these reports are likely to be a poor indicator of whether or not you need the help.

Even if the media report is correct in its facts, such a report may still be a misleading indicator of whether you should outsource. As we explore in Chapter 14, outsourcing often isn't a better choice. A common problem is that many organizations lack the skills to consider and make outsourcing choices for difficult tasks. Here's an example: When a wine company looked at industry economics, the owners correctly understood that more profit was earned in low-priced wines by making bottles than from making wine. The owners read lots of accurate horror stories about how hard it was to learn to make glass bottles. As a result, the task was outsourced to a joint venture with a proven bottle maker. Unfortunately, the wine company didn't know how to negotiate such a contract. The wine company thought that by limiting the partner's compensation to a fixed percentage of costs, the wine company was protected. Instead, the wine company had unintentionally granted a license to print money for its partner who could find never-ending reasons to escalate costs — hardly what the wine company had in mind.

It seems like a no-brainer to be focusing on choices that provide huge savings. How can you go lose? Well, often you won't, but *sometimes you will miss better savings opportunities by being on the wrong track.* For instance, if you are in an area where costs will rapidly decline anyway, your potential outsourcing supplier may simply be quoting you low current prices that are high when compared to the average cost over the duration of the contract. The outsourcing company's plan is to lose some money now and make a killing later at your expense. Or you may simply be the world's biggest incompetent at whatever you are doing. Put both circumstances in place, and today's lowest cost outsourcing choice may not be in your organization's best interest. Here's an example: When Electronic Data Systems (EDS) was led by Ross Perot, the company displayed a genius for finding very incompetent data processing organizations and quoting long-term prices based on a small percentage saving over the current mess. Between EDS's ability to improve data processing operations and the rapid declines in computer equipment costs, these contracts often created enormous profits for EDS. Within 2 or 3 years, such an organization could have found any number of vendors who would have completed the work at a lower price than EDS was charging at that time. But it was too late. EDS had already locked up the business with 10-year contracts so the organization doing the outsourcing had no choice.

If your own operations are poorly run, letting someone else work on the problem may be a great solution. That's true if your outsourcing resource's people are brilliant at fixing messes. We encourage you to be a little skeptical about how helpful outsourcing will be in such a situation. In our experience *most organizations are better at starting a new activity on the right foot than in cleaning up a mess.* We observed a great example of this point: Ecolab has industry-leading expertise in eliminating pests and various kinds of contamination from food preparation activities. When it contacts a potential new customer, Ecolab usually finds that the food preparer is already outsourcing most of its needs. In doing a performance audit, Ecolab often finds that despite these outsourcers having promised to keep out the vermin and bacteria, the premises are shockingly unhealthy and the costs are no bargain. We had an opportunity to see an Ecolab outsourcing proposal for a large food handler, and the report on how well the current outsourcers had been doing was appalling. Yet the company's management didn't even know the company had a mess. The operating managers around the country had informed senior management that past messes had been solved by the various outsourcing vendors that had been selected. Obviously, no one had been paying attention to the actual performance compared to the lip service that had been received in the outsourcing proposals.

Look for Better Reasons to Use Outsourcing

If the previous excellent-sounding approaches aren't surefire methods, where should you look for outsourcing assistance? While the right answer will differ from organization to organization, we have some suggestions that few consider, but that may be your biggest outsourcing opportunities:

- Use outsourcing to advance your most important tasks.
- See outsourcing as a temporary device to enhance your ability to do more yourself.
- Achieve leadership of your market faster by leveraging outsourced expertise.
- Consider outsourcing as a financial tool.

- Attract capabilities through outsourcing that you couldn't hire internally.

Purchase Outsourcing That Advances Your Most Important Tasks

Many people will tell you that you should never consider outsourcing for those areas that are most important to your success. These authorities argue that you'll give away parts of your competitive strength and will become vulnerable as a result. While vulnerability may sometimes be created and exploited, having outsourced important tasks can also lead to greater success. For instance, when Hewlett Packard introduced the first mass-market laser printer for personal computers, that printer used Canon print technology and was directed by Hewlett Packard software. For more than two decades that technical marriage was the greatest source of Hewlett Packard's profits.

Here's another issue to consider: Have you ever found yourself with a list of more important things to do than you could possibly attempt, let alone master? That's not an unusual circumstance for organizational leaders and those with important responsibilities at any level. Work on one important task, however, and that may leave other important responsibilities uncovered.

When that's the case, stop to consider whether outsourcing could make a difference. Let's begin with an obvious opportunity. You're really busy now but will have more time in a few months. In that situation, consider whether some work can be done now by skilled people outside of your organization so that progress can be made while you're busy. Here's an example: Many tasks cannot be defined until someone does basic data gathering and analysis. If you spare a few hours now, you can probably participate in designing that preparatory work so that it can be undertaken immediately. Done carefully, such a project may develop better information than you would have otherwise gained … especially if you engage people with specialized skills for the type of data gathering and analysis you need.

A more typical problem is that you are pursuing an important series of innovations. You aren't quite sure how to approach the opportunities. In fact, your organization may lack some of the perspectives you need. Rather than outsource the whole task, outsource the elements that require the diversified perspectives that you lack. You can engage professionals or service firms that have relevant knowledge in those areas who can complement your internal efforts. In other cases, do what Hewlett Packard did and work with a potential supplier or partner to fill in part of the gaps.

If the opportunity is a substantial one, you should consider inviting experts to compete to find solutions as Goldcorp and Procter & Gamble have done. Beyond that approach, is there an opportunity to permanently engage stakeholders to develop the opportunity such as occurs with open source software?

In considering places where you might find outsourcing advantageous, look at what no one has ever done in your organization before and think about how outsourcing could make the process go better. Here's an example: Increasingly, new business models engage in providing services that are provided as a consequence of someone using an organization's product. For instance, the new vehicle's owner may consider purchasing an extended warranty. A powerful twist on that approach can be to offer other products because someone buys the service. Because of the extended warranty purchase, the owner seems to be indicating that the vehicle will be operated longer than average before resale. Such an owner is a good candidate for purchasing vehicle refurbishment items that show the most wear such as carpets and interior door handles. Perhaps you should be designing your vehicles to make it easier and more attractive to make such refurbishments. As a vehicle manufacturer, you have a lot more knowledge about how to produce millions of cars than you do about how to make an older car look nicer, one unit at a time. Those with refurbishment design skills might help you generate a highly profitable product business that you can market to all of your extended warranty purchasers.

Learning is another opportunity. Organizations whose business models are relatively unique sometimes find that it's hard to develop helpful learning experiences for employees, distributors, users, and other stakeholders. Standard materials don't apply, and the internal organization doesn't have the skill set to create certain kinds of learning experiences such as simulations. Under such circumstances outsourcing simulation development could be a good move. Many people learn best from simulations. After finding out what can and cannot be learned from simulations, you'll know a lot more about what other kinds of learning experiences you need to develop. If the simulation covers everything, you've just eliminated big chunks of the potential task.

Acquisitions present a special opportunity. Most acquisitions fail to work out well because the purchasers make all kinds of incorrect deductions about how the two organizations might be meshed together. As a result, a company may make a wrong purchase. That mistake is often compounded by coordinating the two enterprises in the wrong way. Those mistakes are somewhat unavoidable when research into acquisitions only begins after a bidding war starts. No matter how hard you work, there's only so much you can learn in a few weeks. Skillful acquirers are increasingly likely to identify the organizations that they may want to buy someday and to outsource the task of checking each one out well in advance of any potential bidding. Without the last-minute rush, this work can be done better and less expensively. If you have learned about a potential acquisition in advance, you'll know whether to join in the bidding when such organizations become available. The money you spend can save you the cost of enormous mistakes and missed opportunities. And the best part is that you don't have to divert much time and attention by your existing staff to make these advance preparations.

Add more top talent and your organization is bound to be more successful. Specialized search firms can help you define new positions and negotiate attractive offers that will help bring the talent into the fold. Naturally, you still need to do your own due diligence on the prospective employees. But having great candidates to choose from makes you aware of how you can build your organization to pursue more of the most important tasks.

Use Outsourcing to Learn How to Do-It-Yourself

Years ago, many service organizations jealously guarded their expertise from their clients. The thought behind this caution was that otherwise you would lose the opportunity to sell the same expertise over and over again to that and other clients. The best a client could hope to do was to hire some people from the service organization after the engagement and hope to transfer needed skills and knowledge that way.

Knowledge and skills become obsolete very rapidly now. Many such service organizations realize that they will have to add totally improved skill sets every few years. Under such circumstances, the chances to resell the same expertise to a client are more limited. If the client wants to learn those skills, that's often a bigger assignment than merely applying the skills once for the client. As a result, more kinds of expertise can now be learned from state-of-the-art practitioners in service organizations.

From the client side, these frequently expensive learning programs can be a turnoff. The courses often take lots of time, and the learning can be rapidly lost if the skills aren't used every day. A better approach is to establish internal positions that require the new skills and knowledge, and then hire service organizations to work as part of the teams with those in the new positions. By learning on the job through the teams, people in the new positions will become productive sooner. By having experts available to your people on a daily basis, knowledge transfer will also be accelerated.

Sometimes your organization doesn't have enough skill to pursue the approach just described. When that's the case, you can still arrange for those you want to become more effective to shadow the service organization while it does its work. At a minimum, this activity will help improve the focus onto what your organization wants to accomplish. External experts may know their fields better than you do, but you know your organization and the stakeholder needs you serve better than the experts.

If there is going to be an ongoing need to collaborate to add new knowledge and skills, consider a joint venture as a way to facilitate that learning. Many people believe that such combinations have to become large entities before anyone will pay adequate attention. Contrary to that belief, most prosperous joint ventures work well because of long-term relationships among people in both founding organizations. If you focus on putting the right people together and give them interesting things to work on, you'll be surprised how productive even a small joint venture can be.

Volunteering for nonprofit organizations is increasingly used to develop executive and management skills. When you enter a nonprofit organization, you find yourself in a world where there is usually high motivation and few resources. If you can succeed in a nonprofit organization, you gain an understanding of how motivation can make a difference in your own for-profit organization. Someone who works in a nonprofit organization is not likely to understand how you access major resources. Have nonprofit personnel perform volunteer work in a for-profit enterprise, and new perspectives will soon be apparent for how to assemble and apply resources. A wise organization may realize that there are great learning benefits from having appropriately related for-profit and nonprofit entities that work in mutually beneficial ways. For instance, imagine that your organization needs more information technology (IT) workers but is based in a community that doesn't have enough information technology training available. An allied nonprofit foundation could pursue ways to add more training while developing foundation leaders and enhancing the training of entry level IT employees who come to work for you.

Step Up to Being the Best in the World Through Outsourcing

Most organizations will tell you that they are the best in the world at what they do. In most cases, that's more pride talking rather than reality.

Over the years, we have conducted many worldwide searches for organizational best practices. Invariably, we find that most organizations are well above or well below average in each particular practice. You can picture this occurrence as a steep bell curve around a median that's well below the average performance. The bell curve also has two long tails with one spread more to the upper side of performance reflecting that the performance spread between the best and the median is much wider than the spread between the median and the worst. The curves are also skewed so that there are many more below average performers than high performers. In essence, such a bell curve is no more than a graphic expression of Pareto's Principle that 20 percent of the efforts will account for 80 percent of the results.

Why, then, do so many organizations overestimate how well they are doing? The answer usually lies in two types of ignorance:

1. Organizations usually don't know how well they are doing in a given activity.
2. Organizations rarely know which other organization is best at any activity, how well the best does, and how that organization achieves the enviable result.

But we learned an even more important point from these studies: Where an organization ranks in performance for its activities is randomly related to how important that activity is to the organization's success. For instance, a business in a low-priced commodity business that will flourish only because of low costs may instead be performing best at providing sturdy packaging, something that doesn't improve its cost position nearly as much as would top skill in most primary processing activities.

Why does that mismatch occur between capabilities and needs? Once again, the foundation is ignorance: Organizations seldom measure themselves to find out how their effectiveness compares to the best-in-the-world for their important activities. To be fair, busy operating people aren't likely to have the time, skill, or knowledge to pursue such investigations.

As a result, a good place to add valuable outsourcing help is in making these measurements. The measurements will probably reveal something important: No one else is very good at all the critical activities. By seeing how your competitors stack up at the same time, you should be able to identify a few areas where improvements by you can create decisive advantages. Otherwise, you'll be pushing everyone in your organization to get a little better on everything while ignoring the opportunity to concentrate on the largest part of your untapped potential.

Outsourcing can provide an additional step in making rapid progress: Engage the best at what you need to do well. Hire these organizations to outsource for you or provide the learning you need. Here's an example of how much difference that decision can make: For special fund-raising events, Habitat for Humanity will build a completed home in a few hours. Yet that same activity usually takes months for commercial builders. Ironically, those who organize these speed builds are often the same people who work as supervisors for the commercial builders. What's different? Habitat studied the lean manufacturing methods employed in the automobile industry and applied those best-in-the-world processes to home building for this special promotional purpose. You can put that accomplishment into context by remembering that many rural communities during frontier days in the United States completed a barn raising in a single day. The barn would usually receive its paint on another day, but the rest of the construction would be accomplished by the neighboring farmers working together for a few hours. A key organizing principle for speedy performances was having all of the materials in place and ready to be used in the right order by people who knew what needed to be done next.

There's an unexpected advantage to this approach of using outsourcing to direct your outsourcing focus: Even leaders who know little about a company's operations can still direct the organization to great operational improvements. When an operating expert who heads a business or company wants to devise her or his own solutions, those internal solutions are likely to fall short of what the less informed leader can accomplish by finding the best answer outside the current organization.

Eliminate Capital Drains with Outsourcing

Increasingly, organizations see many fixed assets and virtually all working capital as drags on performance rather than as strategic advantages. Why is that view taking over? To understand that shift let's make a contrast between Henry Ford's day and the automobile industry now. When Mr. Ford started his breakthrough of the assembly line, there were few suppliers who could provide parts that would work interchangeably enough to permit an assembly line to function. If the part didn't fit, someone had to file it down, weld on something, or make other time-consuming alterations. Meanwhile, the assembly line either had to shut down or send through cars that were missing lots of parts. Mr. Ford realized that he would have to supply himself to make the assembly line work. In its heyday, the Rouge plant in Michigan was a marvel of modern steel-, glass-, and parts-making methods. For the applications that Mr. Ford was addressing, the Rouge plant was usually the best in the world.

Today, many would instead tip their hats to Toyota for the vehicle production model to emulate. Toyota does whatever it can to avoid having fixed assets and working capital. In fact, Toyota doesn't have an assembly line at all. Toyota knows that it can build a better vehicle by adapting itself more to the customer through its team assembly process. With this method, Toyota can primarily assemble cars from constantly shifting combinations of parts to fit custom orders rather than building lots of undifferentiated cars it hopes to sell. As a result, Toyota needs smaller plants and less inventory, and has less money tied up in unsold vehicles. If the best way to manufacture vehicles advances to something else that requires different flexibility, Toyota will be more financially able to make the shift by having been sparing with its capital.

Some companies have taken this approach a step further and outsource all of their manufacturing. This practice is common, for instance, among those who develop electronic components and products. Few such companies are large enough to master the complexities of best practices in semiconductor manufacturing or to learn how to set up state-of-the-art facilities in the lowest cost country. Contract manufacturers, by comparison, can put complementary products from different clients into the same facility, operate more efficiently from shared scale, and learn from many other facilities how to provide short-lived products. Both the product's designer-marketer and the outsourcing manufacturer gain. Capital intensity is less for both, but the designer-marketer gains the most from this specialization. It's not unusual for a company that outsources its electronic production to only require one-third of the capital of an organization with the same level of sales that does its own manufacturing.

But it's not just manufacturers who can outsource; service providers have their own opportunities. If, for instance, a service company's information technology operations are outsourced, the outsourcing provider owns the facilities and the equipment and is paid for only after providing the services to the client. The outsourcing provider will probably be able to pool fixed assets in ways that will provide advantages to itself and its clients.

Add Unique Capabilities with Outsourcing

The largest organizations can hope to attract top talent and create unique organizational resources; everyone else can only be jealous of that opportunity. But outsourcing is increasingly leveling the playing field for smaller organizations. Globalization drives up the value of being the world's top talent as more people can potentially employ that talent. You see this situation in the entertainment industry where worldwide stars earn 20 or 30 times what someone does who is a star in only one country. As a result, top talent often seeks the freedom to provide services to the highest bidder. This move usually increases the scarcity value of their skills versus working as an employee for one organization. The exception is where the talented person can add more value to one organization than to all others combined, and that's rare. Even in those circumstances, compensation is more likely to rise for the talented person if the possibility exists of other people hiring him or her.

You can expect that highly capable individuals and organizations will increasingly operate like freelancers do in providing professional services. These talented individuals will be available to the highest bidder. But with the world at their feet, such talent will need to be coddled wherever it is found. For instance, top internal groups are finding that they are being given increased freedom to serve clients and customers outside of their own organizations. Such expanded roles sharpen internal skills and help retain talented people who are looking for new challenges.

We were reminded of this point recently when one of the world's leading Internet marketers, Alex Mandossian, explained how he uses outsourcers to do virtually everything for his organization. In that way, he doesn't even have to learn very much about how to organize his marketing efforts. Mr. Mandossian can focus instead on how to sell more products. He keeps at least four different top outsourcing organizations busy with each aspect of his various activities and switches back and forth among these vendors as his needs and their workloads vary. Mr. Mandossian credits his suppliers with earning him as much as a million dollars in a week. His hourly income from leading teleseminars, as a result, rivals that of the highest paid professional athletes in the world for their competitive performances. His network of suppliers also tips him off to new best practices he should try. As a result, Mr. Mandossian has an enviable reputation as one of the best teleseminar marketers.

But Mr. Mandossian isn't satisfied. He encourages his vendors to learn how to become Internet teleseminar marketers and leaders as well, knowing that these outsourcing vendors will deliver even more profits when they better understand his business.

Many people will tell you they wouldn't like to manage outsourcing vendors for small organizations: They favor the closeness that colleagues develop in a larger organization. We wondered about that preference, however, as we heard vendors talk about how devoted they are to Mr. Mandossian. Two of their children have been named after him ... and one of those was a girl! We cannot remember the last time we heard of people who work for a company naming their children after the CEO except when the parents were the CEO's relatives.

In describing what he looks for in an outsourcing vendor, we were impressed to learn that these vendors mostly run Mr. Mandossian's business without any guidance from him. On a day-to-day basis, each one primarily works with Mr. Mandossian's other vendors. If a problem arises, the vendors usually decide among themselves who will take the lead in working things out. As a result, a project moves through to successful completion despite occasional hiccups along the way.

But, how could hiring all of these talented people be cheaper for Mr. Mandossian? It all depends on what you measure. Certainly, the hourly cost of employing outsourced top talent is going to be higher than employing ordinary people ... or doing the work yourself. Done carefully, however, the cost as a percentage of sales should be quite a lot lower. Let's look a little deeper into the teleseminar business as an example of this point. The cost to develop the marketing for such a teleseminar is more or less fixed until you reach the point of buying or renting lists. But the response to a marketing campaign can vary from selling nothing to selling millions of dollars of information services and products. Spread the cost of paying even three times as much to develop that marketing, and you're still way ahead when your revenues expand even faster than the development costs do.

Let's start by considering a hypothetical example of someone who does all the marketing preparation by herself. She spends nothing except her own time in the process. Let's also assume that she is reasonably good at marketing and is able to sell $30,000 worth of products and services. Let's also assume the costs of delivering those products and services are quite low. In that case, the profits can be as high as $25,000 ... before putting any value on the her time.

Let's now assume that Mr. Mandossian pursues the same marketing opportunity. We'll create a hypothetical example for him as well. Let's as-

sume he spends 5 hours on the preparation while our do-it-yourselfer probably spent 100 hours. But Mr. Mandossian also has to pay a lot of expensive
people to do the rest of that work. Let's assume that he has to buy 150 hours
of other peoples' time at $150 an hour (probably more than he spends). If
Mr. Mandossian can sell $100,000 worth of products and services, his gross
profit before the extra expense is probably around $83,000. If we deduct his
added marketing costs, Mr. Mandossian's profit is over $60,000 while the
do-it-yourselfer earned $25,000.

Let's analyze the profits per hour. Mr. Mandossian earned $60,000
in profit contribution for 5 hours of marketing effort. The do-it-yourselfer
earned $25,000 in profit contribution from 100 hours of marketing effort.
Assuming they each then spend another 10 hours to deliver the services, Mr.
Mandossian earned $4,000 an hour while the do-it-yourselfer earned around
$223 an hour.

Next, let's assume that Mr. Mandossian has a large number of marketing projects he could pursue, and he spends the 95 hours he saves doing six
other marketing projects. If each one is equally successful, he earns an extra
$395,000 over the $25,000 the do-it-yourselfer gained.

If you were operating like Mr. Mandossian in this hypothetical example, would you care that your top-of-the-line vendors were earning $150
an hour? Probably not.

Here are questions to help you use outsourcing to make breakthrough
gains in cost reductions:
- How can you use outsourcing to advance your most important
  tasks?
- What kinds of outsourcing can allow you to make gains while
  you are busy?
- Which outsourcing approaches can help speed you to industry
  leadership?
- When should you use outsourcing as a financial tool?
- How can outsourcing allow you to attract people you couldn't
  hire to be employees?

Chapter 14

Pump Your Own Gas
Replace Expensive Outsourcing

Well-found consultants can stay in a company forever;
moving from one divisional trouble spot to another ....
— Robert Heller

We often consider outsourcing's practical limits while visiting our neighborhood gas station. That station gives you the choice of outsourcing gasoline refueling … or not, as you prefer. There are four pumps for full service and four pumps for self-service. Rarely are all the pumps busy.

There's an additional charge for full service, which amounts to about 25 percent of the self-service price per gallon. Let's assume we decide on full service. Here's what the experience is like: The attendants are located inside the station, which is about 40 feet away from the full-service pumps. There's a delay of at least a few seconds until they notice us and cross over to the pumps. The attendants double as cashiers and also answer the telephone. If the attendants are busy at these tasks, we have to wait longer for someone to arrive. Once there, we tell the man what grade of gasoline we want to purchase. He starts the pump and heads back inside. We wait until the tank is full. Whenever the attendant notices that our tank is full and he's not busy in one of his other roles, he comes back out to take our payment. If the payment requires a receipt or change, he goes back inside and waits if the cash register is being used to serve another customer. The attendant then rings in our sale and brings back the receipt and any change. How long has this transaction taken? It's usually about twice as long as serving ourselves.

Unless we ask, no other service will be provided. Our windshield will still be dirty and our oil may be low.

At the self-service pumps, we stick a credit or debit card into a slot and activate the pump in about 15 seconds. We put the nozzle into the tank, set the pump to stay on, and head to the self-service station for cleaning our windows. Armed with a squeegee and paper towels, we clean the windows while the gasoline is pumped. When we hear the pump stop, we finish the windows and go over to push a button for a receipt. We are usually on our way again within four minutes. In a typical fill-up, we save at least four minutes, give our vehicle a better window washing than any attendant has ever given us, and keep over $5.00 that would have been paid for the full service.

There used to be a drawback to self-service that discouraged many: Your hands smelled like gasoline for the next two hours. But our station now has handy towelettes next to the pump that effectively help remove any dirt and smell.

Why does anyone use full service? We're not really sure except if someone is physically handicapped and the task is difficult to accomplish.

Before you laugh this example off, consider that many organizations are using outsourcing that's helping them about as much as full service is helping customers at this gas station. Why does that happen? The most common cause is closing the door to self-service.

Another neighborhood gas station takes that approach. You can only purchase full-service gasoline at that station. If you like full service, you should use that station. The attendants stay by your car while the gasoline is being pumped. They will measure the air pressure in your tires if you ask them and politely inquire if you want your oil level checked. These attendants always clean your windows, and they do almost as good a job as you would. What are the drawbacks? It still takes about two minutes longer than self-service and costs about $2.00 more than self-service at the other station. They try to give you full service, even if you don't want it. Your already clean windows will receive another cleaning. You will be asked about your oil level even if you just changed the oil at that station an hour before.

As you can imagine, this full-service-only station isn't nearly as busy as the station that offers four self-service pumps. The lack of business creates a cost problem for the owners. Oil companies base their prices to gas stations in part on the volume that is purchased. In addition, the station's overhead has to be paid from pumping fewer gallons. To offset these prob-

lems, the full-service-only station specializes in repairs while the first station offers no repairs. Because of these differences, the station with four
self-service pumps is usually priced at least 7 percent lower for self-service gasoline than this full-service-only station's gasoline. Undoubtedly the
lower volume plays a role. Providing superior service is probably part of the
mix too. It must cost more to have these dedicated, capable attendants.

Here's how companies create the equivalent of all full-service gas stations for their organizations: Someone makes a rule that you have to follow
a certain procedure. Before long, the procedure provides an excuse to layer
on costs. You can, of course, help yourself anyway. But you may just help
yourself into hot water. These rules are often compounded by creating still
other rules until you've created a silly way to accomplish things, whether on
an outsourced basis or internally by self service.

We saw an example of rule making one day at *The New York Times*
that led to unnecessary costs. That venerable publication had a rule that its
reporters could not accept so much as a cup of coffee from sources. But
for an extended interview, it's helpful to be able to escape the newsroom's
noise. Having a cup of coffee together is a natural thing to do while chatting.
The closest location to the newsroom for coffee is the company cafeteria.
The reporters guided us there and ostentatiously bought the coffee. We sat
at a table and had a nice conversation. At the end of the interview, we each
picked up our cups to carry away. The reporters politely asked us to leave
the cups behind. It turns out that the reporters and the cafeteria staff belong
to labor unions. The reporters have been asked by their fellow unionists to
leave their dirty dishes and trash behind on the tables in the cafeteria. The
idea is to add more work for the cafeteria staff. In this way, there will perhaps be one or two more jobs for clearing off tables. There's another risk,
too. People cleaning up after themselves might lead to a union conflict, and
reporters could find themselves facing a picket line at the front door. As
union members, the reporters would be expected to stay out of the building
and not cross the picket line. Management presumably wants its reporters
investigating and writing articles rather than standing outside observing cafeteria workers' picket lines. As a result, you don't clean up after yourself in
the cafeteria at *The New York Times*.

Without all of these rules, we could, of course, have either brought coffee or offered to meet the reporters for breakfast or lunch at a pleasant place.
It would have been nicer that way. I doubt if the reporters' integrity would
have been compromised by the price of a latte, omelet, or BLT. Without the
rule, costs for treating us would have been eliminated. We might even have

given a better interview while relaxing in more comfortable surroundings.

Editors and unions aren't the only sources of such practices. Lawyers can easily make up dozens of such rules. For instance, many organizations are justifiably concerned about proper handling of hazardous substances. Otherwise, someone who is injured by those materials might sue for millions in damages. There are special containers for such substances, which outsourcers pick up. Typically, the substances are incinerated at a high temperature in a self-contained environment in which the fumes are also cleaned. That sounds like a desirable practice, doesn't it? But consider the alternative. The kind of incinerator that you need is neither large nor expensive. Why many organizations could afford to incinerate their own hazardous materials. Why? Most of the cost of the outsourcing comes from picking up and carrying around the contents of all those special containers to far away locations. If you incinerate right where the hazardous materials are being used, there's not much cost for picking up and carrying the materials.

Keep Outsourcing Relationships Short Term

Consider outsourcing and you'll find eager companies and suppliers lined up to offer you long-term contracts. Why? Assuming that the outsourcing provider performs as promised, you are locked into using their service ... even if a better alternative arises. The more profitable the arrangement is for the provider, the more that organization will want you to sign a long-term deal.

All kinds of reasons will be offered to justify a long-term arrangement. A typical explanation goes as follows: The supplier has to make a capital investment to start serving you and needs you to stay with the supplier long enough to allow the company to recoup the costs. While that's highly desirable for the supplier, you have to also consider if it's equally desirable for your organization. Can the capital investment be used by a large number of other customers? If yes, why should a long-term contract be required? If not, what would be a fair payment be during a shorter contract to compensate the supplier for having made the initial capital investment?

Others will tell you that they lose money during the first year and need several years to recover that cost. What they may not be telling you is that a lot of those costs are selling expenses that the outsourcing provider should be absorbing.

As consultants, we've often seen other consulting firms become established inside companies much in the way that Robert Heller describes. They seem to live permanently inside the client. Under such circumstances it's not unusual for the consulting firm to have a five-year contract in exchange for a modest discount in hourly rates. Long before the contract term is over, consultants priced at over $300 an hour may be doing work that could have been supplied elsewhere at $10 an hour. No matter how discounted the consulting price is, the client didn't get a good deal.

This kind of arrangement can be pretty hard on organizational morale, especially during hard times. Staff members often complain bitterly when they see wasteful spending on consultants. Every decision in the company may find its way through the consultants, both slowing down progress and making progress more expensive as the consultants find ways to grab pieces of the workload. We've heard people who haven't had a raise in two years say that they would be glad to do the same work on their own time for $15 an hour just to get a little extra income. It's pretty galling to see relatively inexperienced MBAs strolling around charging consulting rates when they typically know less about the issues than the people who work in the organization.

Sometimes, overly expensive long-term relationships sneak in the back door as a way to accomplish some other purpose. Before such relationships were restricted by legislation in the United States, accounting audit firms could sell clients other types of professional services. If the auditors found a process problem while reviewing internal controls, the auditors would prepare a proposal to solve the problem on an outsourcing basis. Because other outsourcing firms didn't know about the problem's background, it often seemed logical to hire the auditing firm to do this work at full price.

Although auditing contracts were usually for a single year, public companies were generally reluctant to change auditors very often. Such changes could create a public presumption that the old auditor turned up some sort of accounting problem that the public company wanted to keep quiet. As a result, most public companies worked with the same auditors for a decade or longer. The longer those relationships lasted, the bigger the outsourcing bills became.

There was another subtle influence at work in some cases. CFOs who wanted to use questionable accounting methods would be sure to spend plenty on the auditing firm's latest outsourcing ideas. The accounting firms would often find accounting methods that deferred, capitalized, or otherwise kept their fees from hurting current profit levels. With so much money at stake for the auditing firms, some accounting partners became more focused on the auditing firm's profits than on the integrity of the organization's books they were auditing.

A parallel pattern of excessive influence showed up in many public companies' relationships with U.S. investment bankers. Journalists have reported that some senior executives in public companies were allotted large numbers of shares in hot initial public offerings (IPOs) by investment banking firms seeking more business from the executives' firms. These executives could in some cases flip the IPO shares for a 200 to 300 percent gain in a single day, making as much as several hundred thousand dollars. Some would call such accommodations nothing less than bribery. These same executives also received a lot of their compensation in the form of stock option grants. Investment banks were in a position to encourage their security analysts to write more favorable reports about public companies that spent more on fees with the investment bank. In fact, the security analysts were often in the dual role of salespeople for outsourced investment banking services and security analysts for the public investors. A senior executive who wanted to earn more often found it to be beneficial to reward investment banks with higher fees. Like the accounting firms, investment banks found ways to package these fees so that they did not affect current earnings (and lower executive bonuses).

This pattern of using outsourcing to gain other purposes shows up in other parts of organizations. Local plant managers have often used outsourcing contracts to reward relatives of local officials who were in a position to aid or harm company efforts. In other cases, this prerogative was abused by being used instead to gain personal favors for the manager's family.

What all of these back-door relationships have in common is that they don't receive much scrutiny, aren't well understood by any but a handful of people in the organization, and are seldom compared to alternatives. It's no wonder that long-term outsourcing relationships often become tainted by bad apples.

Use Scenarios to Retest the Need for Outsourcing Before Signing a Contract

Let's assume that you've moved past silly rules and individuals pursuing "I'll scratch your back, if you'll scratch mine" at the company's expense. There's a seemingly legitimate outsourcing offer on the table. You've investigated all of the reasonable bidders and looked carefully at what you are doing now. Outsourcing seems like the way to go. But you know a lot of people have been burned in the past. How can you test your thinking before you sign on the dotted line?

Many organizations have found that scenarios are helpful that consider the extreme possibilities of what could go wrong. The wisdom of this approach was validated a few years ago when an earthquake damaged many electronic manufacturing facilities in Taiwan. If you had outsourced all of your production to firms on that island, you could have been left very short of finished inventory. A scenario built around the possibilities of natural disasters would have counseled in favor of selecting at least two geographically dispersed outsourcing providers who could handle all of your needs in a pinch.

Any scarcity that can affect performance should be investigated and considered. For instance, is the supplier dependent on the availability of one or two key people? What could happen if those people were injured or left the company?

Technology substitutes should be carefully evaluated. Many outsourcing contract offers suddenly become very competitively priced when the old technology is about to become obsolete. It's a chance for the outsourcing firm to dump equipment, products, or services with little or no value onto a customer. Within two years of the switch from analog to digital copiers, for instance, the pricing was very aggressive among those offering ways to outsource print shop and copying activities. Otherwise, a lot of analog machines would not have been placed. The clients, of course, ended up paying more in total despite the lower prices per unit. Why? The digital copiers could eliminate some of the need for paper copies through electronic access and distribution.

Examine the penalty clauses through scenarios as well. Many outsourcers depend on their customers making lots of mistakes to turn a money-losing contract into a gold mine. Printing is a typical problem area for this practice. Most organizations will rely on a printer to take care of most publications, forms, and routine documents. To protect themselves against high prices, the customers usually put the jobs out to bid. Customers receive a fixed price before various "discretionary" items such as authors' alterations and overtime. If you switch printers, you can be sure that there will be more mistakes than usual in getting the work done properly and on time from our organization's staff. Why? Your organization has to become used to a new process. Those errors and delays will probably, however, end up on your bill as "discretionary" charges.

Role-playing exercises involving scenarios can be a quick and easy way to spot such vulnerabilities. Have people in your company who are good at persuading your customers to spend more play the role of the new outsourcing provider. Let your team that will work with the outsourcer play themselves. Encourage the outsourcing role players to find ways to increase their profits by suggesting things that your team will be eager to do. Here's an example of what you may find: If the outsourcer makes packages, you'll be astonished by how many new packages are being developed and used. Why? There are usually all kinds of custom charges that can be added that aren't affected by the agreed-upon quantity discounts for mass-produced items. After you've run the role-playing exercise, have those playing the outsourcers explain their strategies and ask your financial staff to calculate what those strategies would have cost your company.

Another sort of scenario-based role playing can be helpful as well. Put yourself in the role of key stakeholders who could be harmed by the out-sourcing. Experience how it feels to receive bad treatment and find out that an outsourced supplier was part of the problem. In many cases, you will feel let down twice: Once because you had a bad experience and twice because the organization felt like it made more sense to cut costs in this area than to meet your needs as well as possible. Many firms that outsource answering customer service calls probably wouldn't do so if they had gone through this exercise first.

Examine How New Processes
Can Eliminate Expensive Outsourcing

Much outsourcing is based on comparing what you do now to what another organization would charge and promises to achieve. That's too narrow a way to consider your alternatives. By outsourcing, you may simply be turning a bad process into a permanent feature of your organization's operations. Instead, consider if you should switch to another process to replace some or all of the outsourcing. This evaluation is helpful both before and after an outsourcing decision, but offers the greatest payoff if you find a better alternative to outsourcing in the first place.

Here's an example: Many companies have moved from having large internal legal staffs that do everything to hiring specialist law firms as need-ed for unusual litigation. Done properly, you may have more experienced lawyers on your side, and the total cost can be less because these lawyers don't have to get up to speed like the staff lawyers would have to do.

But assuming that litigation is the only process you can use in cases involving harm is a mistake. Two primary alternatives can slash your costs and be more beneficial to those who were harmed by your organization. The first alternative is to create and act on a reasonably predictive model of what's likely to happen to a given case if you pursue litigation. Let's assume that the answer is that both sides will incur $65,000 in legal fees and your company will pay $100,000 in damages 62 percent of the time. The total expenditure before looking at nonlegal staff time and other expenses for you and the litigant is $230,000. If the litigation succeeds, the litigant clears $35,000 before any value for their own time. If you prevail, you still spend $65,000 before nonlegal staff time and expenses. If you lose, you pay $165,000 in total while incurring your other expenses.

Under these circumstances, some will settle all such cases where legitimate harm seems to have occurred for $50,000. In all cases, both the harmed party and your organization are better off. Only the external lawyers lose some potential revenue. And such a procedure could be handled efficiently through some simple investigatory process. Verify that someone is injured, make a reasonable offer, and pay those who agree. If such legal matters are pursued through a good process, you won't need those specialty litigators nearly as often.

If the other party won't settle, you still have a second alternative. You can propose using alternative dispute resolution methods. These processes are faster and cheaper than litigation, and you may not need specialty litigators.

Companies are most likely to pick a poorly designed process to outsource when faced with a new challenge. When such issues arise, take a little extra time to consider what the best practices might be for addressing that new challenge. Chances are that your first reaction to get the best help you can isn't the right one. Once outsourced, you will have created great inertia to keep the process as is through the outsourcing provider's vested interest in keeping the process going that provides the most profits for itself.

Encourage Your Staff to Find Do-It-Yourself Improvements to Outsourcing

Rarely does an outsourcing mistake occur without someone in the organization realizing the mistake before the decision is made. But even more rarely does the organization ask its people to come up with better alternatives to outsourcing before signing on the multiple-year dotted line. What's going on? Those closest to the problem usually identify key issues deserving consideration that are easily missed by those who only consider the big picture. Those who understand the details should call the shots, shouldn't they?

But those who are closest to the problem are generally low-ranking staff members, people who are usually encouraged to do what they are told rather than to create solutions. After all, thinks senior management, if those low-ranking people were so smart, wouldn't they be high-ranking executives? Not necessarily. Many engineers (a group of capable problem solvers in many organizations) aren't listened to by senior managers because those leaders can't easily understand the engineers. It's easier and more ego satisfying to just make decisions and let the chips fall where they may. That attitude makes leading easier for big-picture thinkers, but it can cost your organization a fortune.

That kind of communication's block is an example of the sort of problems you may encounter when you ask for new solutions. You need to encourage teams containing those with all the relevant skills and detailed knowledge to define and evaluate outsourcing choices and alternatives. When the teams are done, they will need to communicate simply to more senior management. In addition to gaining better choices to expensive outsourcing contracts, this approach may also help you find future leaders you don't know you have in the organization.

If you later decide to outsource by following a recommendation such a team has made, morale will be a lot higher because the decision will have more credibility. Your organization will know that you are seriously interested in doing the right thing. As a result, you may hear from these same people on future occasions when outsourcing is a bad idea and you didn't realize it.

Hire an Outsourcing Evaluator
to Advise You on Do-It-Yourself Options

There are times, however, when your internal team simply won't have the skill or experience to realize that better do-it-yourself options can comfortably replace expensive outsourcing arrangements. If you think that lack of skill or experience might be the case, you are a good candidate for hiring an organization that does outsourcing evaluations to describe what your best internal process choices are.

To avoid potential conflicts of interest, make it clear that under no circumstance will you hire this organization to do any outsourcing for you related to the issue at hand. You should also tell the evaluating organization that you will not hire it to locate outsourcers if the do-it-yourself choices are not chosen.

With those potential conflicts of interest out of the way, you have placed yourself into a happy situation: People who are familiar with industry best practices can evaluate what you really need and how else you might supply those needs. How can you provide a valuable reality check on this thinking? Insist that the outsourcing evaluators add some of your staff members with relevant knowledge and experience to the team.

As an early step in the process, ask your outsourcing evaluators to propose what your measurable objectives should be for either your internal process or outsourcing relationship. Much of the potential benefit you can gain comes from this reframing of what the objectives should be. Going back to the litigation example, the internal legal staff may be focusing on winning cases or reducing the annual cost of payments to litigants. Reducing company expenses in helping those who have been harmed from mistakes already made is a better goal. But it might take someone who isn't a lawyer to spot that way of framing the issue. That's the sort of new thinking that may help you to see the possibility for new processes. Better goals can shift your organization's mental framework into a more helpful focus..

Before you take the best do-it-yourself option this evaluation turns up, find a way to run some simple tests of how well do-it-yourself may work. Otherwise, you may find yourself undercutting your purposes. A fashion designer could certainly save a lot of money by using company employees to model the newest designs. But the glamour effects of having just the right models might be critical for creating the desired impression for one-of-a-kind designs of expensive apparel.

Here are questions to focus your attention on ways to avoid unjustifiably expensive outsourcing:

- What are the right objectives for the activity?
- What rules are you using that force unnecessary expenses, whether from outsourcing or from do-it-yourself?
- How can you reduce the duration of outsourcing relationships to increase your flexibility to hire other outsourcers or to do it yourself?

- Who can help you design scenarios to test the appropriateness of your outsourcing and do-it-yourself choices?
- Where can you find ideas for new processes that will eliminate both expensive outsourcing and internal work?
- Which staff members are likely to see good do-it-yourself options that no one has considered before?
- Where can you find expert resources to identify and evaluate the best do-it-yourself alternatives?

Chapter 15

Buy a Lifetime Warranty
Ask the World to Compete to Find Breakthrough Methods

Competitive advantage is based not on doing what others already do well, but on doing what others cannot do as well.
— John Kay

What organization can afford to stand still? Most would agree that focused improvement is critical to staying competitive or gaining new advantages. If you are trying to accomplish something well beyond the future best practice, you'll need to be cautious in your spending, as well. Going to the next level of performance can be extraordinarily expensive. But find ways to innovate at below normal costs, and exciting panoramas of opportunity open up.

For a vehicle owner, one such option is to buy a lifetime warranty on parts and labor. In that way, should any of the parts fail you have no additional expense. That's a good deal for those who keep their vehicles on the road for a long time. Parts soar in price the older your vehicle is. You're also covered if the vehicle maker has designed a part that keeps failing.

Why should you want to keep the same vehicle? The biggest expense you have is driving a new vehicle off the dealer's lot and turning it into a used machine. The decline in value can be over ten thousand dollars. Keep that vehicle on the road for many years, however, and that cost becomes a modest annual depreciation expense. At the same time, you also avoid incurring the additional depreciation expenses of taking another new vehicle and turning it into a used one.

Savvy buyers also know that you can buy used vehicles in the first place and avoid most of that depreciation. If you buy your vehicle from the dealer where it received regular service, you can also be reasonably sure that there have been no accidents and few problems. That dealer will also inspect the used vehicle and sell you a warranty on it for parts and labor.

A key advantage of buying a warranty is that you never face an unaffordable vehicle repair bill. Should many parts fail at the same time, especially if they include key parts of the engine and transmission, the cost can be in the thousands of dollars. Yet you can drive off most used vehicle sales lots by paying only a few hundred dollars down. To conserve cash flow, many vehicle owners will opt for the lower near-term cash flow option of not buying a warranty … even if it is much more expensive in the long run.

Without a warranty, many people will scramble to pay the repair bills to keep their vehicles running. That outlay will mean some major belt tightening in other aspects of what they do. Vacation may be day trips to the beach rather than a winter jaunt to Florida. Bag lunches will be replacing salads from the local deli.

How do these lessons apply to your organization? Chances are that your organization has exploited most ways of creating new advantages that you already know how to do. Running up against such a limit in capabilities, many organizations choose to scale down their improvement standards. When that happens, it's as though the organization has developed a permanent disability that will hinder future progress. That artificial limitation will remain until higher improvement standards return.

See the opportunity differently! Consider how few of the world's best thinkers and doers have worked on creating your breakthrough competitive advantages. From that perspective, the surface opportunities have barely been explored while the deeper potential advantages remain hidden. When you involve more of the world's best people, it's as though you had a lifetime warranty for making organizational improvements.

A good way to accelerate improving competitive position is to set progress goals to move years ahead of what anyone else has been delivering. An even better idea is to set goals that represent astonishing and important breakthroughs. Such a goal might mean shooting for a 10,000 percent solution in cost reductions while employing minimal resources. What's the benefit? Higher goals force you to consider new ways to accomplish tasks. You may even discover that lower cost choices exist that you didn't know about.

Here's a space exploration example that shows how seemingly impossible goals can lead to creating stellar performance … on a tight budget. This example demonstrates that playing safe may be the most dangerous thing you can do. Instead, shoot for perfection on a slightly increased budget and you may exceed previous accomplishments by hundreds of times.

Ever since people began looking at Mars through telescopes, observers have seen areas that appeared to be canals and bodies of water. That appearance led generations of science fiction authors to create stories about life on Mars. With better telescopes, it soon became apparent that there were no canals and bodies of water. Instead, there are places on Mars that look like rivers, lakes, and seas might have been present at some time in the past. In addition, there are two nonaqueous polar ice caps that increase and decrease in size with the seasons.

When *Mariner 9* successfully reached Mars orbit in 1972, river and channel-like features were confirmed. Viking spacecraft landed on Mars in 1976 and made it even clearer that there might have been water on Mars at one time.

That event was important for another reason: An undergraduate at Cornell, Steve Squyres, was hooked on the question of whether there had been water on Mars after seeing vivid *Viking I* and *II* orbiter images that looked like dry river beds. He wanted to find out about when and how much water might have existed earlier. That fascination led him into a career in science at Cornell. Not satisfied to read the results from others' experiments, he began assembling teams to propose Mars missions that would answer his questions.

Until 1999, Professor Squyres didn't get anywhere. NASA had been pursuing the least expensive ways to explore Mars. Those methods didn't allow for the kind of science experiments the professor and his colleagues wanted to pursue. But in the face of double disasters for its bargain-basement experiments in 1999, NASA decided to go for the more expensive option: Launch a breakthrough attempt in 2004 to explore for water on Mars and gather other valuable information. Because of its improved understanding of how risky Mars missions are, NASA asked the Squyres team to send two identical rover vehicles and instruments in separate spacecraft to attempt landings in different Mars locations. Hopefully, at least one rover would arrive and function properly.

There were several problems in pursuing NASA's vision. Little time remained to create even one instrument package and there was very little budget. Looking around, the team soon realized that it could do better with a worldwide team rather than a solely U.S.-based effort. For instance, combining resources with others would allow the mission to fly a Mössbauer spectrometer that had already been developed with German funds. The team also reused engineering solutions from the Viking landers.

Before long, engineering problems started to creep into the project. There was no time to test the landing system in the surefire way of having a dummy payload drop from a high altitude to Earth. Instead, the team found a wind tunnel in California where the parachutes could be tested for how well they deployed. This step saved months of testing and millions of dollars. Without this cheaper, faster way of testing, the mission would probably have been scrubbed.

Still, the team was falling further and further behind schedule. The vehicle assembly operations rethought the way that mission packages are prepared and found ways of assembling the two vehicles that cut the elapsed time for both. This approach meant, for example, assembling the vehicles in different sequences to allow for testing different things at the same time. This novel approach speeded assembly and discovery of design faults.

As problems were uncovered, the *Mars Exploration Rover* mission team was firm in its desire to accomplish more scientific investigation than ever before. As an example, NASA's minimum standards for the mission called for the rovers to remain powered up and operating for just a few weeks. Knowing that dust from storms on Mars could easily cover the solar panels that would provide new energy for the rovers, the team pushed for a way to add many more panels within a tiny space and limited weight allowance. While many just smiled at this seemingly impossible request, other engineers found it to be a remarkable challenge. Through a combination of a novel design and adding more weight to the payload, the higher energy potential objective was met. That one decision turned out to be an important line in the sand in creating breakthrough potential.

Having pushed for maximum science and trying to ensure minimum results with as much redundancy as possible, the team could only wait after the two successful launches. Once on Mars, who knew what might happen?

The story has an astonishing ending. Both rovers landed safely on Mars and operated well past their minimum lives. The solar-panel decision turned out to be decisive in enabling this longevity. As a result, these missions were able to make enormous numbers of investigations, measurements, and images. At this writing, both rovers continue to operate successfully with in-service periods more than 10 times their designed lives and even more impressive increases in mileage covered. It's as though the new vehicle you just bought turns out to run just fine without maintenance for 5 million miles.

As this remarkable accomplishment continues, NASA is likely to reach the point where it will have accomplished 20 times the usual amount of science from the mission it set out to pursue. The result has been to reduce the cost of this kind of exploration by over 95 percent while avoiding the risk of failure that dogged earlier low-cost efforts. The combination is essentially an infinite increase in scientific information.

And what about water on Mars? Both rovers hit the jackpot. Definitive evidence of water having been present was found at both exploration sites. One of the sites probably deserves additional exploration with a more advanced set of instruments since it appears to have had a past with the kind of wet environment that could have led to life beginning.

What's the lesson? Another team with more modest goals would probably have spent almost the same amount of money and would have accomplished much less. The high goals pushed the team to find low-cost, rapid solutions that were possible, but didn't seem plausible.

If you would like to read the fascinating story of how this achievement occurred, see *Roving Mars* (Hyperion 2005) by Steven W. Squyres. If you are curious about Mars, then visit NASA's Web site to see the latest research from the mission.

Pick Critical Elements That Can Lead to Breakthrough Cost Reductions

Those who analyze systems understand that a process can only operate as well as the least effective activity. Mr. Ford's assembly line couldn't go any faster than the slowest step in the process. If Ford broke the steps down into too many elements, the assembly line itself became longer and the whole process slowed down. Somewhere between too much speed and too many steps lay the optimum solution for one of his assembly lines.

Consider performance constraints from another perspective. To do that, let's look at a used vehicle. Chances are that many of the parts are in virtually new condition. For instance, the rubber doughnut that serves as a temporary spare tire will be flawlessly clean and shiny if you haven't had to use it. If you seldom have passengers in the back seat, the upholstery and carpets there will be remarkably fresh. Look under the hood and you'll notice that the container for windshield wiper fluid is just as functional as the day you left the dealer.

But at some point, you will sell or give away your vehicle. Often the reason will relate to mechanical unreliability. For instance, you may start to experience mysterious episodes of the engine shutting down while you are driving. Or you have to replace the engine because someone forgot to add oil. Naturally, vehicle breakdowns occur more often in some areas than others. Understanding this point, many purchasers check out the maintenance records of new and used models before selecting a vehicle.

Unlike the Mars rovers, terrestrial vehicle makers aren't really in the business of providing transportation that will last as long as possible. That feature would mean selling fewer vehicles. Also, the makers know that many people will sell their vehicles long before they cease to run. Spending less to make the vehicles allows both lower prices and higher profits.

Working in a for-profit or nonprofit enterprise, in many cases you have a different incentive than a vehicle manufacturer. Certainly, you would like your solutions to require as little maintenance as possible. That approach makes solutions less costly and saves time. If there is a large economic benefit from providing a more reliable, longer lasting offering, you will accomplish more if you supply that benefit. For example, even vehicle makers who produce more reliable, durable trucks that are used for long-distance commercial hauling will probably earn more.

Start by verifying that greater performance is a good idea. Then begin to identify those elements of current offerings that fail most often and cause the most problems when they do fail. For a vehicle, engines and brakes will be high on the list.

The Mars rovers provide a good metaphor for identifying problems. Unlike on Earth where you can go into a gas station and refuel, these rovers can only refuel by using their solar panels. Leave the rover in the shade or at the wrong angle towards the sun, and the power would soon be gone as batteries are drained. But if you create a vastly increased capacity to gain that power (as the rovers did with the unusual solar panels), you have lots more room for error. It's as though a terrestrial vehicle had a fuel tank large enough for a nonstop trip of 3,000 miles. Seldom would such a vehicle run out of fuel while looking for a gas station.

The conventional solution for such a vehicle is a bigger gas tank. This vehicle might look something like a gasoline tanker truck. If the gasoline sloshed in the wrong way on a turn, the vehicle might easily roll over and ignite itself. Who would want to drive around in such an ungainly moving bomb?

But the goal of making long trips without adding fuel is a good one. Here are other examples of conventional thinking for incremental gains. Many alternative technologies could help … including those used in hybrid vehicles (such as the Prius), and those that provide for carrying lots of stored energy in batteries charged by flywheels and solar panels at home or work. Reducing energy consumption helps, too. Every so many years, gasoline prices spike. When that occurs, more people want fuel-efficient models. Make the vehicle fuel efficient enough and you've added new value for owners who will pay more for the benefit. If your engine is also less polluting, those who are concerned about cleaner air will prefer your vehicle and may pay a premium for it. Some technologies offer the potential to use less fuel *and* pollute less. For instance, there are promising ideas for storing braking energy in batteries. Most of these technologies are not yet as efficient as most drivers would like, but the technologies offer the potential of being more reliable sources of power for vehicles that are otherwise likely to run out of fuel. As you can see, this line of thinking has taken us to where the major vehicle companies are experimenting. But that's still incremental improvement, rather than breakthrough progress.

Let's look at the problem of providing breakthrough results by applying the thought process of the Mars rover designers. They might start from scratch to consider all vehicle elements to see how to sparingly supply more of what's most critical to performance while cutting back on what's unneeded.

Here's one insight: What's a big part of the joy of having a vehicle? It's often the sense of freedom and excitement that the driver feels from high-performance jaunts. With ever more crowded roads pitted with more potholes and less time for joy rides, a different route to joyful ownership may offer more promise. Perhaps adding a little more joy driving could replace much of the urge for long drives.

Vehicles don't need to be as big as they are today to provide high-performance experiences. After all, didn't the rover team miniaturize everything that was carried to Mars and accomplish more as a result? How can that principle apply here? Having driven the tiny versions of Grand Prix race cars, we were astonished by how exciting it was to run those twisting loops at little more than go-cart speeds. A drive once around the teeny track brought more exhilaration than driving across country in a full-sized vehicle.

An entrepreneur who wanted to create a breakthrough driving experience efficiently might skip making conventional vehicles. Undoubtedly a great version of the scaled-down sports cars could be developed to sell for around $7,000 that would be much more fun to drive than any $150,000 sports car is at legal speeds on regular roads. Naturally, the driving experience wouldn't be as prestigious, but that's a separate opportunity. Such cars would operate on teaspoons of fuel per lap around a race track rather than gallons per trip on the public roads.

Without an interesting place to drive such vehicles, however, there wouldn't be much demand. The manufacturer could put a variety of challenging tracks in major metropolitan areas. The mini race cars would be transported to and fro in tiny trailers towed by any conventional vehicle with a trailer hitch. For those who wanted to race more often, mini garages could be rented next to the tracks for a few dollars a month.

Suddenly, some families would double or triple the number of vehicles they owned to take advantage of these improved driving experiences. Make the engines fun to tinker with and a whole new generation of auto mechanic buffs would emerge. Fewer long-distance trips would beckon to such owners, and fuel use would drop while driving enjoyment would soar.

Set Goals Beyond What Seems to Be
the Theoretical Best Practice

Assuming that you've found an exciting element to optimize at reduced cost, what kind of a goal should you set? Most people can imagine creating some pretty astonishing performance with unlimited funds. But that's not the real world. Even the U.S. space program has to economize these days. With that restriction in mind, many people will set quite low performance targets. When you do that, all you accomplish is to put the same time and effort into creating a minimal solution that could probably instead have led to a maximum solution.

Imagination is one of the biggest limits to cost-based progress. If you asked someone in the automobile industry in 1921 what a car could eventually do, their forecast would have fallen well below what we see the worst vehicles do today. In 1921, car makers also felt little incentive to work on many of today's most important innovations. For instance, with gasoline selling for a few cents a gallon in the United States during the 1950s, auto makers emphasized big, heavy cars with powerful, fuel-guzzling engines.

Much of the learning about fuel efficiency was delayed by this perception that the best practice was to deliver enhanced feelings of status and power.

In attempting to reach beyond the perceived theoretical best practice, one perspective is to look for ways to reach large multiples of that practice. Why? We've constantly been amazed to find out how pessimistic people are and how little they know about what's already being accomplished in related fields. Ask a leader in a typical organization to set a standard to approach the theoretical best practice, and the new goal is likely to be something that most organizations exceeded in the 1950s. Yet the leaders usually feel great stress for having selected what seems to them to be a stretch goal. Overcome this self-limiting pessimism and you may glimpse possibilities so wonderful that your mind will conceive of unconventional ways for providing those benefits.

As we mentioned in the preceding section, driving on regular roads can be pretty, well, pedestrian as you creep along in traffic jams. On the one hand, that's good. It means that drivers are focused on a simple task and are less likely to make mistakes that cause injuries. On the other hand, drivers also spend a lot of time being bored. As a result, you see more and more vehicles where the drivers and passengers are entertaining themselves with nonstop cell phone conversations, portable music players, satellite radio stations, videos, and electronic games. The driving experience becomes more dangerous as drivers are lulled into forgetting that they are supposed to be paying attention to driving. At 10 m.p.h. that's no problem. At the increasingly rare higher speeds, the danger is palpable.

We have a suggestion that can create value for drivers while driving down the lifetime cost of accidents that harm vehicles and people: Create a more intense, yet safer, driving experience. This experience might be achieved by providing heads-up displays of the vehicle's instruments and the environment around the driver, warning sensors for dangerous conditions, and ways of monitoring the quality of one's own driving. While those things may sound dull, imagine that the new displays look like those used by jet fighter pilots or that they feature images of family members and friends to draw attention to safety needs.

To keep things interesting, the displays could provide valuable information based on your actual driving experiences. Here's one for your new teenage driver who likes to tailgate: The display might update her continually on what her chances are of stopping in time if the car ahead of her brakes suddenly. Pretty soon, driving is more interesting and safer, too! Parents could get a readout of the driving experience and review good and bad habits with their inexperienced offspring.

Let's explore another opportunity to extend your understanding of setting exciting goals that provide a multiple of the perceived theoretical best practice by turning our attention back to space. One of the big costs involved in Mars exploration is carrying the payload in a large rocket to escape the Earth's gravity. As a result of that high cost, there's only enough money to do one or two Mars missions about every two years when orbital interception opportunities are best. An advance beyond the theoretical best practice would be to conduct experiments on Mars as though Mars were in the neighborhood. How might that be done?

Thinking past today's perceptions of the theoretical best practice, our exploration planner might conceptualize a string of continual shuttles going back and forth between Earth and Mars. These shuttles would never land on either planet, but simply carry payloads to Mars. If such shuttles were fueled with nuclear reactors, they would run for years without refueling. Because the shuttle vehicles wouldn't have to be lifted away from Earth's gravity each time, a large increase in the size of payloads could be sent to Mars. Portions of the final payload could be brought up from Earth using conventional launch vehicles. Final assembly and loading could be conducted at the international space station or by docking with a shuttle from Earth.

If you can now send hundreds of times as much material to Mars on each mission, how might that circumstance change your view of how to conduct experiments? One possibility is that you could dispatch hundreds or even thousands of rovers from a single Mars shuttle. Because you are producing so many, the cost of each rover would drop to being a tiny fraction of the cost of producing only one or two. Based on typical experience curve effects (a way of estimating how rapidly costs decline due to learning), the average cost of producing each of 4,000 rovers should be much less than 5 percent of the average cost of making two. Using the latest intelligence about which sites on Mars are of interest for specific purposes, you would select sites to insert these rovers after you arrived in orbit. This situation would be a big improvement over relying on what you knew years before the launch. If atmospheric conditions were less than optimal when you arrived, you could also delay insertion until winds and atmospheric pressure were better for safe and precise landings.

Another possibility is that you might stockpile large quantities of redundant instruments, parts, and testing chemicals on Mars. Rovers might be designed so that they could be repaired and updated by using robotic repair kits that draw on the extra materials at their Mars base. You could also send robots that could be manipulated at a distance through radio signals to make fine-tuned repairs and adjustments to instruments.

What's the concept here? It's basically to set yourself up to explore Mars in the same way you might explore the Sahara desert on Earth if you had enough robot vehicles to do the job. Instead of having a two-year delay between choices for what research you do next, you would be able to adjust to explore new options every few days should that be appropriate. Imagine one of those warrior-droid-filled space ships from *Star Wars: Episode II* as you think about this way of exploring.

Although it's not as good as H. G. Wells's time machine, this way of eliminating payload limitations can certainly shrink the time delays involved in taking the next steps in our investigations of Mars while minimizing the expense of gaining significant new information.

Launch Redundant Searches for Solutions

When you're trying to do something no one's ever thought about doing before, where do you find the best solution? Chances are that you cannot predict what the best information and knowledge sources will be. Think back to the Goldcorp and Procter & Gamble examples of engaging more resources through running worldwide contests that succeed because no one knows in advance who will provide the best answer. Otherwise, you could just hire that person or organization. But you need to move beyond the idea that worldwide contests will drive you well past the theoretical best practice. Why? Because there's probably a way to improve on the results enjoyed from those contests.

Instead of starting your search for improvement based solely on your own organization's thinking, step back and have a contest to identify the optimal goals for your organization. Your goals may be directed at the wrong performance areas. Your goals also may be too modest. The bigger your organization or the less confident you are, the more likely you will set goals like NASA's minimum case for the Mars rovers that would operate for just a few days.

Next you need to identify where the development should be located. Most organizations assume that they or one of their primary suppliers will coordinate everything. That assumption might be faulty. If Ford made that assumption today about reforming its manufacturing, it might be a tragic mistake that could doom the company. Ford could instead find itself greatly advantaged by joint venturing with a non-U.S. competitor to access the kinds of manufacturing expertise that Ford might require years to develop. In such a joint venture, it would certainly make more sense for the manufacturing planning to occur in a stronger competitor's shop rather than Ford's.

But Ford cannot count on a stronger competitor wanting a partnership. Also, who's to say that lean manufacturing using teams is the ultimate best way to make vehicles? Ford should explore organizations that are checking out other manufacturing processes that have higher potential. In many cases, these processes may be found outside of the vehicle production industry. Currently, there's a lot of custom manufacturing work done in electronics. Exploring those options might open the door to improved directions for vehicle manufacturing.

Ford also shouldn't assume that existing organizations will have the best answers. The vehicle industry hasn't exactly been knocking down the doors of the world's finest thinkers to find better ways to produce. Further, Ford is hampered with many legacies of past thinking that hinder its effectiveness. It may well be that Ford should shrink its business model so that the company no longer produces its own vehicles. Someone without those legacies could probably accomplish more than Ford can.

Like potential Mars missions delivering thousands of rovers that can be deployed to reflect opportunities, Ford should also explore these alternative development paths simultaneously. Conceptual thinking to create breakthrough gains costs pennies compared to the dollars involved in retaining or putting inappropriate processes in place.

But wait. That's still not enough. The major costs of a vehicle are borne by an owner, not by Ford. No matter how good Ford or its suppliers are at manufacturing, those improvements are not very likely to make a big dent in an owner's costs. The multiple searches for cost reductions must primarily look for ways to benefit the owner's purse or wallet. Let's look at a few potential examples.

When a vehicle runs for more miles, that extra use normally reduces the operator's cost per mile. But many vehicle owners favor experiencing vehicle variety over low cost. How might you provide both? Imagine, for example, if vehicle interiors could be refurbished by their owners with new colors and designs for $500. While that's a major expense, someone who spends a lot of time in the vehicle might welcome the opportunity to experience a new vehicle aroma, a nicer look, a more appealing color, and the pleasant feel of new fabric. Those who like to be fashionable would be changing their interiors long before the old ones showed wear. The extra

$500 every so often is a lot less than the cost of switching vehicles.

An odd thing happens to older vehicles. Long before they are ready for the junk heap, the value of their used parts soars to well over the vehicle's market value. A manufacturer could stimulate faster turnover of older vehicles by providing services that allow owners to turn trade in vehicles for a high percentage of the used parts' value. This service would, in turn, help owners to reduce their costs per mile.

When gasoline prices are rising or are high, vehicle purchases and values are affected because most motorists don't have the assets or expertise to hedge the cost of gasoline over the expected life of their vehicle. Vehicle companies do have such assets and skills. The vehicle manufacturers could provide futures hedging services to owners that fix the rate paid for gasoline and diesel fuel. If a vehicle manufacturer wanted to do provide such services, the organization should also explore whether an integrated petroleum company wanted to provide a similar product. By owning the raw materials, the petroleum producer might be able to make long-term deals at a lower cost to vehicle owners.

Taking this thinking a step further, a vehicle manufacturer could consider becoming backward integrated into petroleum production. This strategy would provide a major source of profits when energy prices are high that could be used to provide incentives to purchase vehicles … such as free gasoline for the first few years that you own your vehicle. Obviously, acting on this opportunity to invest will work best if pursued during low-price periods for petroleum rather than in high-priced markets.

If a driver is permanently injured in a vehicle accident and cannot return to work, the lost income from that disability could cost the driver more than all of the vehicles that he or she will ever purchase. Yet most people don't have income-coverage disability insurance related to vehicle accidents. If you're hit by someone who is uninsured, you won't even have a chance to collect through a lawsuit. Large manufacturers of vehicles would again be in a good position to provide such a financial service at a low cost by spreading the development and overhead costs over millions of drivers.

Be Flexible with Resources

Detroit fell in love with robots in the 1980s. Led by GM's Roger Smith, robots seemed to offer the promise of improving quality, eliminating dangerous jobs, and making Detroit more competitive with Japanese manufacturers. However, robots of that era had some drawbacks. If you wanted to shift the robot to do a slightly different task, the setup time wasn't very fast and engineers had to make the changes. When the robot's purpose was to eliminate lower cost jobs, the savings often weren't so great. In addition, the robots tied you into assembly-line methods in many cases. Because technology was advancing rapidly, the robots also had to be replaced pretty frequently with better robots.

By contrast, robots make a lot of sense for exploring Mars. It's much more costly and difficult to send a person there than a robot. On Earth, however, people often have the edge over robots because people can adapt so much more rapidly and inexpensively than robots can.

Many organizations make a mistake when they commit all their resources in one direction. What was the stroke of genius in one era can be the competitive vulnerability of the next era. Consider lean manufacturing. That sounds hard to beat, doesn't it? But if you design offerings to be more modular, customers and consumers can customize their own offerings to flexibly fit their circumstances. That do-it-yourself option will often be preferred by customers and consumers where they gain major cost and time advantages, as shown in the self-service gasoline example in Chapter 14. In fact, more modular decorating choices would probably attract buyers to vehicles because owners would prefer such truly custom cars.

In other cases, lean manufacturing doesn't apply or could be a hindrance. If you keep a vehicle long enough, there are going to be many parts to repair and replace. Since labor in repair shops often carries a charge of over $80 an hour, designing vehicles so that they are less expensive to repair could save a vehicle owner hundreds of dollars. If that design meant that the original manufacturing cost a bit more, the owner is still better off with this trade-off.

Vehicle companies love to load up their offerings with various extras for which they can charge a high price compared to the cost. Thus a standard vehicle with a stripped down price of $14,999 may actually sell for $24,999 with all of the geegaws. Since most vehicle manufacturers primarily produce vehicles for unsold inventory rather than to order, the decision of what extras to add can layer unnecessary costs on vehicle owners. When demand is weak, these vehicles may sit rusting on the dealers' lots. With a different design for such extras, dealers would have the option to remove some extras from vehicles and add the extras to another vehicle … or to ship the extra items to another dealer or the manufacturer. Or if the automobile design is modular enough, the owners could do some of the removal work for themselves and resell the extras online.

How can a manufacturer stay flexible? Run high quality experiments of totally different approaches for delivering stakeholder value. Here's an example: The Detroit manufacturers have labor and retiree agreements that the vehicle makers feel are too expensive. At some manufacturers, thousands of auto workers show up to simply sit in a room for the day and still draw full pay for their "guaranteed" jobs. Obviously, the union wants those people protected. Equally obviously, the companies would like to pare those costs. Rather than trying to keep splitting an ever smaller pie as Detroit's market share plunges, the two sides might do better to investigate how they could retrain these surplus workers and healthy retirees. For instance, those employees might wish to work as automotive technicians for dealerships and repair shops. Although such jobs pay much less than what automotive workers receive, the subsidy paid by the vehicle companies would be substantially reduced ... even after providing incentives to switch from doing nothing. Certainly, workers who like to keep busy would enjoy the change.

But you also have to be cautious about experiments with strategic consequences that may tie up resources. Here's an example: General Motors launched its Saturn brand as a way of learning how to succeed with low-priced, good gas mileage cars. In making that decision, the company failed to appreciate that a successful experiment could mean adding a full lineup of Saturn vehicles ... requiring additional investments in the billions of dollars. The result of the experiment's success has been to make Saturn more like GM. At the same time not enough has been done to make GM more like the successful aspects of Saturn. Was this experiment a net gain? It's too soon to tell. Had the same resources gone into trying the same experiment with Chevrolet, you cannot help but feel that GM's strategic benefits would likely have been larger.

There's a tendency to treat each decision as being totally disconnected from every other decision. But some decisions have large implications for future commitments. New Orleans and the Netherlands were committed to maintaining levees and dikes just as soon as they began to build on land that was below sea level. Discounted cash flow analysis is supposed to deal with this problem of taking care of long-term needs in economic ways, but that measurement doesn't usually do so because decision makers often ignore liquidity and opportunity costs. Here's why those factors are important. Great opportunities show up in discontinuous fashion. Let's look at the stock market as an example. You could buy almost any U.S. stock in August 1982 and make a fortune over the next 17 years. If you had bought almost any U.S. stock in 1973, you would probably not have seen any profit for more than 10 years. The wise organization keeps access to lots of resources so that huge opportunities can be pursued whenever they randomly appear. But that doesn't mean it makes sense to chase the top of the market. Here's a specific example: Mercedes-Benz bought Chrysler through a stock swap for a price of $37 billion in 1998. The purchase has been viewed by some as a major failure. Within a few years, the combined companies were trading for a value lower than Mercedes enjoyed when it made the purchase while Chrysler experienced steep losses. A weak Chrysler, by comparison, could have been purchased by anyone in 1978 for less than two billion in stock, and you would have benefited from having Lee Iacocca lead the turnaround with K-cars and minivans.

Resist All Expensive and Slow-Developing Choices to Pursue Opportunities

What is a slow-developing opportunity? It's almost always an opportunity that you don't know how to pursue yet. What's a slow-developing, expensive opportunity? It's an opportunity for which you've spent a lot of money without yet knowing how to pursue the opportunity. The only difference between the two is that more money is spent in the latter case.

What's the lesson? Focus on learning what you can for as little cost as possible and as quickly as possible. That intention seems obvious, doesn't it? Yet organizations make enormous mistakes in this direction every day by pursuing cost-reduction opportunities while not learning very much from their efforts. Why? Here are some of the reasons: For one, organizations may make promises they cannot meet, especially about future growth and profitability. The more promises the leaders make, the more they feel like they need to do something that may fill the gap between the promises and reality. In the absence of a clear option that's working, leaders may be tempted to throw money at the opportunities that seem the largest … and hope for the best. This approach may buy some time, but it rarely fills the cost-reduction gap. In some cases, such an organization will undergo an ill-conceived belt-tightening that will delay and reduce the effectiveness of good cost-reduction projects. That strategy is like trying to drive your vehicle for another 100,000 miles without a ring job after your engine starts using a quart of oil every 200 miles.

Making promises that cannot be kept hurts most when those who are pursuing the opportunities subscribe to achieving unrealistic accomplishments. In such a circumstance, the money and time are diverted from learning into ever larger gambles to make a quick breakthrough. That approach is like a pyramid investment scheme. Each promise requires a bigger payment down the road, but there's a limit to the cash flow that's available to make things happen. Seeing their careers potentially suffering damage, such leaders may become desperate and hide the depths of their problems, a step that also hurts learning.

For another thing, some organizations are paradoxically not too well organized. Some of these enterprises are little more than poorly coordinated baronies run by people who aren't held accountable for specific results. Ask a leader in that sort of organization to accomplish some new task, and that leader may be off hiring people and launching programs before setting objectives. It's facetiously called "Fire, ready, aim." Even in well-run organizations, most leaders have no experience in developing the large cost reductions that we've been exploring in this part of the book. As a result, the instinct will be to duplicate the sorts of cost-reduction programs that they have used in the past — most of which will be inappropriate.

Slow development of cost reductions can be related to a number of causes. Whenever you run into such slow developments, check what's going on to diagnose what the causes might be. Here are some potential causes to consider as you investigate:

- Lack of appropriate measurements to define what the potential is
- Undefined performance objectives
- Ignorance about current and future best practices
- Inability to project future best practices
- Misunderstanding what the theoretical best practices are
- Lack of knowledge about how to explore choices for approaching the theoretical best practices
- Staffing weaknesses
- Unmet learning needs
- Conflicts between incentives and objectives
- A slow cycle for repeating the 2,000 percent solution process
- Premature commitment of resources before the opportunities are validated
- Misunderstandings about the strategic process involved in creating 2,000 percent solution-based cost reductions.

Like most such circumstances, it makes sense to think things through before taking action. That old carpentry adage comes to mind: "Measure twice. Cut once."

With any of these causes, start by being sure that your organization is well versed in initiating major cost-reduction programs through the 2,000 percent solution process. Next, make sure that stalls are identified, stallbusters are designed and tested, and the eight process steps are all pursued and reported on before any significant implementation commitments are made. Rarely will more than 100 hours of effort will be required to scope out the potential opportunity, which should supply sufficient understanding to decide if further investigation is warranted. By having multiple teams working on alternative approaches to 2,000 percent cost reductions, you should be able to further shrink the elapsed time needed to find high potential, rapid-implementation opportunities.

Here are questions designed to help you apply the lessons developed in this chapter for engaging the whole world to achieve astonishing cost reductions:

- Which critical elements of your business model or operations could lead to cost-reduction breakthroughs?
- For the most promising of such opportunities, what are inspiring goals to urge people past the theoretical best practices for cost reductions?
- What is the most effective way you can launch deliberately overlapping global solution searches?
- How can you be more flexible in maintaining resources to apply to your best opportunities when they arise?
- Are you prepared enough to learn from pursuing these cost-reduction choices?

Chapter 16

Have 30,000 Mile Checkups
Repeat the Cost-Reduction Steps

Don't look back. Something might be gaining on you.
— Satchel Paige

When you buy most vehicles, they come with an owner's manual that describes routine checkups and maintenance. The purpose of such checkups is to see that everything is working properly and, if necessary, to bring your vehicle up to safe and efficient standards of operation. While a few items like oil changes need to be done frequently, most types of vehicle maintenance occur every 30,000 miles. You are usually told to change the air and fuel filters, as well as the spark plugs. You are also encouraged to rotate and balance the tires and align the vehicle. In addition, you inspect critical parts such as the engine, brakes, and battery. On some 30,000 mile checkups, you are also told to replace the coolant, if you have a radiator, and the transmission fluid. For some vehicles, the dealers can also do extensive electronic checks to see if any other function has degraded to below critical performance levels.

We have a different kind of checkup in mind for you in pursuing greater cost reductions for stakeholders. This checkup allows you to streak exponentially past the 2,000 percent solution level of cost-reduction success. Our checkup has two purposes:

1. To refresh and strengthen your cost-reduction capabilities as an organization after a success in implementing a 2,000 percent solution

   2. To lift your organization to new heights of cost effectiveness, much like the second stage of a rocket launches the payload to a higher altitude by adding to the momentum provided by the first stage

Let's look at the astonishing size of the potential benefits from this checkup. First, you may be able to open up important new markets. Many people are inclined to leave well enough alone after having reduced costs by more than 95 percent for some stakeholders. After all, the absolute size of taking that cost down by a second 95 percent is a pittance compared to the prior cost reduction. That's certainly true, but that's also not the end of the story.

You should see the opportunity differently. Here's why: If you reduce the costs enough, at some point you begin adding important benefits. Consider this example: You provide some kind of education that learners can apply to make money. Let's assume that you've reached the point where the value of that education to learners does not change as a result of further cost reductions. That change can instead often be accomplished by pruning away the unnecessary aspects of the education and improving the most valuable parts. Transfer that essential experience into a virtually costless business model, and you've created a superior offering ... even though its cost is much reduced. For example, many people assume they must spend money for educational resources that are unnecessary. They envision classrooms, teachers, people marking papers, and examinations. But did very many people learn to speak their first language in that way? With electronic distribution and automated feedback mechanisms, delivery of learning experiences can be virtually costless.

Let's assume your original educational offering cost learners $300,000. After you apply 2,000 percent solution, the education still costs learners $15,000. That's way beyond what 80 percent of the world's people can afford. If you take that cost down again by 95 percent, you reach $750. That's great, but still too expensive for most people. Take that cost down by another 95 percent and you reach $37.50. Now you've added tens of millions who can afford the education. Take that $37.50 down by another 95 percent and you reach $1.88. At this level, hundreds of millions can afford your offering. Take that $1.88 down to $0.04 and nearly everyone can use what you have to offer. Somewhere along the way, you will also reach a tipping point where you unleash other forces that will aid your efforts.

Here's one possibility of what that tipping point could be: If the income gains from the education are large, you've also created a happy customer who will want to invest a substantial portion of the new income to gain additional education from you. If that additional education also helps create more income gains, even more education will be purchased. As long as the value is high enough, your student will buy more. With low marketing costs, you can look forward to selling lots of services and having the opportunity to find lower costs to provide those other forms of education. You've created a virtuous cycle that makes growth and profit gains automatic, and you can serve most people on Earth, which allows for the potential of having an enormous enterprise.

That example may seem frivolous and unrealistic to you; forgive us if it does. But some people have seen such cost reductions occur within their own lifetime. For instance, the computing power of a $4.00 solar-powered calculator today cost more than $30 million in the early 1950s. That change is identical to reducing the cost of a $300,000 education to $0.04. How much of the economic progress we've enjoyed since the 1950s came as a result of more people being able to make more calculations? No one knows, but clearly the effects must have been quite large. Certainly, we've seen the computing industry grow from less than $100 million in annual sales then to hundreds of billions of dollars today.

The second benefit of such a checkup is that further cost reductions may allow current customers to make greater use of your offering. When such greater use follows, your sales increase and your potential to reduce costs further improves. For instance, consider a city that adds border-to-border wireless service for computer users with a time-based connection fee. Much of the cost of such a capability is involved in acquiring computers and equipment, installing transmission towers and dishes, renting transmission sites, and putting the system together. When such a wireless service has only a few customers, the operating and overhead costs may be identical to when the service has 100,000 customers. In other words, there's some minimum scale involved in just setting up the business. Because of the high startup cost, the initial service coverage is likely to be a minimal one. The connections won't work in a lot of locations, much like the dropouts that people experience now with cellular telephone coverage. As the service adds customers, the provider can afford to put more towers and dishes in place so that connections work in more locations. That improvement, in turn, stimulates more usage by existing customers, which lowers the cost of providing connection time to the average customer.

The third benefit of such checkups is that tackling tough cost-reduction challenges can hone your organization's skills. With improved skills, you can move on to bigger opportunities competing against or acquiring organizations that aren't as effective as you are. Let's look at how acquisitions can be used to gain such benefits. We saw that approach effectively taken by Coca-Cola and PepsiCo for many years as they purchased weak bottlers. Turning loose their best operating people, these operations would soon emerge as much more effective and with lower costs. When those new approaches were well understood by the bottler's management, these bottlers were then resold for a tidy profit while they remained more valuable members of the soft drink companies' distribution networks. Companies with such cost-reduction skills may also be able to become outsourcing providers.

With those benefits in mind, let's now consider how such checkups might be best done. We draw from our extensive experience with organizations that have developed 2,000 percent solution cost reductions to clarify the ideal approach to such checkups.

Square Your Recent 2,000 Percent Solution Cost Reductions

When clients and students describe their first 2,000 percent solutions, they always acknowledge that repeating the process will be a good idea. When the improvement has been related to reducing costs, however, few set a date for that repetition. We strongly encourage you to set such a date … and consider making the time to begin again sooner rather than later.

We had a recent experience that led us to think that frequent repetitions might be a good idea. See what you think after you read this story.

The 2,000 percent solution involved a large nongovernmental organization (NGO) that provides relief activities for poor people. Because of the scope of the organization's activities, each step in obtaining and distributing aid resources needs to be carefully coordinated. Otherwise, people would be waiting around for resources that weren't yet available. To create such closer coordination, the organization saw an opportunity to upgrade the quality and frequency of its status reports on resource availability by location. The savings would be over a million dollars a year in a single unit of the NGO.

When the person working on the problem first explored the solution options, he reported that the only choice was to hire expensive database experts. This solution meant a cost of over $340,000 to create the necessary reporting and communications' capabilities. While that might be a

2,000 percent solution over time, we were skeptical. Surely, the software and systems would have to be redone every few years. If each update cost $340,000, this might be an 800 percent solution, but it probably wasn't a 2,000 percent solution. We suggested that the solver look for cheaper ways to put the information technology in place. With the help of a colleague, a reputable local supplier was found who charged only $50,000 for the information technology. Within a year of beginning to use that technology, it looked like this NGO had a 2,000 percent solution for reducing costs. Naturally everyone was happy.

The very same week that this solution was devised, a different person working for a government organization in another country reported on his progress with a similar problem. Major projects in the government organization were being delayed because it took the staff so long to accomplish each step. Everyone else was waiting for the information in the meantime. Yet the information could be easily summarized, reconfigured, and communicated by sending out e-mails containing answers from Excel spreadsheet calculations. Because the government group had no budget to work on the solution, the solver wrote the necessary formulas in Excel and trained the person working on this activity how to use Excel to make the calculations. He spent about 50 hours on this task. At the end of that work, his organization was able to make the necessary calculations and communicate them in less than 1/20 of the time traditionally spent.

As we applauded this second excellent solution, we couldn't help but think about the first solver in the NGO. His reports and communications could probably also have been provided through an Excel spreadsheet attached to e-mails. But the first solver hadn't thought of that option. Instead of spending $50,000, he could probably have gotten the job done for 50 hours of someone's time who is good at writing Excel formulas. If that alternative were truly available, the NGO had another 2,000 percent cost solution waiting in the wings for the next time it needed to update its software and reports. If the first solver happens to pick that software update as a cost-reduction checkup date, the second solution can be created. Otherwise, another $50,000 (plus inflation) will be spent. By setting the first software update as a checkup point now, the first solver is more likely to repeat the process then and create a 2,000 percent squared cost-reduction solution for this reporting.

What are the lessons? Clearly, you should set a definite checkup date before you will have to spend money again. But if you normally have a lot of staff turnover, you may run the risk of that checkup never taking place. If you are the problem solver and later leave that part of the organization, who will repeat the cost-reduction process? The odds of the timely repetition are greatly improved if everyone involved in that aspect of the organization learns about creating 2,000 percent solutions during the first solution-finding process, and you create a consensus among the group about when the repetition should occur. A further benefit could come in agreeing during the first solution process on some hypotheses about how the next round of 2,000 percent solution cost reduction might take place. In the case of the NGO, such hypotheses could include amending the reports to allow for better coordination of expensive activities, locating less costly information technology solutions, and looking for more problems to solve through improved reporting.

An even more valuable lesson is to hold more frequent checkups. If the group could find a second 2,000 percent cost-reduction solution soon after the first, that would impress everyone with the full potential of this important discipline. Such an approach would also mean that the skills of everyone in creating 2,000 percent solutions would expand a lot faster.

We have a radical suggestion that may shock you: *Shoot for a 2,000 percent squared cost-reduction solution on the first application of the 2,000 percent solution cost-reduction process.* If you don't succeed with going past a 2,000 percent solution, you will have only spent a little more time than if you had sought a regular 2,000 percent cost-reduction solution. But if you make a little more progress, you may well end up with a 2,300 or 2,800 percent solution as a reward for relatively little more consideration. If you succeed, the benefits are, of course, magnificent. You have a 40,000 percent cost-reduction solution. In addition, you'll have created a capability for additional cost solutions in other areas that will probably be unmatched in your industry or activity.

Expand Your Focus to Locate
Previously Unperceived Targets for Cost Reductions

New 2,000 percent solution cost reducers often lack confidence when they begin. As a result, they pick some area of glaring inefficiency as an easy target. In such activities, it's not unusual for a 2,000 percent solution to be possible by simply applying methods known since the 1920s. That approach is unfortunate because the solver often gets a sense that 2,000 percent solutions for cost reductions only exist in a few places where horrible results are occurring.

However, move this attention into an organization's most important activities, and you can have more impact with one solution than with a thousand small activities. Think about the toy industry as an example. A new 2,000 percent cost reducer might focus on locating lower-cost suppliers for low-volume toys 20 times faster. If the toys account for less than one-tenth of 1 percent of an organization's sales, these savings might only succeed in eliminating a few salaries.

Compare that potential to making the sales of new toys 20 times higher from the same development efforts, and you can see the point about how much more valuable such a focus would be. We encountered a recent example among dolls that impressed us with the availability of better development methods in what seem to be mature industries. Barbie® dolls had dominated the U.S. toy market for over 50 years. These dolls were made to look somewhat like Donald Trump's second wife, Marla Maples. If scaled up to adult size, Barbie® would have been about six feet, two inches tall. Her measurements on an adult woman's scale would have veered towards the unrealistically large for chest and bra sizes with a waist that barely existed. If you saw someone in real life like Barbie®, she would have been in danger of falling over frontward. Clearly, that version of Barbie® didn't look like any little girls anyone had ever seen. Girls tended to play with Barbie® like they would have with a pretty Mommy doll.

MGA Entertainment was a small factor in the toy business but was on the lookout for ways to grow. The company's owner noticed that his not-so-young daughter didn't find Barbie® dolls appealing when she wanted to play dolls with her friends. At the 7 to 11 age level, girls more often like to pretend that dolls are friends who are doing activities together. Barbie® clearly looked like a Mommy, not a friend. MGA decided to bring out a line of dolls that would facilitate this friend-oriented play. Bratz™ dolls have huge heads, teenager-like bodies, and lots of teenage clothes. They also come in all hues of skin color and hair, just like real girls. Girls in the "tween" stage, between being little girls and teenagers, quickly adopted these Bratz™ with a vengeance. Within three years, Bratz™ became the number-one selling doll brand in the United States, and annual sales exceeded one billion dollars. That's quite a hit for the tiny toy company.

By shifting its focus from developing toys like other toy companies did to studying what children found lacking in current dolls, MGA Entertainment was able to reduce its cost of developing a new toy by more than 95 percent as a percentage of sales. Notice that by making such a critical activity more effective, MGA also expanded its revenues so much that other cost-reduction opportunities are much larger now, as well.

Observe, too, from this example of improving product development that not all 2,000 percent cost reductions entail spending less for something. You may spend about the same amount, but accomplish more than 20 times as much. In the case of MGA Entertainment, the shift allowed the company to accomplish over 50 times as much.

As you can see from this example, making new product or service development more productive can be one of the most highly leveraged areas for 2,000 percent cost-reduction solutions. Yet most organizations seldom look at becoming more effective at developing new offerings as a cost-improvement opportunity.

Traditionally, most people think of cost-reduction opportunities as being most concentrated in operations that provide offerings, in initiating outsourcing, and in improving information technology. Those initial reactions of where to focus attention for cost reductions usually reflect stalled thinking. Here are the highest potential places for cost reductions in most organizations we've studied:

- Developing new offerings
- Accelerating customers' trial of offerings
- Expanding awareness of offerings
- Increasing availability of and access to offerings
- Reducing capital intensity of offerings
- Raising low cost capital
- Eliminating flaws that harm customers and other stakeholders

As a result, we encourage you in establishing your checkup scheduling to be sure that all of these areas receive 2,000 percent solution cost-reduction attention on a frequent basis. Naturally, you should add other areas that might be more important for your organization than for most other organizations.

Add 2,000 Percent Solution Cost-Reduction Capability

Most organizations have only one person in them who knows how to create 2,000 percent solutions. Why? These individuals have usually learned about and created 2,000 percent solutions on their own, away from the spotlight that normally surrounds major new initiatives. Such 2,000 percent solutions are what we like to call "stealth" initiatives, which talented organization members are using to create increased organizational effectiveness.

However, when isolated from organizational sponsorship, these individuals are highly unlikely to expand this problem-solving knowledge within the organization. Why? These talented solvers have valid reasons not to do so, unless they happen to own the firm. Here's one reason: Most careers are helped by being able to produce truly astonishing results that no one expects. By keeping quiet about the source of their success, these 2,000 percent solution cost reducers are able to climb quickly up the organizational ladder from one promotion to another. Their organizations appreciate and reward the results they see without understanding the source of the results. At the same time, the organizations fail to understand that virtually everyone in the organization could be producing similar results in a multitude of areas. If the problem solver lets everyone in on the secret, there goes the easy route to the top. It's a rare individual who will take that step.

There's also a disincentive for problem solvers to become involved with educating others. Most problem solvers just want to get on with accomplishing something important. Training others often feels to talented 2,000 percent solution creators like not doing anything very useful. There's another hurdle: Even if you understand how to do something, you may not be able to explain what to do to someone else. Since most such problem solvers have little background in helping others learn, the solvers are naturally reluctant to put effort into extending their skills in this new way. If solvers prove to not be very good at educational assistance, they have just created a failure on their record. Why would anyone want to take that risk of failure unless they owned the firm?

Another barrier is crossing functional lines. A few confident problem solvers simply share the opportunity with colleagues in other parts of the organization and engage their support. Most solvers, however, stick to improving activities pursued by those who report to the solver. As soon as problem solvers run out of areas where they can make direct improvements, the solvers are done with making 2,000 percent solutions.

A more significant barrier is avoiding embarrassment to others. If you show someone else they could be doing the work 20 times faster or better, in many cases you've made the person feel incompetent. If the people involved are notoriously thin-skinned, few will propose improvements because of the potential to be caught in a backlash from those who feel embarrassed. Yes, some organizations do shoot the messenger.

How might these barriers and limitations be avoided without drawing all of the fuss, skepticism, and expense that comes with an officially sponsored activity? Undoubtedly, there are more ways to do this than we've thought of or seen, but let's start you off with a brief list of opportunities that have worked well:

- Find a life-saving application.
- Explore an injury-avoiding opportunity.
- Identify a way to avoid environmental pollution.
- Present the process as a possible methodology for a task force that's unclear about how to proceed.
- Introduce the methodology to those who are missing their goals by a wide margin and are likely to be demoted or fired unless they quickly improve.
- Use the methodology to deal with a crisis that requires quick action.
- Make courses based on the 2,000 percent solution methodology available to those with budgets in your organization to pay for personal learning.

For entrepreneurs, there are some additional choices worth considering:

- Build improved business models around 2,000 percent solutions for expanding the market size, customer acquisition, and cost reductions.
- Direct mandatory training and assignments in creating 2,000 percent solution cost reductions.
- Offer training to partners, suppliers, distributors, and other key stakeholders with incentives for improved performance.
- Hold contests for the public to propose 2,000 percent solutions for key activities.

Use 2,000 Percent Solution Cost Reductions as a Management Development Tool

In larger organizations, developing the candidates to fill key positions in the future is a key management task. Depending on the organization's circumstances, those with different kinds of skills are likely to be favored. For example, when the economy is weak, those with cost-reduction skills will be in favor. When times are robust, those with sales talent will be considered more seriously. When interest rates are volatile, financial acumen and experience are more highly valued.

We have a different idea for you. Consider having everyone who wants to be a senior member of your organization demonstrate skill in creating 2,000 percent solution cost reductions. This approach has several potential advantages:

- This skill will be seen as more desirable by those with upper management ambitions.
- Experience will be gained more rapidly in all functional areas.
- You will create a common language and understanding of the subject that will allow cross-functional 2,000 percent solution cost reductions to be developed more often.
- The organization will have one point of common comparison among all of its top candidates for key jobs.

Naturally, you can also push this tool deeper into the organization so that people experience 2,000 percent problem solving earlier in their careers. For many organizations, cross-functional task forces of younger people are often assembled in part to see who can do what. These task forces could become 2,000 percent solution cost-reduction proving grounds for those who want to show their aptitude to move upward from technical, analyst, and support positions into managerial roles. A reward for good performance on such task forces could be assignment to the team that implements the 2,000 percent cost reduction. In that role, those with primarily analytical skills can have a chance to show what they can do in managing change.

Here are questions to help you apply the lessons found in this final chapter for building on 2,000 percent solution cost reductions to make greater progress:

- How can you schedule and ensure repetitions of 2,000 percent solution cost reductions in the same areas?
- What can you do to expand the focus of your cost-reduction activities into higher potential areas?
- Which barriers to expanded use of 2,000 percent solutions for cost reductions do you need to remove?
- How can you expand your organization's ability to generate and implement 2,000 percent solutions?

Epilogue

There are three things which the public will always clamor for sooner or later, namely, novelty, novelty, novelty.
— Thomas Hood

It's the nature of some people to be out looking for something better when most people haven't gotten around to trying the best of what's available. Hopefully, *The 2,000 Percent Squared Solution* has provided a helpful outlet for the former group while providing a worthy subject for the people who haven't yet gotten around to mastering all of the improvement processes they would like to learn.

It's with an eye to both groups that we now take a cautious look into the future. Where is the novelty going to be for creating 2,000 percent solutions after this book is mastered? While we cannot say for sure, we can certainly share with you the frontiers that we are busy exploring.

First, recent evidence has convinced us that the threshold for many improvements should be higher than 2,000 percent. While improvement potential may not always be as high as 40,000 percent, clearly 4,000 percent seems to be usually just as available as 2,000 percent is for a solution.

Second, if you can have 2,000 percent squared solutions, why not have 2,000 percent cubed and fourth-power solutions? Assuming that the solutions have been designed to create full-scale multiplier effects for access to resources by creating surpluses that can be applied elsewhere and to expand benefits, we see no limit to the potential multiplier effects of complementary 2,000 percent solutions.

While those greater benefits are truly mind-boggling to consider, it seems clear to us that those who want to pursue 800,000 percent and 16,000,000 percent solutions in the near term will need direction from us. To this end, we have started this direction by establishing The Billionaire Entrepreneurs' Master Mind, a group of entrepreneurs under our leadership that is looking at how to create such solutions for new enterprises. While it's too early to report progress, we are encouraged by what we've experienced so far. When the time is right, we'll publish again to share what we've learned.

Stay tuned!

About the Authors

The oldest books are only just out to those who have not read them.
— Samuel Butler

Donald W. Mitchell is chairman and chief executive officer of Mitchell and Company, a management consulting firm established in 1977 to specialize in business strategy. He is also cofounder of Leading Executive Organizations 100, Inc., which facilitates advanced executive learning by CEOs, CFOs, division presidents, business development executives, corporate planners, and investor relations executives. Prior to cofounding Mitchell and Company, Mr. Mitchell served as corporate director of strategic planning for Heublein, Inc., where he was also responsible for acquisitions and divestitures. After graduate school, he worked as a project manager at The Boston Consulting Group, Inc., in Boston under the direction of well-known strategist, Mr. Bruce D. Henderson.

Mr. Mitchell has contributed to many business process innovations that have been used successfully by companies to establish improved business models. These process innovations address improved ways to profitably gain market share, adjust prices, reduce costs, add new customer benefits, develop a more profitable customer and offering mix, lower the cost of capital, expand the stock-price multiple, develop a more compatible shareholder base, and anticipate stock market reaction to corporate decisions and performance.

He has led strategic assignments for several hundred major companies during four decades. He often speaks before groups of CEOs and CFOs.

Mr. Mitchell coauthored *The 2,000 Percent Solution* and *The 2,000 Percent Solution Workbook*, designed to help companies make faster progress by creating outstanding solutions for their most significant problems and opportunities; *The Irresistible Growth Enterprise*, focused on how to benefit from unpredictable changes in business, economic, and social trends; and *The Ultimate Competitive Advantage*, which shows companies how to gain lasting competitive advantages by continually improving their business models. He has authored dozens of articles in professional publications about business management. He is listed in a number of biographical references, including *Who's Who in the World*.

He graduated magna cum laude with an AB degree in modern European history from Harvard College and holds a Juris Doctor degree from Harvard Law School. He attended Harvard Business School to study marketing while a second year student at Harvard Law School, receiving a Distinction for his second-year marketing project for *New York Magazine*. He is a member of the bar in Massachusetts.

Mr. Mitchell has served on the board of Literacy Volunteers of Massachusetts, has been treasurer of the Harvard Law School Association, and was a member of the boards of the Harvard Alumni Association and the Harvard Cooperative Society.

He was born and raised in San Bernardino, California, and now resides in the Boston area with his family.

Carol Bruckner Coles is cofounder, president, and chief operating officer of Mitchell and Company. She has spent more than 29 years designing management processes to help companies develop the strategic potential of their businesses and improve their market value. Prior to 1977, Ms. Coles served as manager of strategic planning for Heublein, Inc., where she was responsible for developing and installing the strategy audit process and involved in acquisition and merger activities.

She is coauthor of *The 2,000 Percent Solution*, *The 2,000 Percent Solution Workbook*, *The Irresistible Growth Enterprise*, and *The Ultimate Competitive Advantage*. She has frequently been quoted in the business press about the future direction of major corporations and the stock market. Ms. Coles has been a guest speaker at annual conferences for *Business Week's* CFO Forum, *Institutional Investor*, the National Investor Relations Institute, and YPO. She has been listed in *Who's Who of American Women* and served as a director of the Boston chapter of The Planning Forum.

Ms. Coles has a BA degree from New York University and an MA in economics and education from Columbia University.

She was born and raised in New York City and now lives in the Boston area with her family.

Donald W. Mitchell and Carol Bruckner Coles may be reached at ultimatecompetitiveadvantage@yahoo.com.

2,000 Percent Squared Solution Products and Services

Benevolence is a natural instinct of the human mind; when A sees B in distress, his conscience always urges him to entreat C to help him.
— Sydney Smith

Turning the ideas in a book into a 40,000 percent improvement in profits or performance requires more attention and effort than many people find they can muster by themselves. To provide more support for your solutions, we offer some products and services for which we charge clients professional fees that may be of help. Feel free to contact us at 781-647-4211 during normal business hours in the eastern United States with your questions about these fee-based products and services.

Creating a 2,000 Percent Squared Solution: The Custom Workbook

Tell us what you want to accomplish, and we will produce a custom workbook for you that will guide you in creating your 2,000 percent squared solution.

Individual Online Tutorial in Creating a 2,000 Percent Squared Solution

Donald Mitchell will provide individual online guidance as you develop a 2,000 percent squared solution.

Task Force Online Tutorial in Creating a 2,000 Percent Squared Solution

Donald Mitchell will provide online guidance to a task force group as you develop a 2,000 percent squared solution.

Telephone Coaching in Creating a 2,000 Percent Squared Solution
Donald Mitchell will speak with you on a regular basis to review your progress and help you think through the best ways to deal with your remaining issues.

Keynote Speech about 2,000 Percent Squared Solutions
Donald Mitchell will be pleased to address your company, industry group, or organization to explain this exciting improvement opportunity.

On-Site Workshops in Creating 2,000 Percent Squared Solutions
Both coauthors are available to introduce and provide hands-on experiences with the 2,000 percent squared solution process.

Consulting Support for 2,000 Percent Squared Solutions
You or your organization may not be in a position to pursue all of the eight steps in the 2,000 percent solution process to your own satisfaction. One of the coauthors will lead a consulting team to provide expertise to fill in any gaps in what you can accomplish for yourselves.

Busy organizations may also wish to develop more 2,000 percent squared solutions than they have time to do for themselves. In those circumstances, one of your coauthors will lead a consulting team to work with key personnel in your organization to define and implement 2,000 percent squared solutions that you choose to pursue.

Certification Training in 2,000 Percent Squared Solutions
You may wish to develop an internal consulting group to facilitate 2,000 percent squared solutions. We are pleased to provide the training necessary to receive a certificate of competency in this discipline.

Licensing of the 2,000 Percent Squared Solution Process
We will be glad to provide you with the resources and experience you need to become an official licensor of this process so that you may deliver services in this discipline to other organizations.